ENERGY, ECONOMY AND EQUITY INTERACTIONS IN A CGE MODEL FOR PAKISTAN

To Ammi, Abbu and Amna

Energy, Economy and Equity Interactions in a CGE Model for Pakistan

FARZANA NAQVI

Ashgate

Aldershot • Brookfield USA • Singapore • Sydney

Published by
Ashgate Publishing Ltd
Gower House
Croft Road
Aldershot
Hants GU11 3HR
England

Ashgate Publishing Company
Old Post Road
Brookfield
Vermont 05036
USA

British Library Cataloguing in Publication Data

Naqvi, Farzana
    Energy, economy and equity interactions in a CGE model for
    Pakistan
    1. Energy policy - Pakistan 2. Power resources - Pakistan -
    Costs 3. Pakistan - Economic conditions
    I. Title
    333.7'9'095491

Library of Congress Catalog Card Number: 97-74460

ISBN 1 85972 169 9

Printed in Great Britain by The Ipswich Book Company, Suffolk.

Contents

Foreword

Readers of this book will find that Farzana Naqvi has built a sophisticated model of Pakistan's economy and has applied it in an outstanding study of energy pricing issues. Included in her work are detailed specifications of:

(a) substitution possibilities between different energy products and between energy products and other inputs to production;

(b) production functions for the main energy producing and using industries;

(c) the operation of price regulations for energy and other products;

(d) rural-urban migration; and

(e) income distribution and social welfare.

Dr. Naqvi did most of the research underlying her book in a two year period as a visitor to the Centre of Policy Studies and the IMPACT Project. That she achieved so much in such a short time attests to her ingenuity, perseverance and determination.

General equilibrium modelling, the approach which Dr. Naqvi adopts, has become a major component of policy analysis in Australia. It found its way into Australian policy circles about twenty years ago, mainly through the efforts of two far-sighted public servants, Alf Rattigan and Bill Carmichael.

Rattigan and Carmichael had responsibility for Australia's Industry Assistance Commission (IAC). The role of the IAC was to advise the Australian government on industry policy, e.g. the levels of tariff and subsidies. Rattigan and Carmichael realized that industry policies should be analysed in a quantitative, economy-wide framework. They understood that restrictions on the import of cars would stimulate activity in the domestic car industry but would also have effects on other industries. They rejected the then popular input-output model which suggested that stimulation of one industry would stimulate all other industries via increases in demand for intermediate inputs. They saw that import restrictions on cars would increase costs and could have adverse effects outside the car industry.

In 1975, Rattigan and Carmichael organized the IMPACT Project. Their objective was to obtain an economy-wide model capable of tracing out the links between different industries arising not only from flows of intermediate inputs but also from competition for the economy' scarce resources, e.g. labour in different skill categories, capital, urban and rural land, foreign exchange and the pollution carrying capacity of the air and water. They appointed as director of the project Alan A., Powell, a young, energetic and highly distinguished econometrician. I was fortunate enough to be Powell's deputy.

Under Powell's leadership, the IMPACT Project met Rattigan and Camichael's requirements by producing a series of general equilibrium models, the best-known being ORANI. Because of its connection with policy advising, the IMPACT Project was, and continues to be, intensely practical. It is also very open. During his long period as director, Powell insisted that models used in policy advisory must be fully documented and available for critical assessment.

A spin off from Powell's devotion to openness is that the IMPACT Project has spawned other modelling efforts in Australia and overseas. These efforts have been facilitated not only by documentation of IMPACT models but also by the GEMPACK programs created at IMPACT by Ken Pearson.

Dr. Naqvi's general equilibrium model of Pakistan is in the best traditions of the IMPACT Project. It provides a quantitative, economy-wide perspective on a policy issue (energy pricing) of intense practical importance. In this book, her model is meticulously documented making it available both for critical assessment and further development.

At CoPS/IMPACT, we all hope that Dr. Naqvi's work receives the attention in Pakistan and elsewhere that it richly deserves.

Peter B. Dixon
Director,
Center of Policy Studies/IMPACT Project
Monash University
Melbourne, Australia
June 1997

List of abbreviations

AGE	Applied General Equilibrium
CES	Constant Elasticity of Substitution
CET	Constant Elasticity of Transformation
CGE	Computable General Equilibrium
CIF	Cost, Insurance, Freight
CPI	Consumer Price Index
DGNRER	Directorate General of New and Renewable Energy Resources
FO	Furnace Oil
FOB	Freight on Board
GDP	Gross Domestic Product
GE	General Equilibrium
GE-PAK	Computable General Equilibrium model of Energy, Economy and Equity Interactions in Pakistan
GEMPACK	General Equilibrium Modelling Package
GOP	Government of Pakistan
HSD	High Speed Diesel
HSSW	Harberger, Scarf, Shoven and Whalley
IEA	International Energy Agency
IMF	International Monetary Fund
KWh	Kilo Watt hours

LDO	Light Speed Diesel
LES	Linear Expenditure System
MCFT	Million Cubic Feet
MSG	Multi Sectoral Growth
OCAC	Oil Companies Advisory Committee
PDB	Pakistan's Data Base
ROW	Rest of the World
Rs	Pakistani Rupees
SAM	Social Accounting Matrix
TOE	Tonnes of Oil Equivalent
WAPDA	Water and Power Development Authority
WPI	Wholesales Price Index

List of tables

List of figures

xix

Preface

In the last three decades, Computable General Equilibrium modelling has emerged as an established field of applied economics. CGE models have been widely applied to analyse a variety of issues faced by the economic planners and policy makers. Starting from the well-known issues of public sector policies, such as taxes and tariff, CGE applications have been made to look into the new emerging issues such as formation of the trading blocks, emission of greenhouse gases and degradation of environment. There are two major factors that have popularised this methodology. (1) It allows implementation of large-scale models capturing interaction and interdependence between various sectors. (2) All relationships are derived from micro-economic theory, hence, its application does not depend on historical time series data. Consequently, CGE models facilitate simulation of policy shocks which have no precedent.

This book presents a CGE model developed for Pakistan with the hope that it will lay down a foundation for application of general equilibrium modelling for policy formulation in Pakistan. As the country is being driven swiftly to become an open market economy, it becomes vital to find out the policy measures that can foster the objectives of economic planning, such as social equity, with the minimum loss of the efficiency gains from the open market resource allocations.

It is not possible to build a model for practical use that can do justice to all sectors of the economy in modelling of their peculiar features. The CGE model developed in this book focuses on the energy sector. Energy is considered as one of the basic needs and an essential input to economic growth. Hence, energy policy has multiple criteria to meet. In this book, a case study has been carried out to analyse energy pricing policy in Pakistan using this CGE model of energy, economy and equity interactions. Hence, the book also demonstrates how researchers can model the fine details of one sector given the core structure of a CGE model.

In the development of the CGE model for Pakistan, the earnest desire was to incorporate some peculiar features of Pakistan's economy. But this effort should be looked at as only a starting point rather than an accomplishment. The model has been developed in a framework which allows modification and expansion in a very convenient manner. Thus, this model provides a template to the academics and researchers to meet the challenges posed by the theoretical limitations of the existing CGE models, in general, and the model for Pakistan presented here, in particular.

Input data preparation is one of the tedious tasks faced by CGE model builders. One chapter has been devoted to discussion of the data base preparation for the Pakistan model to show how the researchers can get around the data problem.

I hope researchers, academics and research students will find the model a useful addition to their "kit of methodologies", and that this book will be a useful guide in future modelling of Pakistan and other countries.

The book was made possible through the intellectual contribution of Professor Peter B. Dixon and Dr. Mark Horridge, Monash University, Australia, to computable general equilibrium modelling over more than a decade. My gratitude goes to them. I am especially thankful to them for their encouragement and guidance during my Ph.D studies on which this book is based. Special thanks are due to Ms. Louis Pinchen (Centre of Policy Studies, Monash University, Australia) and Messrs Matloob Qureshi and Jehanzeb (Applied Systems Analysis Group, Pakistan Atomic Energy Commission) for their assistance in word processing.

Farzana Naqvi
Islamabad, June 1997

1 Introduction

1.1 Energy planning issues in Pakistan and a need for a general equilibrium model

Pakistan is one of the South Asian economy that has maintained a high economic growth during the last 15 years. Between 1980-81 and 1994-95, the average growth rate of Gross Domestic Product (GDP) was 5.2 per cent *per annum.* Owing to the high population growth rate, however, *per capita* income grew at only 2.3 per cent *per annum.* Pakistan continues to rank amongst the low-income developing countries.

Like in many developing countries, economic liberalisation and the privatisation policies have been pursued in Pakistan. Particularly, since the early 1990s, ample incentives have been given to the private sector in the energy policy to enhance private investment in the energy sector including the electricity sector which has traditionally been a public monopoly.

Despite these recent developments in the energy policy, the energy sector's management remains one of the government's responsibilities. The public sector supplies, or directly supervises the supply of, all commercial energy products except coal. The functioning of the energy industries and most of the related industries is mainly regulated by the government policies and plans which include setting of energy prices. In Pakistan, much effort has been devoted to the formulation of policies and plans for the energy sector. A recent example is the appointment of the Prime Minister Task force on energy (GOP, 1994a). The recommendations of the Task Force became a part of the current Eighth Five-year plan (1993-98). The scope of energy planning activities varies from the design of an integrated energy plan to the appraisal of a single project. The energy planners face a number of problems and policy issues. These problems are similar to those faced by all the developing countries who are net importers of energy, *i.e.*:

1. Meeting of the rapidly growing energy demand.

1

2. Setting of energy prices to meet multiple objectives.
3. Mobilisation of resources to meet the high investment requirement for energy projects.
4. Reducing of the high dependence on imported oil.
5. Management of the capacity shortage in the electricity sector.

Table 1.1
Macroeconomic and energy indicators of Pakistan

	Per capita gross domestic product[a]		Per capita primary energy[b] consumption		Per capita electricity consumption		Energy Intensity			
							Primary energy (per 10^6 Rs.)		Electricity (per Rs. 10^3)	
	Rs.	Index	TOE	Index	kWh	Index	TOE	Index	kWh	Index
1980-81	2956	100	0.18	100	192	100	61	100	65	100
1985-86	3504	119	0.22	122	262	137	63	103	75	115
1990-91	3920	133	0.26	144	361	188	66	108	92	142
1994-95	4188	141	0.28	155	418	217	67	110	100	153

a At constant factor cost of 1980-81
b It includes all commercial fuels and electricity

Source: GOP (1996a, 1996b) and GOP (1985).

In 1994-95, total primary energy demand in Pakistan was 59.18 million tonnes of oil equivalent (TOE) comprising 61 per cent commercial energy products and 38 per cent non-commercial fuels. Over the last 15 years, the demand for energy has been growing rapidly and the share of commercial energy has been rising. As a result, the commercial energy demand has been growing at a high rate, *i.e.* 5.6 per cent *per annum* which is higher than the GDP growth rate in the same period. In particular, the demand for electricity has been growing tremendously; registering 8.3 per cent *per annum* growth over the 15 years period. Table 1.1 shows the trends of *per capita* consumption of commercial energy and electricity. Despite a significant increase in the *per capita* consumption of both commercial energy and electricity, the present consumption level is quite low; only 0.28 TOE *per capita* of commercial energy and 418 kWh *per capita* of electricity.

Table 1.1 also shows energy (electricity) intensity, *i.e.* units of energy (electricity) used per unit of GDP during 1980-95 at the five-year intervals. There has been a steady increase in electricity intensity which registered about 53 per cent increase in this period. Contrary to this, there has been a small increase in primary energy intensity.

Up till now most of the planning efforts in Pakistan have been directed towards commercial energy supply planning — in particular towards the expansion in the electricity sector. Although, various measures of energy demand management, particularly rationalisation of energy prices, have been recommended from time to time but research studies have not been carried out to evaluate the socio-economic effects of these measures.

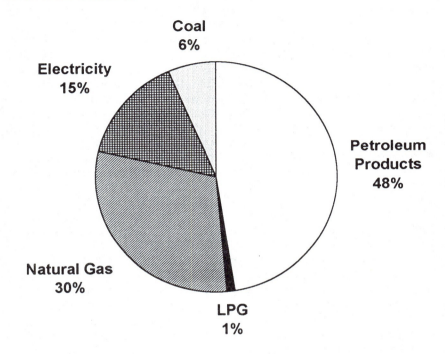

Figure 1.1   Composition of final commercial energy consumption 1994-95

Source: GOP (1996a).

Fig. 1.1 shows the shares of energy products in Pakistan's total commercial energy consumption in 1994-95 (GOP, 1996a). Petroleum products and natural gas accounted for more than 70 per cent of the total energy demand, while the share of electricity was 15 per cent. Coal had the smallest share in the total demand accounting for only 6 per cent share.

Thus, petroleum products, natural gas and electricity are the major forms of commercial energy used in Pakistan. The supplies and prices of these 3 types of energy products have been administered by the government. Within the energy sector, public corporations and private companies work for the given government-regulated energy prices/profit margins. The public sector also has a significant share in the production of cement and chemical fertilisers. The production processes of these two commodities are highly energy intensive, and their prices are also set by the government.

Coal industry is the only energy industry in which the private sector has a large share in production and investment. Market forces determine the consumption, production, and price of coal. A small quantity of coal is produced in the public sector, and its price is set in line with the market determined price. Coal, however, has a dwindling share in total commercial energy consumption; its share declined from about 15 per cent in 1971-72 to only 6 per cent in 1994-95 (GOP, 1996a).

The prices of petroleum products, natural gas and electricity have been administered by the government to promote equity, to stabilise prices (of both energy and other commodities), to generate revenue, and to discourage import of certain energy products. As a result, the energy prices diverge from the levels which would be obtained under a free-market regime. It is possible to think of these divergences as a series of implicit taxes and subsidies on energy products. After the 1970s and 1980s oil crises, studies were conducted to analyse and estimate the level and nature of distortions in the administered energy prices in developing countries (for example Sidayyo, 1983; 1988 and Kosmo, 1989). There were two such studies for Pakistan. Kuijper (1982) examined petroleum product prices of 1979-80, while Sabih (1986) analysed electricity prices. These two studies were carried out in a partial equilibrium framework to compute the social welfare loss arising from the distortions in the energy prices. Although such analyses are important to estimate the inefficiencies of the regulated energy prices and the resultant loss to the society, their scope is limited. Most importantly, such analyses do not evaluate the micro and macro economic impacts of removing the distortions from the regulated energy prices. Furthermore, because of the partial equilibrium framework, the complex interrelationships of energy, economy and equity are overlooked. Last but not least, such analyses do not show to what extent the distortions in the energy prices (in the form of implicit subsidies and taxes) actually further the above listed multiple objectives of the energy pricing policy.

It has been generally accepted that energy prices play a major role in macro economics in the long term. Only after the first oil shock in 1973, energy pricing was given its due weight in the short-term policies by all countries; developed or developing. Energy prices affect the economy in various ways which we now discuss.

Energy plays a dual role of consumption good and an essential intermediate input. It is demanded both for direct use (private consumption) and indirect use (input into production and transportation). Besides income, the major determinants of energy demand from households are prices of both energy using and producing sectors' outputs. An increase in energy prices reduces real expenditure of households leading to the reduction in their demands for energy as well as non-energy commodities in the first round. Consequently, on the production side, this reduces the demand for labour, and real wages decline. On the supply side, the

4

increase in energy prices makes two conflicting effects on all production sectors: (i) an increase in the production costs as a result of a rise in the price of energy which is used as an intermediate input, and (ii) a decline in the costs as a result of the reduction in wages. Thus, one expects changes in the prices of all commodities. The direction and magnitude of the change in the price of a commodity depend on factors such as labour and energy intensities in its production and its related industries, and substitution possibilities of the energy input. The changes in the prices of exported goods affect their demands in the foreign markets, while the changes in the prices of import-competing and non-traded commodities affect the households' consumption pattern, and thus affecting the domestic market. These feedback effects from the domestic and foreign markets induce changes in the production pattern of the economy. The ultimate impacts are the net effects of all these changes which are measured in terms of the effects on real GDP, balance of trade and government revenue.

In the short term, since capital stock is fixed, changes in output prices and production levels affect the rental value of capital stock in all industries. While changes in output prices (from the demand-side) relative to the cost of primary factors determine demand for labour. Labour wages and the levels of employment in various industries then depend on the labour market conditions and labour intensities in these industries. Hence, the households' income changes with changes in returns to primary factors.

Indirect taxes and surpluses from the public corporations are the major sources of government income. Changes in energy prices affect the surpluses of public corporations and government departments related to the energy sector. Changes in the prices of and demands for non-energy commodities also affect government revenue from indirect taxes on these commodities. On the other hand, the government expenditures are also affected due to the changes in the prices. All these elements determine the overall budget deficit. The revenue implications of changing energy prices, therefore, should be analysed taking into account all these linkages.

Since, the demands for exports and imports are determined by the relative prices of domestic and imported goods, any change in the domestic prices and demands affect the trade balance. Management of the trade deficit is one of the major tasks of the government, and the effects of changing energy prices on the foreign trade of the economy should be analysed.

Turning to the equity objective, the cost of the commodity bundle of the poorer section of society is one of the major considerations in the regulated pricing policy in Pakistan and many other developing countries. As pointed out earlier, changes in energy prices affect factor incomes in a complicated way. Changes in household incomes along with changes in commodity prices affect real consumption of households. This aspect ought to be analysed carefully for any purposeful evaluation of energy pricing policy.

The discussion so far shows that the energy pricing issues cannot be looked at in isolation. A general equilibrium model which considers the immense complexity of the linkages of the economy is required.

Furthermore, the regulated energy prices have multiple announced objectives, hence, any reform or proposed changes in energy prices should be analysed considering their effects on all these objectives. A general equilibrium analysis allows us to simultaneously examine, in a consistent framework, all the effects of any reform in energy prices on these objectives.

1.2　Survey of developments in CGE models

This section briefly surveys CGE models in general and energy models in particular. CGE modelling is a growing and vibrant area of applied economics. The objective here is not to provide a comprehensive discussion of a model of a particular type, but to introduce various types of CGE models. Neither will a comprehensive bibliography be provided, but rather only citations of illustrative works. The focus here is on CGE models of the 'neo-classical' type. We divide this section into two parts. In subsection 1.2.1, we discuss distinctive approaches to applied general equilibrium modelling, and introduce the CGE model developed for Pakistan in this book. We list the main features of the model to show its commonality with the approaches discussed for CGE modelling. In subsection 1.2.2, we give a brief survey of general equilibrium approaches to energy policy modelling, fitting our own model into a wider perspective.

1.2.1　Approaches in general equilibrium modelling

In a recent survey, Bergman (1990a) has reviewed developments in CGE modelling. Bergman's survey identifies four main branches of CGE models on the basis of their main characteristics and uses. In the following paragraphs, we briefly discuss these four major approaches.

Johansen's Multi Sectoral Growth (MSG) model (1960) is essentially a model of the sectoral allocation of capital and labour as well as of the distribution of sectoral output between uses. Models using the Johansen approach originate largely from the literature on economic planning and input-output analysis. The two branches of CGE models originating from Johansen's MSG model are: (i) ORANI and its various versions, and (ii) CGE models for developing countries focusing mainly on income distribution issues. Models in Adelman and Robinson's study (1978) and Dervis, de Melo and Robinson's work (1982) are examples of the latter branch of the CGE models.

Harberger-Scarf-Shoven-Whalley (HSSW) models have their roots in applied welfare economics. Bergman has pointed out three differences between models from this category and MSG/ORANI models. The first difference is in the level of disaggregation of the household sector. A typical model in the HSSW approach explicitly incorporates two or more types of households, specification of their initial endowments and determination of their budget constraints. The second difference is related to the application type for which the models are intended. The HSSW

6

models are to a large extent aimed at evaluating policy changes in terms of both efficiency and income distribution effects. Moreover, these effects are usually expressed in terms of a one-dimensional welfare measure such as the Hicksian compensating or equivalent variation. The third major difference is related to the way in which Walrasian general equilibrium theory is incorporated in the model. The MSG/ORANI models incorporate some features of the real world which makes them deviate, in the strict sense, from Walrasian general equilibrium theory, while the HSSW models can be regarded, to a large extent, as numerical counterparts of Walrasian general equilibrium model. An example of a large-scale application of this type of model is Piggott and Whalley's study (1977) on the tax and subsidy system of the UK. Owing to the disaggregation of the household sector (100 types of households), the authors were able to elucidate the income distribution effects of a series of hypothetical tax changes.

The third approach to CGE modelling is the econometric estimation approach applied by Jorgenson (1982). The fourth approach is due to Ginsburgh and Waelbroeck (1981) and can be characterised as an extension of activity analysis and linear programming modelling.

An introduction to GE-PAK   The **G**eneral **E**quilibrium model for **Pak**istan developed in this book (from now on called GE-PAK) belongs to the class of MSG/ORANI models, and is in the spirit of ORANI — a CGE model of the Australian economy (see Dixon, Parmenter, Sutton and Vincent, 1982). Nevertheless, it also incorporates some features of the models from the HSSW category. In the following paragraphs, we briefly describe the main features of GE-PAK and its application in this book to identify its commonality with CGE models in other categories. The model is static and its main features are as follows:

1. Multiple-output industries and multiple-industry commodities.
2. Multiple household types.
3. Income mapping equations for multiple households and three types of other institutions: corporations, government and the rest of the world.
4. Disaggregation of the labour market into urban and rural regions and an inter-region labour migration function.
5. Various types of indirect tax variables including the discriminating taxes which are user- and commodity-specific, and implicit taxes on commodities with the regulated prices.
6. Multi-level production structures.
7. Five types of production structures that incorporate factor-energy and inter-energy-product substitutions.
8. A two-level nested electricity supply structure.
9. A social welfare index which is used to compute the elasticity of the social welfare cost with respect to indirect tax revenues generated by increasing the tax rate a commodity.

In this book, GE-PAK has been applied to analyse the income distributional effects of some hypothetical reforms in energy prices, as well as the efficiency gain, on the aggregate, and the effects on the sectoral composition. Thus, GE-PAK shares many distinguished features of other CGE models as well as of ORANI.

1.2.2 General equilibrium approaches in energy policy modelling

In this subsection, we give an overview of GE approaches in energy policy modelling. This review is based on two surveys. Bergman (1988) made a survey of development in energy-economy models based essentially on general equilibrium theory and the neo-classical theory of economic growth. This survey covers energy-economy models for developed countries. Devarajan (1988) surveyed the applications of CGE models addressing the issues related to depletion of natural resources and to taxation in developing countries. In this subsection, we present findings from the two surveys, and comment on the significance of GE-PAK and its application in this book.

Bergman (1988) has identified three categories of numerical models developed to address energy policy issues.

1. Optimisation models: These models have been used for investment and operation planning by firms in the petroleum and electricity sectors.
2. Energy-System Models: These models treat the entire energy sector as an integrated system. Nordhaus (1974) and IEA's MARKAL (see Marcuse, Bodin, Cherniavsky and Sanborn; 1976) are examples of energy-system models. Bergman has classified these models as simple partial equilibrium models; usually specified as linear programming models. For an exogenously given vector of final demands for 'useful energy', an energy-system model determines the cost-minimising patterns of extraction, conversion and distribution for energy resources. Bergman has stated that these models have two weaknesses despite their quite detailed treatment of the energy system. The economic determinants of the demand for 'useful energy' and the mutual inter-dependence of the energy system and the rest of the economy are essentially neglected in these models. Thus, these models have little to say about the impact of changes in the energy supply conditions or domestic energy policies on relative prices and the allocation of resources in an economy.
3. Energy-Economy models: These models are based on general equilibrium theory and the neo-classical theory of economic growth. Much of the public concern on energy issues is related to the possible impact of changing the energy supply conditions on broadly defined welfare measures. Accordingly, these models provide information about how relative product and factor prices and allocation of resources might be affected by increasing energy costs, by the technological change in the energy sector, or by various energy policy measures. Bergman has reviewed a set of energy-economy models within the CGE tradition. These models are grouped into two categories: (a) models with

specific approaches to energy demand within a CGE framework, and (b) models with a more elaborate treatment of energy supply. Bergman has identified four models in the first category: (i) Hudson-Jorgenson's model (1975) of the US economy; (ii) the MSG-4 model of the Norwegian economy (Longva, Lorentsen and Olsen, 1985); (iii) a CGE model of the Swedish economy (Bergman, 1978); and (iv) the ELIAS model (Bergman, 1986). In the second category, Bergman has discussed the ETA-Macro model (Manne, 1977) which incorporates an elaborate treatment of energy supply technologies in a CGE model. In this model an activity or process analysis model of the energy sector is integrated with a model of the rest of the economy. According to Bergman, the integrated models presented by Jorgenson (1982) and Lundgren (1985) are variant of the same approach. Lundgren's model is an elaborated version of the ELIAS model except that the neo-classical production function of the electricity sector in the ELIAS model is replaced by a linear activity model of that sector. Most of these models have been applied to analyse the long-term impact of changes in the energy supply conditions. For example, the CGE model of Sweden has been applied to elucidate the impact on the Swedish economy of a zero-energy-growth strategy (Bergman, 1978). The study used aggregate real consumption as a rough measure of welfare. The Hudson-Jorgenson model (1975) was applied both for projection and policy analysis. Bergman, Jorgenson and Zalai (1990a) has reported this application's results showing the impact of a strategy aimed at eliminating US energy imports in ten years time. Overall, the results of the two studies showed changes in energy supply and consumption patterns without much contraction in the aggregate economic growth.

According to Bergman, the structure of CGE models intended for the analysis of energy policy need not to differ much from CGE models in general. Nevertheless, the representation of the substitutability of different inputs has to be more elaborate in the energy-economy models of the GE type.

Bergman has asserted that such CGE models are useful for two reasons. (1) These models have the capability to test the GDP growth and energy consumption relation. The notion of a generally constant relation between energy consumption and GDP growth cannot be justified by basic economic theory; indeed it can be rejected on empirical grounds through CGE applications. (2) A CGE model has the capability to show the mechanisms through which a change in the energy policy affects the economy; *i.e.*, it provides a rather detailed picture elucidating the working of a number of substitution mechanisms in the economy.

Devarajan also surveyed CGE models related to the energy sector (1988). Similar to the models discussed by Bergman (1988), these models were applied to explicate the energy-economy relation. However, Devarajan focused on the models for developing countries and grouped them according to their application for issues related to natural resources and taxation. The applications of the CGE models to analyse the issues of natural resources were put into three categories: (1) energy management models that highlight the role of natural resources as inputs into the production processes; (2) Dutch-disease models that capture the effects of the windfall that accrues to exporters when the price of oil rises; and (3) optimal-depletion models that take into account the exhaustibility of energy resources and the link between optimal extraction and investment decisions. Devarajan classified CGE applications for taxation into two groups: (1) positive analysis, which sheds light on the link between fiscal and trade policies and the impact on prices and incomes of a change in the tax rates; (2) normative analysis, which computes the 'optimal taxes' in revenue-constrained economies. These 'optimal-taxes' are found to be at variance with proposals for tax reforms that are based on rule of thumb.

Examples of energy-management models of developing countries include those of Blitzer and Eckaus (1983a, 1983b and 1985), Blitzer (1984 and 1986), de Lucia and Jacoby (1982) and Hughes (1986a, 1986b). These and other energy management models were surveyed by Kim (1986). Another use of these models is for determination of domestic fuel prices. Hughes (1986a, 1986b) and Dixit and Newbery (1984) illustrate how the 'optimal' domestic price need not to be the fuel-equivalent world price because of the second-best consideration. According to their results, if there are other distortions in the economy, the optimal domestic fuel price may involve a tax or subsidy to compensate for these other distortions.

Devarajan (1988) has identified two weaknesses of these energy-management models. First, contrary to the detailed treatment these models give to the energy sector, they treat the rest of the economy in a fairly coarse fashion. The feedback effects between the rest of the economy and the energy sector are either missing or rather weak. For example, these models suggest that income in the non-energy and energy sectors affects the demand for energy but do not consider the effect of energy prices on the income. Most of the models do not distinguish between the government's and the private sector's budget constraints. Thus, the effects of variation in tax revenues (often associated with the changes in energy price) are not captured. The second weakness of these models is that they generally have little connection with the theory of international trade. A large number of models assume that the economy is closed to foreign trade at the margin. In some models the economy is 'semi-open' as some imported energy sources compete, albeit imperfectly, with domestic sources. Even so, these models do not capture the implications of the trade deficit on the economy (through appreciation of the real exchange rate).

Examples of Dutch-disease models are the models developed by Corden and Neary (1982), and Benjamin, Devarajan and Weiner (1989). These models provide a useful and interesting picture of what will happen to an economy in response to a boom in its natural resources. But they do not by themselves provide much insight into the types of policies that a government should pursue.

Optimal-depletion models are essentially inter-temporal Dutch-disease models. The oil depletion problem would be independent of the rest of the economy if the capital markets were perfect. Assuming capital markets are not perfect, these models tie the depletion question with the economy's borrowing and investment strategies. Devarajan discussed the application of such a model by Martin and Wijnbergen

(1986). These models are powerful tools to simultaneously discuss a country's resource depletion, foreign borrowing, and investment strategies. According to Devarajan, however, these models hit computational constraints, requiring the model builders to keep the intra-temporal aspect of the model rather simple. Most of these models, therefore, have no more than two or three sectors.

As pointed out by Devarajan (1988), the issues of taxation in developing countries are different from that of the developed countries for three reasons. (1) Limited administrative capacity prevents most developing countries from instituting a consumption tax, or even a viable income tax. Indirect taxes, therefore, are the more commonly used instruments. The assumption frequently made in exercises with models for developed countries, that the tax revenues are rebated in a lump-sum fashion, can no longer be made. After all, if the government has access to lump-sum transfers, it should also be able to levy lump-sum taxes. Hence, the revenue implications of a tax reform become crucial. (2) The effects of a tax change on the distribution of income are clearly important for developing countries. (3) Since most developing countries are open economies, the impact of a tax reform on foreign trade deserves attention. According to Devarajan, only recently have CGE models of developing countries looked at all aspects of a tax reform — namely, the welfare, revenue, equity and foreign trade implications.

The method of examining tax questions with CGE models can be described as either positive or normative. The former simply asks 'what if' questions; the latter attempts to derive optimal taxes for a given economy. For the first category, Devarajan has discussed two models; Devarajan and de Melo (1987) and Bovenberg (1978). Normative models can be viewed as positive models with an objective function; the 'optimal tax' is defined in terms of the objective function. For example, Diamond and Mirrlees (1971) used the utility of consumption in their objective function. It is well-known that the lump-sum taxes are the least distorting, but, as mentioned, they are almost impossible to administer. Diamond and Mirrlees (1971) have shown that without the lump-sum taxes the second best instrument is consumer tax. In many developing countries, however, even consumer taxes are difficult to administer. In this case, a whole array of indirect taxes (producer taxes, export taxes and import tariffs) has to be used. Devarajan has pointed out two problems with the normative models. The first is of making inter-personal utility comparisons. The second is that such models attempt to impose a huge tax on investment goods if utility function includes only current consumption. The second problem can be solved by either imposing a constraint on the taxation of investment goods or by including future consumption as an argument in the objective function. Dahl, Devarajan, and Wijnbergen (1986) adopted the former solution to compute the 'third-best' optimal taxes using a CGE model for Cameroon.

Significance of GE-PAK   In the light of this survey, GE-PAK stands out as an energy, economy and equity interaction model that overcomes many of the weaknesses of the previous energy-economy interaction models for developing countries. In GE-PAK, the energy sector is treated in detail focusing on the demand

11

and supply pattern of petroleum products, electricity and natural gas. On the supply side, there are two multiple-output energy industries (oil and gas and refinery), four electricity industries; each representing a type of electricity technology and a coal industry. On the demand side, the model incorporates various types of production structures that allow substitution between energy and primary factors of production and between energy products.

In this book, we have analysed energy pricing policy in Pakistan using GE-PAK. As stated by Bergman, the usefulness of the energy GE model is its capability to show the mechanisms through which a change in the energy policy affects the economy. In our analysis, for example, the model enables us to trace the factors which affect real consumption of 14 types of households for various hypothetical reforms in the energy prices. The model gives detail information about the effects on various components of nominal income, consumption patterns and the Consumer Price Index (CPI) for each household type separately.

GE-PAK treats all the sectors of the economy in detail. It includes 128 industries and 14 types of households. The model allows imperfect substitution between domestic and imported commodities, and incorporates the upward-sloping export supply curves for the major exports. Thus, in GE-PAK, any change in domestic policy or in the world market affects relative commodity and factor prices and has full feedback effects on both household income and expenditure. In this book, we apply GE-PAK to simulate the effects of some hypothetical reforms in source-, commodity-, and user-discriminating taxes on energy products in Pakistan.

In our study on the energy pricing policy, we examine the taxes on energy products in a positive fashion. We analyse the economy-wide effects of any change in the energy taxes focusing particularly on variables which are related to the government's multiple objectives. Our analysis simply asks the question "Does the energy pricing policy serve its claimed objectives?".

1.3   Introduction to the book

This book aims at giving its readers:

1.   An appreciation of how a CGE model is formulated, solved and applied through building a CGE model for Pakistan.
2.   A concise description of the CGE model of energy, economy and equity interactions in Pakistan.
3.   A case study on energy pricing policy in Pakistan.

In Chapter 2, we review energy pricing policy in Pakistan and analyse historical growth rates of the regulated energy prices during 1971-95. To apply GE-PAK for analysing the energy pricing policy, we choose 1983-84 as the base year. We estimate implicit and explicit taxes on energy prices in the base year, and discuss differences in these tax rates across energy products and consumer categories. Since

12

the objectives of setting energy prices and taxes are not stated precisely by the government, this review helps us to infer these objectives. We formulate scenarios of reforms in the energy prices based on these distortions in the tax structure.

In Chapter 3, we review some of the studies conducted for Pakistan on the issues of energy pricing in a general equilibrium framework, as well as some energy-economy models of developing countries. This review is divided into two parts. In the first part, we present three studies done for Pakistan on energy pricing issues using three types of models. In the second part, we present the main features of some energy-economy interaction models of developing countries which are related to our own study.

In Chapter 4, we present the theoretical structure of GE-PAK, and discuss in detail the equations of the model. The model's equations are divided into 30 blocks, and a section is devoted to each block of equations. We reproduce these blocks of equations in Appendix A for a ready reference. In the model, there are six sets of equations which describe six types of production structures; each corresponding to a set of industries.

In Chapter 5 we discuss the data base of our model and the values of its parameters. Dhanani (1986) developed a Social Accounting Matrix (SAM) for Pakistan for 1983-84. We have modified and expanded it into a data base which is appropriate for our model. In the first part of Chapter 5, we briefly discuss the SAM, and then discuss our modifications in detail. A set of diagrams shows the layout of our data base and the links between various parts of it. In the second part of Chapter 5, we list the parameters of our model and the values assigned to them. We present a brief survey of the literature from which these values have been taken.

For our case study, we constructed scenarios of hypothetical reforms in energy taxes estimated in Chapter 2, and simulated these reforms using GE-PAK. In Chapter 6, we present and interpret these simulation results. Altogether, we conducted 21 experiments to simulate the effects of removing source-, product- and user-discriminating taxes on petroleum products, electricity and natural gas. Conversely, the simulation results indicate the role of these discriminatory taxes in achieving the claimed objectives of the energy pricing policy. In the first section of this chapter, we discuss the short-run closure of the model; this determines the macro economic environment of our experiments.

In the final chapter, we summarise the major findings of the case study on the energy pricing policy, discuss other possible applications of the model, summarise the limitations, and suggest directions for future research.

13

2 Energy pricing policy in Pakistan

2.1 Introduction

The objective of this chapter is to review the energy pricing policy[1] in Pakistan. The prices of three major commercial energy products are regulated by the government. As stated in the *Government Sponsored Corporations* report (GOP, 1985a):

> Active state intervention in the allocation of economic resources is justified by its protagonists on both grounds of efficiency and equity. It is argued that the efficiency of free market forces, which is generated by the pursuit of private interests, is limited by the extent to which private and social interests coincide. Certain economic activities, by their very nature, are characterised by a substantial divergence between private and social interests, commonly described in economic literature as 'externalities'. State intervention in these activities is, therefore, necessary to allow for these external costs and benefits and thereby achieving greater economic efficiency. The equity argument is based on the assumed obligation of the state to assure a certain minimum level of basic consumption for all sections of society. State intervention in critical sectors such as food and petroleum products is therefore necessary to assure stable prices and adequate *per capita* production and consumption.

Thus, the stability of prices and satisfaction of basic needs of all sections of the society are the two motives behind regulation of prices of certain commodities which include energy products. According to the report (GOP, 1985a), formulae for setting producers' prices of energy products are established by consultation between the corporations concerned and their controlling Ministries. There is no policy document which precisely states formulae for and the objectives/motives behind setting of price of each energy product at various stages. Nevertheless, it has been occasionally realised that the regulated prices need to be 'rationalised' (see GOP, 1992b, 1994a, 1994b, 1996b). The objectives of a rational and equitable energy

15

pricing policy have been generally put as (Bahatia, 1984; Munasinghe, 1985; de Lucia and Lesser, 1985; Webb, 1978):

1. Promoting economically efficient allocation of resources both within the energy sector and between it and the rest of the economy.
2. Enabling the utilities to generate sufficient surplus funds to finance their future investment requirements.
3. Reflecting the costs of energy supplies to different categories of customers in the corresponding consumer prices to reduce wastage.
4. Inducing the most efficient utilisation of available energy resources.
5. Providing a certain minimum level of energy to all citizens at prices affordable by the poorest.
6. Encouraging inter-fuel substitutions to achieve desired objectives such as conservation of certain fuels.
7. Increasing energy efficiencies to encounter environmental degradation and climate change.

In this chapter, we examine energy prices in Pakistan to infer the relative weights placed on these different objectives. In our analysis, we examine the historical growth rates of the regulated energy prices during 1971-95 and calculate sales and import taxes on these products for the base year of this study.

Our analysis encompasses the regulated prices of natural gas, electricity and five petroleum products namely— kerosene, High Speed Diesel (HSD), Light Diesel Oil (LDO), gasoline, and Furnace Oil (FO). GE-PAK recognises six types of petroleum products including the above mentioned products and aviation fuel. Owing to lack of data on the price of aviation fuel, our review in this chapter is confined to the first five petroleum products.

The Pakistani government discriminates between various types of consumer groups in setting prices of natural gas and electricity. There have been wide differences in natural gas prices charged to the household, manufacturing and services sectors. Similarly, electricity prices have been different for the household, manufacturing, agriculture and services sectors. We examine, therefore, altogether twelve energy prices: prices of five petroleum products, natural gas prices for three types of consumer groups and electricity prices for four consumer categories.

In section 2.2, we analyse growth rates of the regulated energy prices for the period from 1971-72 to 1994-95. In section 2.3, we describe the pricing mechanism of energy prices and compute the implicit and explicit *ad valorem* sales tax (subsidy) rates on the twelve energy products in the base year.

2.2   Historical growth rates of energy prices 1971-95

In this section, first, we analyse the average growth rates in nominal prices of petroleum products, electricity and natural gas, and then discuss these growth rates in real terms. As shown in table 2.1, petroleum product prices grew by 11 to 13 per cent *per annum* in the period from 1971 to 1995. Among these products, kerosene experienced the most rapid growth in its nominal price, at 13 per cent *per annum*, while the price of HSD grew at an average rate of 11 per cent *per annum*. The major increase in these prices occurred in the late 1970s when world oil prices increased rapidly. Since the late 1980s, the decline in world oil prices have been partly passed on to the consumers.

Table 2.1
Average growth rates of energy prices in Pakistan 1971-95
(in nominal terms)

Prices, CPI & GDP deflator	Average growth rate (per cent *per annum*)
Petroleum products	
Kerosene	12.52
High speed diesel	10.67
Light diesel oil	11.97
Gasoline	11.53
Furnace oil	11.86
Electricity price by consumer categories[a]	
Households	7.3
Agriculture	11.3
Manufacturing	14.4
Services	13.0
Nat. Gas price by consumer categories	
Households	8.93
Manufacturing[b]	13.69
Services	10.93
CPI	9.80
GDP deflator	9.90

a Including all taxes
b Excluding cement, fertiliser and electricity industries

Source: GOP (1989a), GOP (1996a, 1996b), WAPDA (1996).

The structure of electricity tariff has been changed many times during the last 25 years. At present, there are four components of electricity tariff: (i) fixed/minimum capacity charge, (ii) electricity charges, (iii) fuel adjustment surcharge (FAS) and (iv) additional surcharge (AS). Till June 1980, only the first two components were charged. The electricity utilities started charging FAS in 1980 to cover the seasonal changes in fuel costs. These changes are attributed to the decline in hydro power generation and the increase in the peak demand in certain months of the year. The FAS was initially levied on the manufacturing and commercial sectors, and later was extended to the household and agriculture sectors. Since 1993, the AS has been levied on all consumer categories to generate revenues for the government. To analyse the historical growth rate of electricity price, we use 'average sale price' data which is based on revenues collected per kWh of electricity sold inclusive of FAS and AS. Table 2.1 reports these prices.

The average growth rate of electricity prices for the four consumers categories ranged between 7 and 14 per cent *per annum* during 1971-95. The sectors carrying the biggest electricity price increases were manufacturing (14 per cent *per annum*) and services (13 per cent *per annum*). The household sector enjoyed the lowest price increase *i.e.* 7 per cent *per annum growth*; which is only half of the growth rate in electricity prices for the manufacturing and services sectors. The second-lowest growth was in the price of electricity for the agriculture sector; which was 2 to 3 percentage points lower than the growth in electricity prices for the services and manufacturing sectors. Hence, we observe (see table 2.1) the large differences in the growth rates of electricity prices for different consumer categories as compared to the fairly even price increases for petroleum products.

There are similar deviations in the growth rates of natural gas prices. They grew in the range of 9 to 14 per cent *per annum* during 1971-95. As shown in table 2.1, the highest growth rate was in the price for the manufacturing sector (14 per cent). The price for the services sector grew by 11 per cent *per annum* as compared to the price for the households sector which grew by only 9 per cent *per annum*.

Between 1971-72 and 1994-95, the CPI and GDP deflator grew at the rate of about 10 per cent *per annum*. Hence, all energy prices increased in real terms except natural gas and electricity prices for the household sector, and electricity price for the agriculture sector.

Table 2.2 shows the major users of each petroleum product. FO is consumed mainly in the manufacturing sector and kerosene in the household sector. The major consumer of HSD is the public transport industry, while gasoline is mainly used by the household and services sectors for private transport. LDO is mainly used in the agriculture sector for ground water pumping and in some small-scale manufacturing industries.

Table 2.2
Major users of petroleum products

Petroleum products	Major users
Kerosene	Household sector (for cooking and lighting)
High speed diesel	Transport sector
Light diesel oil	Agriculture sector
Gasoline	Household sector (for private transport)
Furnace oil	Manufacturing sector (including electricity industries)

Source: Khan (1986), GOP (1996b).

Fig. 2.1 shows the *per annum* growth rates of real prices of energy products between 1971-72 and 1994-95 for the four major user groups. During this period real prices of electricity for the household sector declined sharply, and there was a small decline in real price of natural gas for them. Kerosene prices to households increased in real terms.

For the agriculture sector, there was an increase in real prices of both types of diesel and electricity, but the increase in the price of electricity is much lower than that for the manufacturing and services sectors.

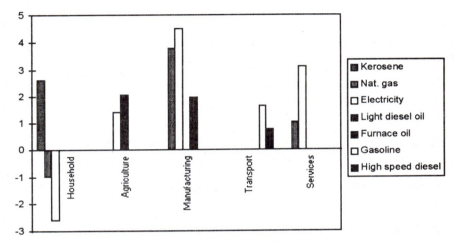

**Figure 2.1   Growth rates in real energy prices 1971-95
(per cent *per annum*)**

Source: Based on table 2.1.

For the manufacturing sector all energy prices increased in real term with the biggest increase in real price of electricity for it. It is noteworthy that real price of natural gas for this sector increased more rapidly than that of FO. Prices of both HSD and gasoline, used in public and private transport, increased by 1 to 2 per cent *per annum* in real term.

Energy prices have undergone considerable changes during 1971-1995. These changes were partly induced by changes in world oil prices and partly by the government policy. For example, rapid growth rates in petroleum product prices in Pakistan during the 1970s were the result of the increases in world oil prices. But during the oil crisis period, the regulated natural gas price for the manufacturing sector was kept constant in real term to protect industries from high energy cost resulting from the rapid increase in real price of FO. As world oil prices started declining from the mid 1980s, this trend was reversed to increase the price of natural gas more rapidly than that of FO during the 1980s.

19

Summary Our analysis of energy prices during 1970-1995 shows that:

1. Real electricity prices declined significantly for the household sector and increased rapidly for the manufacturing and services sectors during this period.
2. real price of natural gas declined for the household sector and increased significantly for the manufacturing sector.
3. Over the same period, petroleum product prices increased more rapidly for the manufacturing and household sectors than that for the transport and agriculture sectors.

2.3 Implicit and explicit taxes on energy products in the base-year

In this section we compute the implicit and explicit tax rates on petroleum products, natural gas, and electricity, and discuss the differences between these rates.

2.3.1 Taxes on petroleum products

In Pakistan, both public and private companies are involved in refining crude oil and the marketing of petroleum products. These companies work under the direct supervision of the government. The government regulates their profit margins and sets prices of petroleum products at various stages. So it is impossible to know the taxes (or subsidies) by only looking at the explicit tax rates on petroleum products. In this section, we compute the magnitude of the 'effective' taxes on petroleum products in 1983-84 which include both explicit and implicit taxes.

The regulated prices of petroleum products in Pakistan have five components: (i) ex-refinery price; (ii) excise/custom duty; (iii) trade margins; (iv) transport margin; and (v) development surcharge. Table 2.3 gives the price structure of petroleum products in 1983-84 showing these components.

The 'ex-refinery' prices are the prices at which the refineries sell their products to the marketing companies. The excise and custom duties are sales[2] taxes levied at the same rate on domestic and imported petroleum products. The government fixes the ex-refinery prices, tax rates, trade margins and transport margin on all petroleum products as well as their sale prices. The sum of the ex-refinery price, taxes and the two trade margins (i.e. distribution margin and dealers' commission) is called the 'prescribed' price.

The difference between the fixed sale price of a petroleum product and the cost of supply (prescribed price plus transport margin) is called the 'development surcharge' which is the tax (subsidy) collected (paid) through the marketing companies. As mentioned, the government regulates return on capital in the refinery industry to protect consumers from the 'monopoly' price. To keep the prices stable, the fixed sale prices are kept at a certain level, and are changed occasionally. But the various components of the regulated prices are revised individually from time to time due to

Table 2.3
Price structure of petroleum products in 1983-84 (Rs / litre)

Petroleum products	(1) Ex-refinery price	(2) Custom /excise duty	(3) Distribu- tion margin	(4) Dealer commi- ssion	(5) Pres- cribed price 1+2+3+4	(6) Inland freight margin	(7) = 8-5-6 Develop- ment surcharg	(8) Fixed sale price
Kerosene	2.44	0.00	0.05	0.00	2.49	0.24	0.02	2.75
HSD	2.97	0.25	0.03	0.03	3.29	0.28	0.43	4.00
LDO	2.41	0.04	0.04	0.00	2.49	0.21	0.05	2.75
Gasoline	4.64	0.88	0.07	0.05	5.66	0.29	0.05	6.00
FO[a]	1355.00	35.20	16.80	0.00	1407.10	308.30	4.60	720.00

a Rs per metric tonne

Source: GOP (1989).

changes in the domestic and international markets. The government uses the 'development surcharge' as an instrument to stabilise prices of petroleum products. Fluctuation in any component of the regulated petroleum products prices is offset by the change in the 'development surcharge' while the sale price remains unchanged. The 'development surcharge' is an implicit tax, and its rate fluctuates with changes in the costs of production, distribution and transportation for petroleum products.

The data on the long-run marginal production cost of petroleum products or the criteria for setting the ex-refinery prices are not available. According to a report on the government sponsored corporations (GOP, 1985a), the ex-refinery prices of petroleum products have been set on the basis of an overall 18 per cent rate of return on paid-up capital in the refinery industry. However, the report does not give criteria or formula for the price-setting for each product. Hence, we can not compute the difference between the actual marginal cost of production and the set ex-refinery price of each petroleum product.

From the structure of prices given in table 2.3, we compute the 'effective rates' for two types of *ad valorem* taxes on the five petroleum products: (i) import tax and (ii) product-discriminating sales tax.

Import tax on petroleum products The custom/excise duty shown in table 2.3 is uniformly levied on both imported and domestic products, so as such no import taxes are levied. However, there is a difference between the fixed ex-refinery price of a petroleum product and its border price, defined as the Cost, Insurance and Freight (CIF) value of imports in domestic currency. We convert the average CIF values of petroleum products in 1983-84, given in US dollars, into domestic currency prices at the official exchange rate of 1983-84 to arrive at the border prices of petroleum products. Columns 1 and 2 in table 2.4 report these values for four petroleum products, while column 3 shows the imported *ad valorem* tax rates on these products corresponding to these border prices.

Table 2.4
Implicit taxes on petroleum products in Pakistan 1983-84

Petroleum product	Ex-refinery price Rs /litre	CIF Rs /litre	*Ad valorem* import tax rate (per cent)
Kerosene	2.44	2.95	-17.0
High speed diesel	2.97	2.80	6.0
Gasoline	4.64	2.98	56.0
Furnace oil[a]	1355.00	2494.00	-46.0

a Rs per metric tonne

Source: GOP (1989).

Table 2.4 shows that there was import tax on two petroleum products, while the other two petroleum products had import subsidies. Gasoline, mainly used in private transport, had the highest import tax rate of 56 per cent, while HSD, used in public transport, had a 6 per cent import tax. Implicit import subsidies on kerosene and furnace oil were 17 per cent and 46 per cent, respectively.

Product-discriminating There are three cost-components of the purchasers' price of each petroleum product: production costs, *i.e.* ex-refinery price; trade margins and inland transport cost (see table 2.3). Since these components are set by the government, any difference between the actual value and the fixed value determines the 'effective' tax rate on a product. In this section, we first determine the actual values of these components for each product, and aggregate them to derive the actual supply cost of each product. Corresponding to these costs, the effective tax rates are computed.

Since data on marginal production costs of the petroleum products are not available, their ex-refinery prices are assumed to be their actual production costs. For the trade margins also, no data on the actual costs are available. But we notice that the trade margins fixed by the government are not uniform for the five products (see columns 3 and 4 of table 2.3). We take the average of these margins as the actual trade margin cost for all the five products (see column 2 of table 2.5).

Until 1991 the inland transport margin on each petroleum product was set by the government. The marketing companies were compensated for the difference between the actual transport cost of the products and that under the prescribed rate. In her study on petroleum product prices in Pakistan, Kuijper (1982) has given actual transport cost for each product in 1978-79. Since data on actual transport cost in 1983-84 are not available, the 1978-79 costs are inflated at the growth rate of the GDP deflator to estimate the 1983-84 transport costs for petroleum products. Column 3 in table 2.5 reports our estimates.

Table 2.5
Implicit *ad valorem* sales tax rates on petroleum products in 1983-84

Petroleum product	(1) Ex-refinery price Rs/litre	(2) Estimated trade margins Rs/litre	(3) Inland freight margin Rs/litre	(4) = (1)+(2)+(3) Actual cost Rs/litre	(5) Fixed sale price Rs/litre	(6) *Ad valorem* sales tax rate (per cent)
Kerosene	2.44	0.06	0.28	2.78	2.75	- 1.0
HSD	2.97	0.06	0.33	3.36	4.00	19.0
LDO	2.41	0.06	0.31	2.78	2.75	- 1.0
Gasoline	4.64	0.06	0.17	4.87	6.00	23.0
FO[a]	1355.00	63.90[3]	346.75	1765.65	1720.0	- 3.0

a Rs per metric tonne

Source: GOP (1989).

Comparison of columns 4 and 5 shows that the fixed sale prices for kerosene, LDO and FO were lower than the cost of supply. For other products, the opposite was the case. Column 6 shows that there were subsidies on three products of 1 to 3 per cent, and sales taxes of 19 and 23 per cent on two products. This pattern of taxes is very similar to that of source-discriminating taxes (see table 2.4), except in two respects. First, the subsidy rates of sales taxes are much smaller than those for source-discriminating taxes. Second, the difference in sales tax rates for HSD and gasoline is very small contrary to the wide difference (50 percentage point) in source-discriminating taxes on these two products.

Summary The analysis of the price structure of petroleum products of 1983-84 shows that besides explicit sales tax rates, there were implicit taxes on them. Furthermore, the effective rates of sales taxes were different from those given explicitly in the price structure. Table 2.6 reports our estimates of these effective source- and commodity-discriminating taxes on petroleum products.

The tax structure described in table 2.6 suggests objectives of the regulated pricing policy for petroleum products in Pakistan as follows:

1. Since kerosene is a fuel for the low-income urban households and a fuel for lighting for non-electrified households, the subsidy on it aims to balance out the inequalities in the income distribution.
2. Since FO is used mainly in the manufacturing sector, its price is kept as low as possible to boost the manufacturing activities.
3. HSD is used for public transport and in the agriculture sector, so there is a tax on it to protect the masses, while the tax on gasoline is significantly high as it is used for private transport by the high income group.

23

Table 2.6
Ad valorem tax rates on petroleum products in 1983-84

Petroleum product	(1) *Ad valorem* import tax rate (per cent)	(2) *Ad valorem* sales tax rate[a] (per cent)
Kerosene	-17.0	-1.0
High speed diesel	6.0	19.0
Light diesel oil	0.0	-1.0
Gasoline	56.0	23.0
Furnace oil	-54.0	-3.0

a   These tax rates are levied on both imported and domestically produced petroleum products

Source: GOP (1989).

Because the early 1980s was the period of the high world oil prices, the import tax structure suggests that gasoline and HSD are highly taxed to subsidise kerosene and furnace oil during periods of high oil import prices. Furthermore, the tax collections from petroleum products in 1983-84 was about 13 per cent of the total indirect tax revenues in Pakistan which suggests that mainly gasoline and HSD are used to generate indirect tax revenues. We also notice that, while the sales tax rates on these two products are not much different, there are wide differences in the import tax rates on them. This suggests that the tax structure is designated to discourage import of these products. The high tax rate on gasoline suggests that the price setting is motivated by the equity concern.

2.3.2   Taxes and subsidies on electricity sales by consumer categories

In this section, we compute the implicit tax (subsidy) rates on electricity sales to four major consumer categories, and discuss the differences between these rates. In Pakistan, up till now, the responsibility for generation, transmission and distribution of electricity mainly lies with two organisations: the Water and Power Development Authority (WAPDA); a fully government-owned corporation, and the Karachi Electric Supply Corporation (KESC); a public-limited company which works under the management control of WAPDA.

Since the mid 1980s the government has given various incentives to induce private sector investment in the electricity sector. As a result, the first private power plant became operational by the end of 1996. Nevertheless, electricity pricing is still regulated by the government. Guided by the private sector policy, the two power utilities are bound to purchase electricity in bulk from the private sector on the prefixed prices [see various policy documents on private power generation; GOP (1996)]. The utilities are responsible for distribution of electricity according to the

24

electricity tariff structure fixed by the government. In the tariff structure, electricity prices for different consumer categories have been fixed to allow the electricity utilities a reasonable rate of return on their capital after meeting operating costs and allowing for depreciation of assets, interest charges and taxes (see GOP, 1985a and WAPDA, 1986). The same criterion of the 'reasonable rate of return' has been adopted for the private power companies in setting the price for electricity purchase in bulk from these companies.

Because of the growing demand for investment funds in the electricity sector and on advice from the international agencies such as the World Bank and the International Monetary Fund (IMF), a criterion for electricity pricing was introduced in 1980s (WAPDA, 1986) for the public utilities. This requires that consumer prices of electricity should be set to generate sufficient revenues for meeting 40 per cent of the trio-annual investment requirement of the electricity utilities. Until now, however, electricity tariffs have not been fully adjusted to meet the 40 per cent investment criterion.

As shown in fig. 2.2, the average sale prices of electricity in 1983-84 for the households and agricultural sectors were lower than the prices for the manufacturing and services sectors.

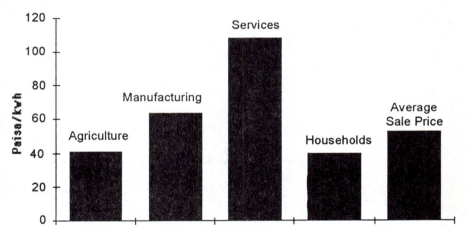

Figure 2.2   **Average sale price of electricity by consumer categories in 1983-84**

Source: WAPDA (1989).

According to the WAPDA's study (1986) on the restructuring of the electricity tariffs, the net-operating surplus of WAPDA in 1984-85 was 6.24 per cent of its capital. In the study, the rates of net-operating surplus were computed for all the consumer categories — using the incurred average cost of electricity sales to these categories and revenues generated on these sales— and it was found that these rates of return for major consumer categories varied between -5.04 per cent to 23.22 per cent. Thus, the prices of electricity for different consumer categories were not proportional to the cost of supplying electricity to these categories. The rates of net-operating surplus on electricity sales to the household and agriculture sectors were -5.4 and 1.25 per cent, respectively. This rate was 15 per cent on electricity sales to the small-scale industries as compared to the highest rate of 19 per cent on the sales to the large-scale industries.

The WAPDA's study also gives revenues by consumer categories required to ensure a uniform 6.24 per cent rate of net-operating surplus on electricity sales to all consumers categories. We compute the implicit tax rate on electricity sales to each consumer category using the required revenues and the actual revenues which are reported in columns 1 and 2 of table 2.7. The computed *ad valorem* tax rates on electricity are given in column 3 of table 2.7.

Table 2.7
Implicit *ad valorem* tax rates on electricity sales by major consumer categories in 1984-85

Consumer category	(1) Actual revenues collected (million Rs.)	(2) Revenues required for uniform rate of return (million Rs.)	(3) = (1 - 2 ÷ 2) *Ad valorem* tax rate (per cent)
Household	1578.0	2768.0	-43.0
Manufacturing sector	2121.0	1454.0	46.0
Manufacturing sector[a]	853.0	535.0	59.0
Manufacturing sector[b]	1268.0	919.0	38.0
Agriculture sector	1401.0	1836.0	-24.0
Services sector	965.0	662.0	46.0

a   Large -scale industries
b   Small-scale industries only

Source: WAPDA (1986), WAPDA (1989).

This tax structure (table 2.7) shows that there were subsidies on electricity sales to the household and agriculture sectors in 1984-85. Contrary to this, there were high implicit tax rates on electricity sales to the manufacturing and services sectors. This discrimination in favour of the household and agriculture sectors on electricity sales is similar to that observed in the tax structure for petroleum products. Since the electricity tariff in 1983-84 was very similar to that in 1984-85, we assume that the implicit tax rates were the same in the two years to formulate a scenario of reforms in electricity prices in Chapter 6.

In Pakistan, the extraction, production, transmission, and distribution of natural gas are performed by government sponsored corporations and private companies, while the government regulates natural gas prices at all stages. According to a report on the government sponsored corporations, the basic price at each level (extraction, production, transmission, and distribution) is regulated in a manner that enables these corporations to execute certain financial covenants of the government's guaranteed loans from the multi-lateral credit institutions (GOP, 1985a). There is an indirect tax on extraction of raw natural gas, but no explicit taxes on its production and marketing.

Fig. 2.3 shows natural gas sales prices by consumer categories in 1983-84. The price of natural gas for the manufacturing sector (excluding cement and fertiliser industries) was about 3 per cent above the price for the household sector and about 44 per cent below the price for the services sector.

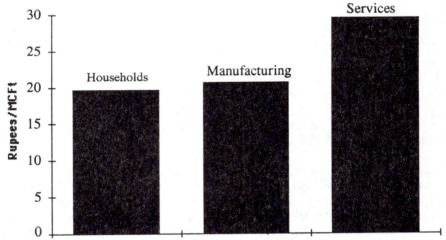

Figure 2.3   Average sale price of natural gas by consumer categories 1983-84

Source: GOP (1989).

Published data is not available on the marginal cost of natural gas sales to different consumer categories. Therefore, we calculate the *ad valorem* tax rates on natural gas sales to major consumer categories, using the weighted-average of purchasers' prices as the basic price which was Rs 18.34 per MMCFT in 1983-84. In table 2.8, column 1 shows the average purchasers' price of natural gas for four major consumer categories, while column 2 contains the *ad valorem* sales tax rates. There was a subsidy of about 23 per cent on natural gas sales to the electricity industry, while there was a high sales tax on its sales to the services sector. The tax rate on natural gas sales to the household sector was lower than the rates for the manufacturing and services sectors.

Table 2.8

***Ad valorem* tax rates on natural gas sales to major consumer categories in 1983-84**

Consumer category	(1) Average sale price Rs /MMCFT	(2) *Ad valorem* tax rate (per cent)
Household	20.0	9.0
Manufacturing[a]	20.63	12.0
Services	29.63	62.0
Electricity[b]	14.20[a]	-23.0

a Excluding electricity industries
b Calculated from data given in WAPDA (1986)

Source: GOP (1989), WAPDA (1989).

2.4 Conclusion

The basic features that emerge from our analysis of the regulated energy pricing can be summarised as follows:

1. The regulated energy prices in 1983-84 had high implicit taxes on some of the energy products and subsidies on others. The weighted-average of the tax rates on five petroleum products shows that there was no import tax on these products on aggregate contrary to the sales tax rate of 13 per cent. The household sector consistently either received subsidies or paid the lowest tax rates on energy products.
2. Energy product sales to the agriculture sector had relatively lower taxes compared to the tax rates the manufacturing and services sectors.
3. The rates of return on capital in the refining and natural gas industries have been regulated by the government. The implicit tax rates on petroleum products and natural gas have been adjusted to ensure the guaranteed rate of returns in these industries.
4. For electricity prices, the gap between the cost of supply and the regulated price affects the rate of return on capital in the electricity sector.

There are four major motives that can be inferred from our analysis in this chapter: promotion of equity, stability of energy prices, management of import of certain petroleum products, and generation of indirect tax revenues. The first two inferred objectives are in line with the announced motives of the government in regulating of prices (GOP, 1985a). Under the first objective, energy prices charged to the household sector are kept low to make energy affordable for the poorest section of society. Thus, energy is considered a necessity and its price is used to counter-balance the income disparities. Under the second objective, energy prices are fixed by the government and any change in the cost of energy supply affects either the implicit tax rate or the rate of return on capital in the sector supplying energy products. Under the third objective, there is a higher source-discriminating tax on gasoline to discourage imports. To meet the two conflicting objectives of equity promotion and revenue generation, there are user-, product- and source-discriminating taxes on energy products.

Notes

[1] Throughout this book until and unless mentioned 'price' refer to purchaser's price of a commodity.

[2] We have divided all indirect commodity taxes into two types: import tax and sales tax. Sales tax is paid on both imported and domestically produced commodities while import tax is paid on imports only. See sections 5.3.5 and 5.3.6. in Chapter 5 for further details.

[3] We convert the set trade margin on furnace oil from Rs. per tonne to Rs. per litre to add it up to other four trade margin costs. Later on we compute the Rs. per tonne rate using the average of all trade margins rates.

3 The review of literature

3.1 Introduction

The 1970s oil crisis stimulated research into modelling of energy policy and planning issues. Since then several models have been developed to analyse issues in this area in both the developed and developing countries. These models vary in their scope of analysis, objectives, analytical techniques, theoretical framework and time horizon. As pointed out by Blitzer (1986), no single model that addresses all the issues in an area can be developed for practical use. Therefore, models have been developed to focus on certain issues, depending on the severity of the problem faced in a country or a region.

The focus of energy models developed for Pakistan has mainly been on projection of energy demand and formulation of the least-cost energy supply plan to satisfy the envisaged demand. For energy demand projection, ENER Petro Tech (1979) and Riaz (1984) have developed econometric models, while IEDC (1983) and Khan (1986) have formulated engineering-simulation models. In these models, energy demand in the medium to long term have been projected for different scenarios of economic development. In the latter type of models, the underlying assumption is that energy demand is stimulated by the pace of economic growth along with changes in production technology. In addition, the trend of household to substitute non-commercial forms of energy by commercial energy products are considered to determine commercial energy demand for each fuel type. In these models, the role of energy pricing is completely ignored. In the econometric models, income and price elasticities of energy demand were estimated, using time-series data over 20 years. The two models developed for Pakistan were used to project energy demand for a scenario of future economic growth. In formulating the scenario, steady growth in energy prices is assumed with out any change in their tax structure — implying a continuation of present energy pricing policies.

There are some models that have incorporated energy-economy interaction in a non-partial equilibrium framework for Pakistan. These models are: Chern (1987);

ENERPLAN (1988); Jalal (1988). In section 3.2 we review these models and their applications. In addition to these, we review some energy management models for developing countries with reference to energy pricing issues and the modelling of energy-economy interactions. Section 3.3 gives this review.

3.2   Energy-economy interaction models for Pakistan

Chern (1987) developed a macro-econometric model for Pakistan to compute the economic effects of the increases in world oil prices between 1973 and 1983. The objective of the ENERPLAN (1988) study was to evaluate the impact of changes in energy prices on prices of non-energy commodities. The analysis was conducted using an input-output model. Jalal's study (1988) analysed the long-term impacts of alternative energy pricing policies, using a CGE model. The following subsections discuss the main features of these three models and summarise the main findings of the studies conducted using these models.

3.2.1 The input-output model for Pakistan

ENERPLAN (1988) conducted a study to find out the impact of increasing electricity prices on the prices of non-energy goods in the period 1986-2000. The study assumed that the real prices of electricity would be increased according to a proposed schedule. These proposed electricity prices were required to support the least-cost development plan for the electricity sector over the period 1987-2010 (UNDP/World Bank, 1987).

In this study, an input-output model of 83 sectors was developed. The model also identifies 11 non-produced inputs including capital, labour, land, foreign exchange rate, taxes or subsidies, profit margins, and four energy products (coal, oil, natural gas, electricity). The prices of these non-produced inputs were assumed exogenous to the system, while the price of each produced input was defined as the weighted-sum of prices of produced and non-produced inputs. Input quantities per unit of output were used as the weights. The model allows substitution between the four energy products.

The 1981 input-output table for Pakistan (Ahmed, 1985) was used in the study to compute the impact of raising electricity price in two cases. In the first case, coefficients of energy inputs were assumed to remain constant over time, while in the alternative case, these coefficients were assumed to change in response to changes in relative energy prices and production technology.

The study estimated increases in commodity prices by sector until the year 2000, starting from 1981 which was the base year of the study. According to the price scenario, the price of electricity was raised in real terms at an average of 9.4 per cent *per annum* over the period 1986-91, and at an average rate of 4.0 per cent *per annum during* 1991 to 2000. The results show that raising electricity prices induces very small increase in the prices of all other commodities. There is an increase of less than 0.5 per cent *per annum* in the output prices of 40 sectors (out of the 83 sectors) during the two periods (1986-91 and 1991-2000). This is despite a 57 per cent increase in electricity price in the first period, and a 43 per cent increase in the second period. Output prices of only 20 sectors rise by more than 1.0 to 1.5 per cent in the two periods. The three sectors with the largest price impact, in descending order of importance, are 'rice milling'; 'cement'; and 'grain milling'. For these sectors, price increases are 6.3, 4.0 and 3.0 per cent, respectively, over the period 1986-1991.

The aim of the ENERPLAN study was to evaluate the pricing impacts of raising energy prices. The study, however, effectively estimated only the initial increase in production costs of commodities due to increased electricity prices. Since prices are affected by both cost-push and demand-pull factors, effects on both costs and demand need to be considered in a simultaneous framework to see the effects of raising energy prices. The model does not incorporate any demand or supply functions for commodities and, therefore, does not allow changes in production costs to affect the demand for and supply of a commodity.

For example, the simulation results of the study showed a significant increase in the production costs of the 'rice milling', 'cement' and 'grain milling' sectors. Rice is one of Pakistan's major exports; cement is one of the major inputs to capital formation and flour (output of the grain milling industry) is a staple food. Since the model did not incorporate an export demand function, the effect on the export demand for rice and its production, and their consequent impacts on other commodity prices were not taken into account.

Similarly, the effects on real consumption of household were not considered when the price of electricity was assumed to be raised by 57 per cent in real terms along with a significant increase in the price of the staple food. Consequently, the effects on the demand for commodities due to the change in households real expenditure and relative prices of commodities were also not taken into account.

As far as analysis of energy pricing policy is considered, the scope of the study is narrow even if we assume that all feed-back effects of changes in electricity prices are small and negligible. Three major weaknesses are as follows:

1. The scope of the study is limited as the effect on real GDP, exports, indirect tax revenues have not been addressed.
2. Second, the study also touches only one of the issues of electricity pricing, *i.e.* raising its level. In electricity pricing policy, a more important issue is the removal of user-discriminating taxes. The ENERPLAN model does not have the capability to address this issue.
3. Third, the model estimated the impact of raising electricity price on the cost of production in isolation from its impact on electricity demand. Will electricity demand keep on rising despite the rapid increase in electricity price? Reduced demand may affect the required increase in electricity prices.

3.2.2 Macro econometric model of energy-economy interaction in Pakistan

Chern (1985) developed a macro-econometric model to find out the impacts of the two oil price shocks on Pakistan's economy. Using the time-series data from 1960-82, the energy-economy relationship was estimated. The model was used to analyse the effects on Pakistan's economy of the oil crises of 1973 and 1980 and to project future energy demand, real GDP, inflation, the balance of trade, and other macro variables for alternative scenarios of growth in capital stock, energy, and export prices (Chern, 1987).

The model consists of seven structural equations which determine energy demand (*per capita* and aggregate), real GDP, energy imports, inflation indicated by wholesale price index (WPI), total exports, and total imports. There are 19 exogenous variables. Growth in real GDP affects the energy demand, while GDP growth itself is determined by the growth in energy and capital. GDP growth interacts with energy imports, total exports, total imports, and inflation.

The model was simulated for the 1973-82 period for two scenarios of world oil price. In the first scenario energy price was assumed to grow at 19.3 per cent *per annum*. This was the actual growth rate of weighted-average energy prices, in nominal terms, during this period. In the second scenario, energy price was assumed to grow at 7.2 per cent *per annum*, in nominal terms, which was the rate registered during the pre-oil-crisis period. The study compared effects on six major macro-economic indicators in the two simulations . It was found that the oil crises had a negative impact on Pakistan's economy. The study suggested that higher energy prices had the following qualitative effects on the economy:

1. Decrease in total and *per capita* energy consumption.
2. Decrease in real GDP growth rate.
3. Decrease in energy imports and total imports.
4. Decrease in total exports.
5. Increase in inflation.
6. Increase in the trade deficit.

The comparison of the two simulations' results showed that, if there had been no increase in oil prices, then in 1982 real GDP would had been 13 per cent higher, the inflation rate 24 per cent lower, and total energy demand 20 per cent higher. Furthermore, Pakistan would had reduced its trade deficit from about Rs. 32 billion in 1982 to only Rs. 2 billion; this implies a 94 per cent reduction in the balance of trade.

Chamber (1985, p. 661) while describing the model stated:

Although the energy-economy interactions are likely to be more complicated than those represented in this model, we face tremendous constraints by the length of the available data series. The degrees of freedom problem prevents

34

us from expanding the model to include more equations and from including more exogenous variables.

Hence, the scope of the model is limited to estimation of energy-economy interrelationships, using only aggregated variables. The model has two types of energy price variables: weighted average domestic and import prices. Both prices are given exogenously. Aggregation of all energy prices into one variable does not allow the model to address the various issues of energy pricing such as source-, product-, and user-discriminating taxes on energy products.

3.2.3 Jalal's CGE model for Pakistan

Jalal (1988) developed a CGE model for evaluation of energy pricing policies in the long term. It is a static model based on a neo-classical representation of economic mechanisms. Each economic agent is assumed to maximise his profit or utility, while commodity and factor prices are determined from the general (Walrasian) economic equilibrium of competitive markets. Basic features of the model are as follows:

1. There are 13 production sectors which produce 17 producer goods. Capital, skilled labour, and unskilled labour are viewed as homogenous primary inputs, and are assumed to be mobile among sectors. A Constant Elasticity of Substitution (CES) production function generates value-added from the primary factors. Each production sector combines intermediate inputs and the composite factor (value added) in a fixed proportion to minimise cost per unit of output.
2. All imports form a single homogenous commodity (*i.e.* foreign exchange) which is produced by the 'trade industry' that uses exports, net remittance inflows, and foreign borrowing as inputs. The last two items are exogenously specified as the government endowments. Foreign exchange produced by exports is represented by a transformation function of traded goods. For production sectors, aggregated imports forms a single non-competitive intermediate input which is used in a fixed proportion. For household consumption, there are six items. Among these only, 'food' and 'energy' are treated as traded goods, and substitution between imported and domestic goods is allowed for these two goods.
3. A fixed coefficient transformation function is used to model an investment activity that produces a commodity named 'capital-in-the-future'. The product is demanded by the household as well as the government. Aggregated demands for the 'capital-in-the-future' commodity from all household groups is set equal to their total savings.
4. The demand side of the economy is represented by six consumer groups, distinguished according to their average income and their rural-urban origin. Each household group has different endowments of capital and labour (skilled and unskilled) which determine its income when evaluated at market prices.

35

5. For each consumer group, there is a two-level nested utility function. On the top level, a CES utility function of present and future consumption is defined. At the bottom level, present consumption is defined by a Cobb-Douglas function of six consumer goods. The demand for each consumer good is derived from maximisation of total present consumption subject to an expenditure constraint. The future consumption is defined as a function of present investment. The demands for the present and the future composite goods are derived by maximisation of the utility function subject to an income constraint. The income constraint states that total present consumption plus the present value of future consumption should be equal to total income.

6. The government gets its income by collecting taxes and renting out its capital. It makes transfer payments in the form of subsidies on production and consumption of certain goods. It uses its remaining revenues to buy investment goods.

7. A fixed-coefficient transformation function converts producers goods to foreign exchange. Any trade deficit is assumed to be met by the government endowment of foreign exchange.

In his study, Jalal focused on the impacts of alternative energy pricing policies in the long-term. Various hypothetical changes in energy prices were simulated, such as a uniform increase in all energy prices, an increase in natural gas price to the import-price level of furnace oil, and increases in the prices of kerosene and diesel to their import-price levels. In all the scenarios, energy prices were raised either individually or cumulatively. In some simulations, these scenarios were made revenue-neutral by introducing either subsidy on 'food' or reduction in the import tax on all commodities.

In the analysis of the simulation results, Jalal focused on two impacts of increasing energy prices: (i) utility indices for six types of household, and (ii) 'inflationary effects' represented by producer and consumer price indices. Summary of the various simulations results are as follows:

1. An increase of 10 per cent in all energy prices results in a 1.2 per cent and 1.0 per cent increase in the producer's and consumer's price indices, respectively. There is a small decline in the utility indices of household, while their total energy consumption decreases by 6 per cent. Total primary energy consumption in the economy declines by 2.5 per cent. The micro- and macro- economic effects of the higher prices and the lower energy consumption are not reported for this scenario. This scenario was made revenue-neutral in two alternative simulations. In the first simulation, a 2 per cent subsidy was introduced on 'food' along with a uniform 10 per cent increase in energy prices. In the second simulation, a reduction of 6.5 per cent was assumed in the import tax on intermediate inputs (except for petroleum products) in place of a food subsidy. The result shows that all the negative impacts of raising energy prices are

cancelled out. There is a small increase in price indices, and an increase in the utility indices of the low-income groups in the two regions.

2. For a 50 per cent increase in natural gas price, there is less than a percentage point increase in the overall producers' price index. The utility indices of household, particularly of the low- and middle-income groups, decrease slightly.

3. A 30 per cent increase in kerosene price has a very small effect (0.5 per cent increase) on the consumer's price index. However, there is slightly more decline in the utility index for the low-income household as compared to the middle- and high-income groups. Again, introduction of a small subsidy on 'food' (0.5 per cent) can make the low-income group even better off. Jalal does not discuss the other economic impacts such as GDP and its sectoral composition, or the balance of trade.

4. The price-scenario of 'elimination of all subsidies' from the energy sector is simulated for four cases. In the first case, kerosene and diesel prices are assumed to become comparable to their import prices (an increase of 30.0 and 6.5 per cent respectively) and the price of natural gas is increased by 50 per cent to make it comparable to the import price of FO. The prices of electricity to household and the agriculture sector are increased by 5 and 10 per cent, respectively.

5. The simulation results show that output in all the sectors declines between 0.2 and 7.6 per cent, while utility indices go down by 0.7 to 1.1 per cent. The 'inflationary' effects are small; the producer's and consumer's price indices go up by 1.83 and 1.51 per cent, respectively. However, there are disproportionate changes in the consumer's price indices if calculated separately for six consumer groups. The consumer price indices for the low-income and middle-income groups show comparatively a bigger increase.

6. This price scenario was modified by introducing three alternative changes in taxes and subsidies given on other goods: the increase in energy price was coupled with (a) an 8 per cent reduction in import duties, (b) a 2 per cent subsidy on 'food', and (c) a 4 per cent decrease in excise duty. In case (a), the reduction in import duties on intermediate inputs is able to reduce the negative effects of the energy price hike. There is a smaller increase in price indices, and output in some of the sectors increases. In case (b), a subsidy on food offsets the negative effects on household utility, particularly for the low-income group. It decreases the CPI and slightly increases the producer's price index. However, there are bigger negative effects on the output of all sectors, except for the agriculture sector. In case (c), the reduction in excise duty on the 'food and beverage' commodity has a more favourable effect on the producer's price index. The increase in the producer's price index, due to a bigger increase in energy prices, is reduced by about 50 per cent compared to the base case. The increase in the consumer price index is cancelled out, and utility indices also show favourable changes for the low- and middle-income household. However, except

for the agriculture sector and the 'food and beverage' sector, there is a bigger reduction in output levels of all other sectors as compared to case (a) and (b).

7. The conclusion of Jalal's study is that elimination of subsidies on energy products will have small 'inflationary' effects but will have negative distributional effects as utility indices for the low- and middle-income groups decline more than that of the high-income groups. However, an introduction of subsidy on 'food' or a reduction in tax on imports can compensate for this decline in the utilities.

In the following paragraphs, we review this study in the light of the energy pricing issues in Pakistan.

Devarajan (1988) pointed out that, in most of the energy-economy models for developing countries, the international trade theory is missing. This is evident from Jalal's model. In his model, all intermediate imported inputs are represented by a single imported commodity which is assumed to be complementary. Import substitution is, thus, completely ruled out in production sectors. Similarly, the export functions are not specified. It is not clear from the model's description whether export volumes or export values are given exogenously. For imported goods, the assumption of homogeneity (among the imported goods), along with non-competitiveness with the domestic goods, is a strong assumption. For a developing country, the assumption of non-competitiveness might be true for some particular products, but this cannot be assumed for all imported commodities. For example, amongst energy products, imported furnace oil is a perfect substitute for domestically produced furnace oil and a good substitute for natural gas.

The formulation of household consumption behaviour by a Cobb-Douglas function appears inappropriate, as almost all the micro-level studies for Pakistan have assumed various forms of Linear Expenditure System (LES) to derive household' demand. The Cobb-Douglas consumption function does not differentiate between the demand for subsistence-level and luxury consumption. Consequently, it does not allow the minimum consumption-levels of essential goods (which include energy). Therefore, the Cobb-Douglas specification allows a higher substitution between energy and other goods, in response to changes in their relative prices, as compared to that in the LES demand function.

In the production function, energy products are treated as the intermediate goods that have fixed input-output coefficients. Therefore, substitution of energy with factors of productions and other inputs is ruled out. As the mix of intermediate inputs does not depend on relative prices, inter-fuel substitution is also not possible. This limitation is critical for the long-term simulation of alternative energy price scenarios as it prevents a certain fuel mix target being attained through changes in the relative prices of energy products.

Though Jalal has grouped household by urban and rural regions, labour input in production sectors is not disaggregated by region. The demands for skilled (unskilled) labour are the simple aggregation of labour supply from the two regions, implying a perfect substitution between urban and rural labour. This assumption may be appropriate in the long term but is arguably not valid in the short term.

Since the equations of the model are not documented, many things are unclear. For example, it is not clear how the exports are treated in the model.

Jalal applied his model to evaluate the impacts of various reforms in energy prices in the long term. In all scenarios, however, the prices of energy products were raised to eliminate subsidies. Hence, these simulations analysed the effects of increasing prices of some of the energy products rather than analysing the effects of removing the distortions in energy prices which are present in the form of product-, source-, and user-discriminating taxes. For example, the price of kerosene was increased to its import-price level but the price of gasoline was not reduced to its import-price level.

The study computed the effects of removing subsidies on energy in the long-term. It is generally perceived by the public, politicians, and policy makers that elimination of subsidies has high adjustment costs in terms of slower economic growth and a bigger negative effects in the short term on the welfare of the low-income group, who are major beneficiaries of these subsidies. Thus, the planners and policy makers are more interested in the short- to medium-term effects of any price change on social equity and 'inflation'.

If we are interested in the effects of an increase in energy price, then the effects on real GDP and the sectoral compositions are important. As mentioned, all the scenarios in Jalal's study assumed increases in the energy prices but the study did not report effects on real GDP, the balance of trade and indirect tax revenues (where simulations were not revenue-neutral) for most of the simulations. Jalal is selective in the reporting of his simulation results. The impact on sectoral outputs are reported for only four simulations. In these simulations, all subsidies on energy products were removed. Though the net effect on GDP is not reported, changes in sectoral output show that there is a decline in output of eight sectors (out of 13) in all simulations. Thus, in addition to the four energy sectors (mining, petroleum, natural gas and electricity), there is a decline in the output of the textile, fertiliser, transport and services sectors in all the three cases. In these results, the effects on the trade balance are not discussed, while the textile product is one of the major exports, and petroleum products are major import items.

3.3   Some energy models of other developing countries

Kim (1984) conducted a survey of energy models of developing countries. The survey reveals a variety of analytical techniques. The scope of the survey is broad, and it categorises the energy models developed for developing countries into six classes:

1.   Project evaluation.
2.   Technology assessment.

3. Energy sector assessment.
4. Macro simulation.
5. Economy wide optimisation model.
6. General equilibrium models.

These models were developed to address a variety of energy policy issues, such as selection of a certain energy project, choosing an optimal mix of energy projects, investigation of particular features of the energy producing sectors, and forecasting of macro variables for the economy. Kim discussed the strengths and weaknesses of each type of model, and listed major features of the selected models from each category. The focal point of our study is the issues related to energy pricing policy, and we intend to evaluate the impact of any change in this policy in a general equilibrium framework. In this section, therefore, we discuss briefly some of the general equilibrium models used for such an analysis for developing countries.

A general equilibrium appraisal of the impact of changes in energy prices was undertaken for Egypt by Nazli (1990); for Jordan by Blitzer (1984); for Sri Lanka by Blitzer and Eckaus (1985); for three types of developing countries by Blitzer (1986); for India by Sarkar and Kadeokdi (1988) and also by Panda and Sarkar (1990); and for Mexico by Blitzer and Eckaus (1983b). For the oil exporting countries, Egypt and Mexico, the studies aimed at finding out the macro-economic impact of the increase in energy prices that would occur if the subsidy on oil was removed. The goal of such a policy change would be to divert the domestic oil supply towards export and away from growing domestic consumption. For Jordan, an oil importing country, the model was designed to make the medium-term forecasts of the economy for two scenarios of energy pricing policy. In both scenarios, world oil prices are assumed to increase at 2 per cent *per annum* in real terms, but in one of the scenarios the government removes the prevailing net subsidies on energy gradually over the medium term. The objective of the study on Sri Lanka was to model the energy-economy relationship in a general equilibrium framework. The model was applied to make the medium-term forecasts of the economy for alternative scenarios of growth in world oil prices and the tariff policies on imported oil.

With reference to the scope of our study, reviewing these models and their applications makes the following points.

1. In none of the models a complete general equilibrium framework based on micro-economic theory has been specified. In all the models, energy-economy linkages are developed in the macro economic framework.
2. As pointed out by Devarajan (1988), the international trade theory is missing in most of the models. Thus, these models do not incorporate import and export demand functions. Currently, most of the developing countries, especially in the Asia, intend to de-regulate their economies and to liberalise their trade policies. Hence, incorporation of import- and export-competition becomes imperative in the economic modelling of these economies. An open-economy model can more precisely measure the micro- and macro-economic impacts of such policy

40

changes. In particular, the analysis of short-term impacts is important to see the effects during the transitory period.

3.   These models are highly aggregated. Most of these energy models treat other sectors of the economy in fairly coarse fashion.

4.   In all the models, petroleum products are aggregated into a single product.

5.   In all the models, the tax rate variables are highly aggregated. There are two types of taxes: sales tax and import tax. Since in these models petroleum products are aggregated into a single commodity, there is no provision to simulate the effects of differences in the import tax or sales tax rates across petroleum products. In the model for Jordan, for example, the subsidy rates and the tariff rates on petroleum products are not given by product types. These CGE models do not allow various types of source-, product-, and user-discriminating tax on energy products.

6.   Most of these models have been developed mainly to simulate the effects of an increase in world oil prices or to project energy demand in the medium term. In respect of domestic energy price issues, the scope of most of these studies is limited to the issue of import tax on crude oil, or taxes on aggregated petroleum products.

7.   The studies for India evaluate the impact of changes in domestic energy prices. In these models, it is assumed that energy prices are set by the government exogenously. The two studies evaluate the impact of increasing these exogenously given prices at a uniform rate for all consumers. Hence, any distortions in the form of source-, user-, or product-discriminating taxes on energy products are not analysed.

8.   The prices in the models for Jordan and Sri Lanka are determined according to three rules: (a) domestic prices for traded goods are a linear function of border prices, tariffs and domestic tax rates; (b) the prices of some of the non-traded goods, such as transport and other services, are set endogenously to clear the market; and (c) the price of electricity is given exogenously. The investment in the electricity sector is exogenously adjusted to ensure that the supply of electricity is equal to demand.

9.   Only in the model for Sri Lanka, the electricity sector is divided into hydro and thermal electricity industries. The model assumes that the total electricity supply is a simple aggregation of electricity generation from the two sources, and investment in the thermal electricity sector is appended exogenously to meet the demand for electricity in the medium term. The model does not take into account changes in the relative prices of production, nor the operational constraints of combining electricity generated from various types of technologies. We discuss the role of these two factors in electricity supply in Chapter 4, where we describe the two-level nested electricity supply structure in GE-PAK.

10. Only in the energy-economy model for India, the income distributional effects are evaluated. The model computes Gini coefficients of the shares of three income groups categorised by agricultural income, non-agricultural wage

income and non-agricultural non-wage income. Since there is only one type of household in the Indian model, this distribution coefficient represents changes in the functional income distribution. The effects of changes in energy prices on consumption and household income are not modelled for multiple income groups.

4 The theoretical structure of GE-PAK

4.1 Introduction

The objective of this chapter is to construct a multi-sectoral CGE model of energy-economy and equity interactions in Pakistan (GE-PAK). The model has been developed in the spirit of ORANI which is an Applied General Equilibrium (AGE) model for the Australian economy (Dixon *et al.*, 1982) and has been widely used by academics and by economists in the government and private sectors.

In section 4.2, we present the schematic representation of the input-output table around which the core structure of GE-PAK is built. Section 4.3 then describes the dimensions of the model. The layout of the model's data-base is illustrated through diagrams in section 4.4. In section 4.5, we explicate the notational system for the names of variables and parameters of the model. Table B1 in Appendix B contains the list of variables and parameters.

Equations of the model are divided into 30 blocks which are discussed in sections 4.9 to 4.39. Section 4.6 gives a list of these blocks. All equations of the model are given in linear percentage change form, therefore, section 4.7 discusses an example of this form to elucidate the transformation procedure. All the equations are reproduced in Appendix A (for a ready reference) except a set of equations discussed in section 4.13. In the model, there are five types of production structures representing certain energy-factor and inter-fuel substitution possibilities, each relevant to a set of industries. Section 4.13 discusses these industry-specific production structures. Besides the five types of structures, there is a special production structure for industries in which energy is a minor input and no particular pattern of its substitution with other inputs is required. Since, the five types of production functions are variant forms of the special production structure, we do not report the former in Appendix A, and instead present only the special production structure there. In the discussion on the industry-specific production structures, we identify equation/equations of the special structure which are replaced by new equations. For every new variable defined exclusively for a type of production structure, there is a corresponding new equation.

In our model, the number of variables exceeds the number of equations. We make the number of endogenous variables equal to the number of equations by assuming a set of variables exogenous to the model; which is referred to as 'closing the model'. Section 4.40 presents a table listing our selected exogenous variables which represents one plausible way to close the model. There are certain rules to be followed to categorise the variables into exogenous and endogenous groups, section 4.40 discusses these rules.

Section 4.41 discusses appropriate interpretation of the model's results for a hypothetical case, while section 4.42 explains the solution procedure of the model. In section 4.43, we briefly describe the steps involved in computer implementation of a model using GEMPACK (**General Equilibrium Modelling Pack**age); the computer software used to implement and solve GE-PAK.

4.2 Model's structure

GE-PAK belongs to the Johansen class of models. It is built around a social accounting matrix (SAM) which contains a detailed input-output table and income-expenditure accounts of 4 types of institutions: households; government; corporations; and the rest of the world (ROW).

The structure of the GE-PAK model is represented by equations describing for the base year:

1.   Producers' demands for produced inputs (commodities) and primary factors.
2.   Commodity demands for capital formation by industry.
3.   Commodity demands for consumption-items formation.
4.   Demands for consumption-items by household group.
5.   Commodity demands for export.
6.   Commodity demands for government consumption.
7.   The relationship of *basic values* of commodities (production cost) to purchasers' prices.
8.   Market clearing conditions for commodities and primary factors.
9.   Incomes of households, and other institutions by source.
10.   Numerous macroeconomic variables.

The demand and supply equations for the private-sector agents (households and producers) are derived from the solutions to the optimisation problems (utility maximisation, cost minimisation) which are assumed to underlie the behaviours of agents in the conventional neo-classical microeconomics. All agents are assumed to be price takers, and producers are assumed to operate in competitive markets which prevent earning of pure profits.

The input demand equations for the public-sector agents (such as electricity producers) are also derived from the solution to the cost minimisation problem. The only difference between the treatment of commodities produced by the private-sector agents and the public-sector agents is in modelling of taxation. All taxes on commodities produced solely by the private-sector agents are levied at certain rates, while there are implicit taxes on commodities produced by the public-sector (see Chapter 2 for details) to model the deviation of the regulated price from the market-determined prices. We have incorporated some commodity- and user-specific implicit tax variables in our model (see sections 4.22 and 4.23 for details).

Along with the above mentioned behavioural equations, there are income determining equations in the model for the four institutions (three domestic and one foreign). Factors of production employed in the industries are owned by these institutions. Each institution's income is determined by its endowment of factors and the factor prices. In our model, there are three types of primary factors: labour, capital and land. Labour is owned only by households, while capital and land are owned by all the four institutions. Every institution gets income from other sources besides returns on factors of production. For example, the government gets indirect tax revenues, and the households receive transfer payments from the government.

For households, a consumption function for each group determines its total expenditures. The demands for commodities are then determined under the expenditure constraint for the each household group. The model incorporates demand functions for 14 types of household groups. There is no budget constraint on the government expenditure. Its demands for commodities (for current expenditure) are assumed to be in direct proportion to real private consumption.

4.3 Dimensions of the model

To define variable names of commodities, industries, consumption items, we have grouped them into eleven sets. Table 4.1a gives the names of these sets, their corresponding subscripts, and their elements. Table 4.1b gives names of the subsets, their corresponding subscripts, and their elements.

4.3.1 Number of industries and commodities

There are one hundred and twenty-eight industries that produce one hundred and thirty-one commodities. Multiple production is confined to the oil and gas, and the refinery industries, while electricity is the only commodity which is produced by multiple industries. Each of the remaining industries produces a unique commodity.

There are 15 industries in the agriculture sector producing primary goods, while the oil and gas industry is the single industry in the oil and gas sector. In the large-scale manufacturing sector, there are 50 industries which include mining industries such as coal, other minerals, agro-based industries such as the sugar refining industry, and manufacturing industries such as the electric goods industry. Some of the agricultural and manufactured goods which are produced at the large-scale are also produced at the small-scale in the household and cottage industries. There are 31 industries in the small-scale manufacturing sector producing such goods. The electricity sector comprises of four industries: hydro electricity industry, gas turbine electricity industry, steam electricity industry, and combined cycle electricity industry. For the fuel supplies, there are gas- and oil-refining industries. The remaining 29 industries belong to the construction, and services sectors. Appendix C gives the list of all industries and commodities.

As discussed, we have defined five industry-specific production structures. Table 4.1b lists names of five subsets of industries corresponding to these structures and their elements.

Table 4.1a
Names of sets and corresponding subscripts for elements

Set Name	Subscript	Elements
IND	j	One hundred and twenty eight industries (see table C1 in Appendix C).
COM	i	One hundred and thirty-one commodities (see table C1 in Appendix C for commodity names).
SRC	s	Source of a commodity supply: (1) domestic, and (2) foreign.
ITM	k	Fifty three consumption items (see table C2 in Appendix C).
REG	r	Regions: (1) rural, and (2) urban.
PRF	p	Groups of professional: (1) skilled and (2) unskilled.
COR	o	Corporations: (1) private and (2) public.
FAC	f	Factors of production: (1) labour, (2) capital, and (3) land.
LND	d	Land types by ownership: (1) non-corporate, (2) private-corporate, (3) public -corporate, (4) government, and (5) ROW.
CAP	c	Capital types by ownership: (1) non-corporate, (2) private-corporate, (3) public-corporate, (4) government capital, (5) ROW capital, and (6) capital in dwellings.
INC	n	Household income groups: (1) self-employed-low-income, (2) self-employed-middle-income, (3) self-employed-high-income, (4) employed-low-income, (5) employed-middle-income, (6) employed-high-income , and (7) others.

Table 4.1b
Names of subsets and corresponding subscripts for elements

Subset Name	Subscript	Elements
ADM	a	A subset of commodities that have regulated prices; natural gas, petroleum products, cement, fertiliser and electricity.
ERG	i	A subset of COM containing all petroleum products, natural gas and electricity.
FUL	i	A subset of ERG containing all its elements except electricity.
MAR	m	A subset of commodities that are used as margin commodities; wholesale and retail, road transport, and rail transport.
NONMAR	m	The complementary subset of MAR.
NONIELE	j	All industries other than the electricity industries.
NONCELE	i	All commodities other than electricity.
IAGR	j	Agricultural industries (see Table C1 for names of industries in this subset).
ICCY	j	Combined cycle electricity industry.
IELE		All electricity industries (see Table C1 for names of industries in this subset).
IGST	j	Gas turbine electricity industry.
IHYD	j	Hydro electricity industry.
IIND	j	All mining, manufacturing and construction industries.
IMFLX	j	More-flexible electricity industries: hydro and gas turbine electricity industries.
ILFLX	j	Less-flexible electricity industries: combined cycle and steam electricity industries.
IRDT	j	Road transport industry.
ISER	j	Services industries.
ISTM	j	Steam electricity industry.

4.3.2 Sources of commodity supplies

All commodities are supplied from two sources: domestic and foreign. Of the 131 commodities, there are three margins commodities which are treated as margins commodities as they are required to facilitate the flows of other commodities from producers (or importers) to users. The subset MAR contains the names of these margins commodities.

47

4.3.3 Number of items

In the model there are fifty-three items which are formed by one hundred and thirty-one commodities supplied from two sources. Households demand these items rather than commodities.

4.3.4 Number of regions

For categorisation of households and labour supply and demand, two regions are defined: (i) urban and (ii) rural. The urban region refers to an area that has access to facilities such as running water and sanitation system.

4.3.5 Labour categories

Labour supplies and demands are categorised by two regions, and within a region by two professions, *i.e.*, skilled and unskilled.

4.3.6 Capital and land categories

In the model, there are six categories of capital and five categories of land. This division is based on ownership of these factors. For example, the private-corporate capital category refers to capital owned by the private corporations (see section 5.3.9 in Chapter 5 for details). These categorisation is used to apportioned rental values of these factors to institutions. At the industry level, all six categories of capital (and five of land) are aggregated into a single entity, and there is a single price of capital (land).

4.3.7 Household categories

Fig. 4.1 illustrates the taxonomy of household types. In each region, all households are grouped into two employment categories, and three income groups in each employment category, while there is a general category including all remaining households. The model recognises these seven groups as seven income groups in urban and rural regions. To define household inter-region migration functions, we further disaggregate these 14 household groups by 'profession' *i.e.* household groups with endowment of skilled and unskilled labour. Since the consumption patterns of the household groups by profession are uniform, we only define 14 types of private consumption functions. Consequently, we discuss the income distributional effects in our results in chapter 6 only for 14 types of household groups.

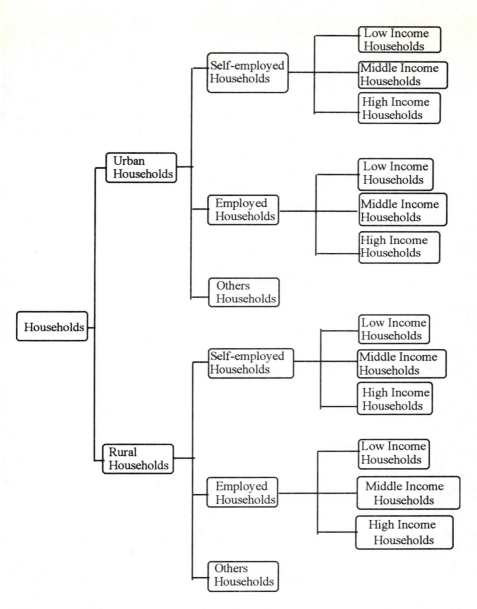

Figure 4.1   Household categories

49

To compute the model, we selected 1983-84 as the bench mark year since the most recent and consistent data set in the form of a 273 × 273 SAM was available for this year (Dhanani 1986a, 1986b).

Because, the SAM for Pakistan, in its original form, was not fully suitable to the GE-PAK's specifications, we expanded and modified it. In Chapter 5, We discuss construction of our data base (built on that SAM), but describe the structure of the data base in the next section.

4.4   Input-output data base

Figs. 4.2 and 4.3 are schematic representations of the model's input-output data base, and they also display names of the data matrices. Figs. 4.4 to 4.6 show various other data matrices which were constructed from the input-output matrices. In the model's specification, names of these data matrices have been used to define coefficients. Familiarisation with the names of the data matrices will, therefore, help the readers to understand the model's equations. In the following paragraphs, we first introduce the input-output data matrices, and then discuss the new matrices built from them.

The columns in fig. 4.2 identify the following user groups:

1.   Domestic producers represented by industries.
2.   Investors represented by industries.
3.   An item producer.
4.   Foreign purchasers represented by an aggregate demand for exports.
5.   An 'other' final consumer representing government.

The first row in fig. 4.2 shows the names of matrices containing production costs (basic values) of commodities for the five user groups. All user groups demand commodities from the two sources except exporters which demand only domestically produced goods. As shown in the second row in fig. 4.2, the matrices V1MAR to V5MAR contain values of m margins commodities demanded by the five user groups. Indirect taxes on commodities are payable by all user groups. The matrices V1TAX to V5TAX contain the sales taxes paid on commodities supplied from two sources (see row three in fig 4.2).

Current goods production requires three types of primary factors: labour, capital, and land. The matrix V1LAB contains the wage bill of labour by profession and region. Similarly, the matrices V1CAP and V1LND contain rental values of capital and land for each industry. The vector of 'other costs' input, V1OCT, gives various miscellaneous expenses in current production by industries.

	Size	1 Producers	2 Investors	3 Items producer	4 Exports	5 Other
		←IND→	←IND→	1	1	1
Basic flows	↑ COM ×SRC ↓	V1BAS$_{isj}$	V2BAS$_{isj}$	V3BAS$_{is}$	V4BAS$_i$	V5BAS$_{is}$
Margins	↑ COM× SRC ×MAR ↓	V1MAR$_{isj}$	V2MAR$_{isj}$	V3MAR$_{is}$	V4MAR$_i$	V5MAR$_{is}$
Taxes	↑ COM× SRC ↓	V1TAX$_{isj}$	V2TAX$_{isj}$	V3TAX$_{is}$	V4TAX$_i$	V5TAX$_{is}$
Labour	↑ REG ×PRF ↓	V1LAB$_{rpj}$				
Capital	↑ CAP ↓	V1CAP$_{cj}$				
Land	↑ LND ↓	V1LND$_{dj}$				
Other costs	1	V1OCT$_j$				

	Joint production matrix
Size	← IND →
↑ COM ↓	MAKE$_{ij}$

	Import duty
Size	1
↑ COM ↓	V0TAR$_i$

Figure 4.2   Layout of the input-output data base

Algebraically, each industry is assumed to produce all commodities. The MAKE matrix contains the values of commodities produced by each industry (see Chapter 5 for further discussion).

Finally, the import tax on a commodity is assumed to be levied on all user groups at a uniform rate. The import tax revenues by commodities are given in the vector V0TAR.

	ITEM formation			Household demand
Size	←COM × SRC →		Size	← REG × INC →
ITM ↑↓	$COMITEM_{kis}$		ITM ↑↓	$VITEM_{krn}$

Figure 4.3   Layout of data matrices of item formation and consumption

For households, it is assumed that they demand consumption items which are formed by the domestic and imported commodities. The columns in the matrix VITEM identify households by region and income group, and its rows represent items. Each cell in $VITEM_{krn}$ gives the value of item k consumed by households from region r in income group n (see fig. 4.3). The matrix $COMITEM_{kis}$ contains values of commodity-use by source for item formation. The rows in this matrix represent items, and columns show commodities by source. For example, each element of $COMITEM_{kis}$ shows the value of commodity i from source s used to produce item k. Demands for commodities for item formation given in V3BAS matrix (fig. 4.2) is then arrived at by aggregating commodity use for all items *.i.e.* $V3BAS_{is} = \sum_{k \in ITM} COMITEM_{kis}$.

Names of the input-output data matrices in purchasers' prices are identified in fig. 4.4. We compute these values by adding up production costs, costs of margins and indirect taxes on commodities. For example, the matrix PUR1 (fig. 4.4) is the sum of the matrices V1BAS, V1MAR and V1TAX.

The vector V1PRM in the first column in fig. 4.4 is the sum of primary-factor costs in each industry *i.e.* aggregation of V1LAB, V1CAP and V1LND matrices for industry j. The total costs of production in industry j is given in the vector COSTS, which is the sum of PUR1 for all commodities from two sources, V1PRM and V1OCT for industry j.

Fig. 4.5 shows that the total sales value of commodity i, is the sum of V1BAS to V5BAS and V0MAR for all user groups. As some commodities are also used as margins goods, the V0MAR vector is added into the sum of V1BAS to V5BAS to arrive at the vector SALES. As shown in fig. 4.7, the vector V0MAR contains the aggregated costs of margins goods consumed by all users.

	Size	1 Producers	2 Investors	3 Items producer	4 Exports	5 Other
	Size	← IND →	← IND →	1	1	1
Values of intermediate inputs in purchasers' prices	↑ COM × SRC ↓	$PUR1_{isj}$	$PUR2_{isj}$	$PUR3_{is}$	$PUR4_i$	$PUR5_{is}$
Value added		$V1PRM_j$				
Other costs	1	$V1OCT_j$				
		$COSTS_j$				

Figure 4.4   Layout of input-output data base in purchasers' prices

		1 Producers	2 Investors	3 Items producer	4 Exports	5 Other		
	Size	←IND→	←IND→	1	1	1		
Basic Flows	↑ COM Domestic ↓	V1BAS (i*j)	V2BAS (i*j)	V3BAS (i*)	V4BAS (i*)	V5BAS (i*)	V0MAR(m)	= SALES(i)
Basic Flows	↑ COM Imported ↓	V1BAS (i*j)	V2BAS (i*j)	V3BAS (i*)		V5BAS (i*)	= IMPORTS(i)	V0TAR(i) - V0IMP(i)

Note: Characters in brackets are subscripts.

Figure 4.5   Layout of data matrices of consumption of domestic and imported commodities

		1	2	3	4	5		
		Producers	Investors	Item producer	Export	Other		
	Size	←IND→	←IND→	1	1	1		
Basic flows	↑ COM Domes tic ↓	V1MAR (i*j)	V2MAR (i*j)	V3MAR (i*)	V4MAR (i*)	V5MAR (i*)	=	V0MAR (m)

Note: Characters in brackets are subscripts.

Figure 4.6   Layout of data flows on consumption of margins goods

The aggregated basic values (*i.e.* cost of supply) of imported commodities are given in the vector IMPORTS. Fig. 4.5 shows that the vector IMPORTS is sum of V1BAS to V5BAS for imported commodities. The cost of imported commodities reported in V1BAS to V5BAS include import taxes. Therefore, the vector VOTAR is subtracted from IMPORTS to arrive at the cost of imports exclusive of import taxes in the vector V0IMP.

4.5 Notational system for variables, coefficients and parameters of the model

Names of all variables in the model are listed alphabetically in Table B1 in Appendix B along with their dimensions and a brief description. Unless otherwise stated, all variables are percentage changes — to indicate this, their names are written in the lower-case letters. For variables that may change sign in the level form, such as trade balance, we prefer to use ordinary change (not percentage); a qualifier, 'del' precedes in the names of those variables. Along with this general principle, the variables are assigned names in a systematic manner. As far as possible, the names of variables conform to a system in which each name consists of two to four parts as follows:

First, a letter indicating the type of variable, *i.e.*,

a	technical change,
c	consumption,
d	dividend rate,
e	endowment,
f	shift variable,
p	price (in Rs.),
t	power of tax,

u	unemployed resource,
v	value,
x	input/output quantity,
y	income;

second, one digit between 0 to 6[1] indicating the user group, *i.e.*,

1	current goods producers,
2	investors,
3	item producer,
4	exporters,
5	Government,
0	all users,

or three characters indicating the type of institution, *i.e.*,

hou	household,
cor	corporations,
gov	government,
row	rest of the world;

third, three letters giving further information, *i.e.*,

cap	capital,
erg	aggregate of energy products in the subset ERG,
frt	fertiliser,
ful	aggregate of fuels in the subset FUL,
inv	investment,
lab	labour,
lnd	land,
mar	margin commodity,
pmp	energy for water pumping,
prm	aggregated primary factors costs,
rev	indirect tax revenues,
tot	aggregate of a variable over all subscripts relevant to it,
wag	wages.

In all the variable names an underscore, *i.e.* '_', followed by one or more subscripts indicates that the variable is aggregated on that subscript or subscripts. For example, the variable $p1lab_{rpj}$ is wage rate for labour of skill type p from region r in industry j. The aggregate wage rate of the two regions is $p1lab\_rpj$.

All the coefficient names are in the upper-case letters. In the model, there are coefficients which are computed from the base-year data. Formulae to calculate these coefficients are put within the equations. We make use of the names of data matrices shown in figs. 4.2 to 4.7, 4.27, and 4.28 to define these formulae. To represent an aggregation of a matrix over a dimension, we append an underscore '_' along with the subscript used for that dimension. For example, the two-dimensional matrix VILABvpj (which contains wage-bill in industry j for profession p from region r from two labour skill categories in the base year) when aggregated over its subscript p is given the name of VILAB_p_{rj}, *i.e*,

$$VILAB\_p_{rj} = \sum_{p \,\in\, PRF} VILAB_{rj}.$$

Coefficients which are not calculated within the equations are listed in table 4.2 with their definitions.

Names of all elasticity parameters are also in the upper-case letters, and begin with the Greek letter 'σ '. In some parameter names, the letter 'σ' is followed by a set or subset name indicating that elasticity of substitution is between elements of that set or subset. For example, 'σFAC' represents the elasticity of substitution between factors of production given in the set FAC. The list of parameters is given in table 4.2. In Chapter 5, we discuss the values assigned to these parameters.

Table 4.2
Parameters and selected coefficients of the model

Equation	Coefficient or parameter	Description
(1.1)	σPRF$_{rj}$	Elasticity of substitution between skilled and unskilled labour from region r, in industry j.
(2.1) to (2.3)	σFAC$_j$	Elasticity of substitution between primary factors in industry j.
(3.1)	σSRCIi	Elasticity of substitution between domestic and imported intermediate input i for current goods production.
(5.1)	σOUT$_j$	Elasticity of transformation between multiple outputs of industry j.
(6.1)	σILFLX	Elasticity of substitution between electricity supply from two less-flexible electricity industries (Steam and Combined cycle).
(6.3)	σIMFLX	Elasticity of substitution between electricity supply from two more-flexible electricity industries (Hydro and Gas turbine).
(6.5) to (6.6)	IELE	Elasticity of substitution between electricity supply from less-flexible and more-flexible electricity industries.

... continued

Table 4.2 continued

Equation	Coefficient or parameter	Description
(7.1)	$\sigma SRC2_i$	Elasticity of substitution between sources of supply of good i for capital formation.
(8.1) to (8.2)	$ALPHA\_I_{krn}$	Share of supernumerary expenditure on item k in total expenditure on item K by household type n in region r.
(8.3)	$ALPHA_{rn}$	Share of supernumerary expenditure in total expenditure of household type n in region r.
(8.1)	EPS_{krn}	Expenditure elasticity of item k for household type n in region r.
(8.2)	$FRISCH_{rn}$	Reciprocal of share of supernumerary expenditure in total expenditure of household type n in region r.
(11.1)	EXP_ELAST_i	Export elasticity of commodity i.
(20.1)	$QCOEF_j$	Ratio of gross (before depreciation) to the net (after depreciation) rate of return in industry j.
(20.2)	$BETA\_R_j$	Elasticity of expected rate-of-return on capital in industry j, with respect to an increase in the planned stock of capital in industry j.
(20.3)	INV_ELAST_j	Elasticity of capital stock in industry j with respect to investment in industry j.
(23.1)	σREG_p	Elasticity of inter-region migration of the household group of profession p.

4.6 Equation system

In sections 4.9 to 4.39, we discuss the model's equations and their underlying theory or assumptions behind them. The equations of the model are distributed into the following 30 blocks:

1. Demand for labour by region and profession.
2. Demand for capital and land.
3. Demand for intermediate inputs by source.
4. Demands for 'other costs' input, a composite of intermediate inputs, and a composite of primary factor inputs.
5. Output mix in multiple-output industries.

6. Electricity sectors structure.
7. Demand for commodities for capital formation.
8. Coefficients in the demand equations for households.
9. Item demands from households.
10. Commodity demands for item formation.
11. Commodity demands for export and government consumption.
12. Demands for margin goods.
13. Purchasers' prices.
14. Various forms of indirect taxes.
15. Implicit taxes for commodities with the regulated prices.
16. Market clearing conditions for commodities.
17. Demands for primary factors.
18. Aggregate demand for final consumption, investment, export and import, and total indirect tax revenues.
19. GDP from income- and expenditure-side and the balance of trade.
20. Allocation of total investment to industries.
21. Various price indices.
22. Factor-price indices for income mapping.
23. Rural-urban migration and real wages.
24. Factor endowments of institutions.
25. Clearing of factor markets.
26. Income of institutions by source.
27. Incomes of institutions.
28. Expenditures and disposable incomes of household groups.
29. Gross National Products (GNP) and the balance of payments.
30. Savings of domestic institutions.

As mentioned, GE-PAK is in the spirit of ORANI. To describe the equations of GE-PAK, we follow Horridge's exposition for ORANI-F (an extended version of ORANI) given in the most recent document of the model (Horridge, Parmenter and Pearson; 1993).

4.7   An example of linear percentage change form

Many of our model's equations are non-linear, for example — demand depends on the price ratio. However, following Johansen (1960) and Dixon *et al.* (1982) the model is solved by representing it as a series of linear equations relating percentage changes in variables of the model. In this section, we discuss the procedure to transform an equation system given in levels into linear percentage change form.

To illustrate the basic principle of linearisation, we consider a very simple equation system that aggregates the rental value of capital in the economy. The rental value of capital in industry j, $V1CAP_j$, is defined as:

$$V1CAP_j = P1CAP_j \times X1CAP_j, \qquad (4.7.1)$$

58

where P1CAP$_j$ and X1CAP$_j$ are price and quantity of capital, respectively in industry j. An aggregation of the rental values of capital in all industries, *i.e.*, V1CAP_j, can be defined as:

$$V1CAP\_j = \sum_{j \in IND} P1CAP_j \times X1CAP_j, \qquad (4.7.2)$$

where IND is the set of industries in the model. Eq. (4.7.2) is turned into percentage-change form by taking the total differential:

$$dV1CAP\_j = \sum_{j \in IND} P1CAP_j \times d\,X1CAP_j + X1CAP_j \times d\,P1CAP_j.$$

Variables in percentage-change forms, *i.e.*, v1cap_j, p1cap$_j$ and x1cap$_j$ are defined *via*:

$$v1cap\_j = 100\,\frac{dV1CAP\_j}{V1CAP\_j}$$

or by rearranging:

$$dV1CAP\_j = \frac{V1CAP\_j \times v1cap\_j}{100}$$

Similarly:

$$dP1CAP_j = \frac{P1CAP_j \times p1cap_j}{100}$$

and:

$$dX1CAP_j = \frac{X1CAP_j \times x1cap_j}{100}$$

Incorporating these definitions, our sample eq. (4.7.2) becomes:

$$\frac{V1CAP\_j \times v1cap\_j}{100} = \sum_{j \in IND} P1CAP_j\,\frac{X1CAP_j \times x1cap_j}{100}$$

$$+ X1CAP_j\,\frac{P1CAP_j \times p1cap_j}{100}$$

which can be rearranged to arrive at:

$$V1CAP\_j \times v1cap\_j = \sum_{j \in IND} (P1CAP_j \times X1CAP_j) \times (p1cap_j + x1cap_j).$$

Using the V1CAP$_j$ definition from equation (4.7.1), we write:

$$v1cap\_j = \frac{1}{V1CAP\_j}\sum_{j \in IND} V1CAP_j \times (p1cap_j + x1cap_j), \qquad (4.7.3)$$

which is the form in which equations of the model are given.

In practice, formal derivations such as given above are often unnecessary for the conversion of equations. Most equations in percentage-change form follow standard patterns. Some of these are shown in table D1 of Appendix D.

One of the advantages of a linearised system is its simplicity. This becomes evident in writing of equations which have complicated functional forms. For example, in the equation system of an input demand function: the CES[2] input demand equations for industry j which produces commodity $X0_j$ using various inputs $X1_{ij}$ (i is the element of commodity set COM) with prices $P1_{ij}$. In levels, the equations are (see Appendix E for the derivation of this demand function):

$$X1_{ij} = X0_j \, \delta_i^{1/(\rho+1)} [\, P1_{ij} / P1\_{ij} \,]^{-1/(\rho+1)},$$

$$i \in COM, j \in IND, \qquad (4.7.4)$$

where:
$$P1\_ij = \left(\sum_{i \,\in com} \delta_i^{\,1/(\rho+1)} P1_{ij}^{\,\rho/(\rho+1)} \right)^{-(\rho+1)/\rho}$$

$$j \in IND, \qquad (4.7.5)$$

and δ_i and ρ are behavioural parameters.

In a linear equation system, the percentage change form of (4.7.4) and (4.7.5) are:

$$x_{ij} = x0_j - \sigma \, (p1_{ij} - p1\_{ij}),$$

$$i \in COM, j \in IND, \qquad (4.7.6)$$

and:
$$p1\_ij = \frac{1}{\sum_{i \in COM} V1BAS\_ij} \sum_{i \in COM} V1BAS_{ij} \times p1_{ij}.$$

$$j \in IND, \qquad (4.7.7)$$

where $V1BAS_{ij} = X1_{ij} \times P1_{ij}$; the value of commodity i input in industry j in the data-base (see Appendix E for this linearisation).

Apart from its simplicity in constructing a model, the linearised approach has two more advantages:

1. It allows free choice of selecting exogenous variables. Many levels' algorithms do not allow this flexibility.
2. To reduce AGE models to manageable size, it is often necessary to use model equations to substitute out matrix variables of large dimensions. In the linear system, we can always make any variable the subject of any equation in which it appears. Hence, substitution is a simple mechanical process. In fact, the computer software GEMPACK (Impact Project, 1993),

that has been used to solve our model, performs this routine algebra for the users. This allows us to specify the model in terms of its original behavioural equations, rather than in reduced form. This decreases the potential of making errors and makes equations easy to check.

4.8   Structure of production

The model allows each industry to produce several commodities, using as inputs: domestic and imported commodities; land, labour, and capital; and 'other costs'. The multi-input and multi-output production specifications are kept manageable by a series of separability assumptions illustrated by the nesting shown in fig. 4.7. The assumption of input-output separability implies that the generalised production function for each industry:

$$F(\text{inputs, outputs}) = 0, \qquad\qquad (4.8.1)$$

may be written as:

$$G(\text{inputs}) = Z = H(\text{outputs}), \qquad\qquad (4.8.2)$$

where Z is an index of industry's activity. This assumption reduces the number of estimated parameters required by the model. Fig. 4.7 shows that the H function is derived from a constant elasticity of transformation (CET) aggregation function, while the G function is broken into a sequence of nested production functions. Starting from the bottom of fig. 4.7, the composite input of regional-labour is a CES aggregation of skilled and unskilled labour from a region. At a level above it, the composite labour is a Leontief aggregation of composite urban-labour and composite rural-labour inputs. At the level above this, the primary-factor composite is a CES aggregation of land, capital and composite labour inputs. Each commodity composite is a CES aggregate of its supply from domestic and foreign sources. At the top level, a Leontief production function combines commodity composites, a primary factor composite, and 'other costs'. Consequently they are all demanded in direct proportion to Z.

Fig. 4.7 shows the special production structure, and its equations are discussed in sections 4.9 to 4.12. We begin at the bottom of fig. 4.7 and work upwards. Section 4.13 discusses the equations corresponding to five types of production structures which allow energy-factor and inter-energy substitutions. The equation blocks which are common to all the production structure are (i) demand for labour by region and profession, (ii) demand for intermediate inputs by sources and (iii) demands for 'other costs', composite primary factors and composite intermediate inputs. These equation blocks are described only once with reference to the special production structure.

61

4.9   Demand for labour by profession and region

The data on the labour force and households in Pakistan can be broadly categorised by rural and urban regions. But, the data on industries are not given by region. The labour employment data in industries show that each industry employs four types of labour: (1) rural skilled, (2) rural unskilled, (3) urban skilled and (4) urban unskilled. The three-dimensional wage-bill matrix $V1LAB_{rpj}$ contains labour wages by region, profession and industry.

In our model, we assume that the pattern of industries' location remains constant over the simulation period. We, therefore, assume that the labour employment in an industry is a Leontief composite of rural and urban labour (see the top level nest of labour demand in fig. 4.7) The substitution possibility in labour demand an industry is only between skilled and unskilled labour available within a region. The input of regional-labour composite is a CES aggregation of skilled and unskilled labour from that region (see two CES production function nests at the bottom of fig. 4.7).

For industry j, the equations for (say) rural-labour demands by profession are derived from the following optimisation problem.

Choose inputs of labour by profession from rural labour:

$$X1LAB_{rpj}, \qquad r = rural, p \in PRF, \qquad (4.9.1)$$

to minimise total rural labour costs:

$$\sum_{p \in PRF} \{P1LAB_{rpj} \times X1LAB_{rpj}\}, \qquad r = rural, \qquad (4.9.2)$$

where:

$$X1LAB\_p_{rj} = CES\left(\frac{X1LAB_{rpj}}{A1LAB_{rpj}}\right), \qquad r = rural, p \in PRF, \quad (4.9.3)$$

regarding as exogenous to the problem:

$$P1LAB_{rpj} \text{ and } X1LAB\_p_{rj}, \qquad r = rural, p \in PRF. \qquad (4.9.4)$$

$P1LAB_{rpj}$, $X1LAB_{rpj}$, and $A1LAB_{rpj}$ are the cost to industry j of a unit of labour (wage rate), units of labour demanded, and the labour-saving technical change, respectively.

The solution to the problem in linear percentage-change form (see Appendix E for the derivation) is given by:

$$x1lab_{rpj} = x1lab\_p_{rj} + a1lab_{rpj} - \sigma PRF_{rj} \left[\{p1lab_{rpj} + a1lab_{rpj}\} - p1lab\_p_{rj}\right],$$

$$r = rural, j \in IND, \qquad (4.9.5)$$

$$p1lab\_p_{rj} = \frac{1}{V1LAB\_p_{rj}} \sum_{p \in PRF} \{V1LAB_{rpj} \times (p1lab_{rpj} + a1lab_{rpj})\},$$

$$r \in REG, j \in IND. \qquad (4.9.6)$$

Eq. (4.9.5) states that demand for rural labour by profession is proportional to: overall labour demand; the profession-specific rural-labour-augmenting technical change; and a price term. The price term is composed of the elasticity of substitution between rural skilled and unskilled labour (σPRF_{rj}), multiplied by the percentage change in a price ratio representing the effective wage of profession p relative to the overall wage for rural labour $p1lab\_p_{rj}$. A change in the relative prices for two professions, induces substitution in favour of relatively cheapening profession. The effective wage term, *i.e.* $\{p1lab_{rpj} + a1lab_{rpj}\}$, accounts for the effect of technical changes. For example, the region-profession specific labour augmenting technical change in industry j at the rate of 1 per cent, *i.e.*, $a1lab_{rpj} = -1$, will reduce the nominal wage rate for this labour type effectively by 1 per cent. The overall wage rate of rural labour, defined in (4.9.6), is a cost-weighted average of wage rate of rural labour by professions.

The matrix $V1LAB_{rpj}$ in (4.9.6) contains the wage bill in the base year of industry j for labour from region r of profession type p, while $V1LAB\_p_{rj}$ is aggregation of the wage bill over the two professions.

The second nest at the bottom of fig. 4.7 shows the demand structure of urban labour which is similar to that for rural labour. Hence, the eqs. (4.9.1) to (4.9.6) are repeated with r = urban.

Total labour demand in industry j, ($X1LAB\_r_{pj}$), is a Leontief composite of rural and urban labour given by:

$$X1LAB\_r_{pj} = MIN\left(\frac{X1LAB\_p_{rj}}{A1LAB\_p_{rj}} \right) \qquad r \in REG, j \in IND. \quad (4.9.7)$$

Consequently, labour demand by region ($X1LAB\_p_{rj}$) is in direct proportion to the overall labour demand of industry j. The Leontief production function is equivalent to a CES production function with substitution elasticity set to zero. Hence, the derived region-specific labour demand eq. (4.9.8) resembles that derived from the CES form but lacks price (substitution) term.

$$x1lab\_p_{rj} = x1lab\_r_{pj} + a1lab\_p_{rj}, \qquad r \in REG \text{ and } j \in IND. \quad (4.9.8)$$

Through substitution of x1lab_prj in (4.9.5) using eq. (4.9.8) we arrive at the labour demand equations given in Block 1.

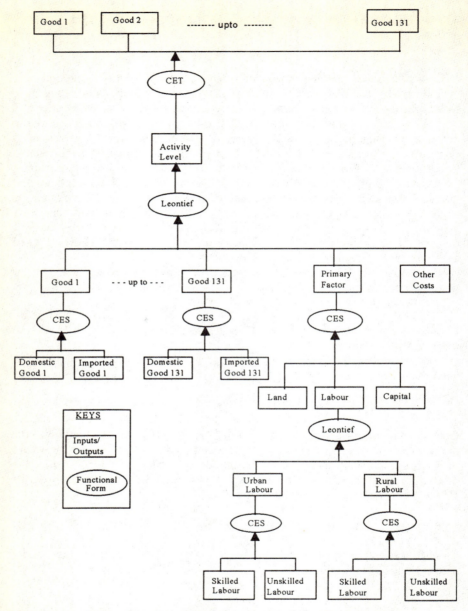

Figure 4.7   Current goods production structure (a special case)

Block 1 Equations for region-profession specific labour demand:

$$x1lab_{rpj} = x1lab\_rpj + a1lab\_prj + a1lab_{rpj}$$

$$- \sigma PRF_{rj} \, [\{p1lab_{rpj} + a1lab_{rpj}\} - p1lab\_prj \,],$$

$$r \in REG, \; p \in PRF, \; j \in IND, \qquad\qquad (1.1)$$

$$p1lab\_prj = \frac{1}{V1LAB\_prj} \sum_{p \, \in \, PRF} \{V1LAB_{rpj} \times (p1lab_{rpj} + a1lab_{rpj})\},$$

$$r \in REG, \; j \in IND, \qquad\qquad (1.2)$$

$$p1lab\_rpj = \frac{1}{V1LAB\_rpj} \sum_{r \, \in \, REG} V1LAB\_prj \times \{p1lab\_prj + a1lab\_prj \},$$

$$j \in IND. \qquad\qquad (1.3)$$

Eq. (1.3) in Block 1 defines the average cost of labour in industry j, which is again a cost-weighted index of the effective unit-cost of rural and urban labour. This average price of labour is used to determine composite labour demand in industry j, defined in Block 2.

4.10   Demands for capital, land and composite labour by industry

As shown in fig. 4.7, total primary factor demand in an industry is a CES composite of capital, land and composite labour inputs. Block 2 (below) contains equations determining demand for these factors.

Block 2 Demand equations for capital, land and composite labour:

$$x1cap_j = x1prm_j + a1cap_j - \sigma FAC_j [\{p1cap_j + a1cap_j\} - p1prm_j] \,,$$

$$j \in IND, \qquad\qquad (2.1)$$

$$x1lnd_j = x1prm_j + a1lnd_j - \sigma FAC_j \, [\{p1lnd_j + a1lnd_j\} - p1prm_j],$$

$$j \in IND, \qquad\qquad (2.2)$$

$$x1lab\_rpj = x1prm_j + a1lab\_rpj - \sigma FAC_j \, [\{plab\_rpj + a1lab\_rpj\} - p1prm_j],$$

$$j \in IND, \qquad\qquad (2.3)$$

65

$$p1prm_j = \frac{1}{V1PRM_j} (V1CAP\_c_j \times \{p1cap_j + a1cap_j + a1prm_j\}$$

$$+ V1LND\_d_j \times \{p1lnd_j + a1lnd_j + a1prm_j\}$$

$$+ V1LAB\_rp_j \times \{p1lab\_rp_j + a1lab\_rp_j + a1prm_j\} \,), \quad j \in IND. \quad (2.4)$$

The derivation of the above equations follows a pattern similar to that discussed for labour demand in the previous section. In this case, total primary factor cost is minimised subject to CES production function:

$$X1PRM_j = CES \left(\frac{X1LAB\_rp_j}{A1LAB\_rp_j}, \frac{X1CAP_j}{A1CAP_j}, \frac{X1LND_j}{A1LND_j} \right), \quad j \in IND. \quad (3.10.1)$$

The coefficients, $A1CAP_j$, $A1LND_j$, and $ALAB\_rp_j$ are factor-saving technical changes in industry j for capital, land and composite labour (uniform for each profession and region), respectively. The solution to the problem in percentage-change form is given by eqs. (2.1) to (2.3) in Block 2 (see Appendix E for derivation). The matrices $V1LAB\_rp_j$, $V1CAP\_c_j$, and $V1LND\_d_j$ in (2.4) contain the costs of composite labour, capital and land in industry j, respectively.

4.11 Demands for intermediate inputs by source

Following Armington (1969, 1970), we assume that imports are imperfect substitutes of domestic supplies. The demand for intermediate input commodity i in industry j ($X1\_s_{ij}$) is, therefore, defined as a CES composite of demands for commodity i supplied from the two sources ($x1_{isj}$) ,*i.e.*,

$$X1\_s_{ij} = \underset{s \,\in\, SRC}{CES} \left(\frac{X1_{isj}}{A1_{isj}} \right), \quad\quad\quad i \in COM, j \in IND. \quad (4.11.1)$$

The total costs of imported and domestic commodity i is minimised subject to the production function given in (4.11.1). Following the derivation procedure given in Appendix E, we arrive at demand equations for intermediate inputs by source given in Block 3.

Block 3 Equations for intermediate input demand by source and industries:

$$x1_{isj} = x1\_s_{ij} + a1_{isj} - \sigma SRC1_i \,[\{p1_{isj} + a1_{isj}\} - p1\_s_{ij}\,],$$

$$i \in COM, s \in SRC, j \in IND, \quad\quad\quad (3.1)$$

$$p1\_s_{ij} = \frac{1}{V1BAS\_s_{ij}} \underset{s \,\in\, SRC}{\Sigma} V1BAS_{isj} \,(p1_{isj} + a1_{isj}\,),$$

$$i \in COM, j \in IND. \quad\quad\quad (3.2)$$

The variable $a1_{isj}$ represents technical-change in the use of commodity i, in industry j, from source s. In (3.1), the elasticity of substitution between imported and domestic commodities is represented by $\sigma SRC1_i$. Lowering a source-specific price, relative to the average, induces substitution in favour of that source. The average effective-cost index, $p1\_s_{ij}$, is again a cost-weighted index of individual prices and technical changes defined by (3.2). The coefficient $V1BAS_{isj}$ is the matrix of basic values of intermediate inputs used by industry j from the two sources in the base year (see fig. 4.2 on the input-output data base).

4.12 Demands for composite primary factor and intermediate inputs in current production

The top most nest of input-demand in fig. 4.7 shows that the commodity-composite, the primary factor composite, and 'other costs' inputs are combined using a Leontief production function given by:

$$Z_j = \frac{1}{A1TOT_j} \, \underset{i \in COM}{MIN} \left[\frac{X1\_s_{ij}}{A1\_s_{ij}}, \frac{X1PRM_j}{A1PRM_j}, \frac{X1OCT_j}{A1OCT_j} \right] \; j \in IND. \qquad (4.12.1)$$

The demand equations derived under the cost minimisation subject to this production function, are given in Block 4. The variable Z_j is the output level in the single-output industries, but is an activity index in the multiple-output industries.

Eqs. (4.1) to (4.3) state that the three inputs are demanded by industry j in direct proportion to its output or activity level and the technical-change variables.

In eqs. (4.1) to (4.5), there are 2 types of technical-change variables. The variable $atot_j$ represents a Hicks-neutral technical change affecting equally all inputs in industry j, while $a1oct_j$, $a1prm_j$, and $a1\_s_{ij}$ are technical-change variables for three inputs: 'other costs', primary-factor composite and intermediate-input composite, respectively.

Block 4 Composite-inputs demand equations:

$$x1oct_j = atot_j + a1oct_j + z_j, \qquad j \in IND, \qquad (4.1)$$

$$x1prm_j = atot_j + a1prm_j + z_j, \quad j \in IND, \qquad (4.2)$$

$$x1\_s_{ij} = atot_j + a1\_s_j + z_j, \quad i \in COM, \; j \in IND, \qquad (4.3)$$

$$p0ind_j - a_j = \frac{1}{COSTS_j} \left(\sum_{i \in COM} \sum_{s \in SRC} PUR1_{isj} \times p1_{isj} \right.$$

$$+ \sum_{r \in REG} \sum_{p \in PRF} V1LAB_{rpj} \times p1lab_{rpj}$$

$$+ V1CAP\_c_j \times p1cap_j + V1LND\_d_j \times p1lnd_j + V1OCT_j \times p1oct_j),$$

$$j \in IND, \qquad\qquad (4.4)$$

$$a_j - atot_j = \sum_{i \in COM} (PUR1\_s_j \times a1\_s_j + \sum_{s \in SRC} PUR1_{isj} \times a1_{isj})$$

$$+ V1PRM_j \times a1prm_j + \sum_{r \in REG} \sum_{p \in PRF} V1LAB_{rpj} \times a1lab_{rpj}$$

$$+ V1LAB\_rp_j \times a1lab\_rp_j + V1CAP\_c_j \times a1cap_j + V1LND\_j \times a1lnd_j$$

$$+ V1OCT_j \times a1oct_j, \qquad j \in IND, \qquad\qquad (4.5)$$

$$p1oct_j = xi3 + f1oct_j, \qquad\qquad j \in IND. \qquad\qquad (4.6)$$

Eq. (4.4) defines a cost weighted average of all input prices. the effective price per unit of output (or activity) in industry j ($p0ind_j$) Given the constant returns to scale, which characterise the model's production technology, weighted-average of input prices is the average cost of industry j's output. Setting an output price equal to its average cost imposes the competitive zero-pure profit condition. The variable a_j in (4.4) is a cost-weighted average index of technical-change affecting the use of all inputs in industry j. Eq. (4.6) states that the price of 'other costs' input is in direct proportion to the Consumer Price Index (CPI) represented by the variable xi3, whereas the variable 'f1oct' represents an exogenous shift in this variable.

4.13   Energy-factor and inter-energy substitutions in current production

In the energy-economy interaction models for developing countries various input structures have been assumed which incorporate inter-energy and factor-energy substitutions in the production sectors.

In a general equilibrium model for developing countries, Blitzer (1986) assumed energy to be a substitute for capital and labour. However, in his model there are only two production sectors: rural and urban. Furthermore Capital, labour and energy were assumed to be substitutes in Cobb-Douglas production function defined for the two sectors. The same specification was applied by Blitzer (1984) in the energy-economy interaction model for Jordan.

In the energy-economy interaction model for Sri Lanka, Blitzer and Eckaus (1985) defined four types of production structures corresponding to four categories of sectors: tree crop and manufacturing, transport, electricity, and oil refinery. In all these production structures, energy has been defined either as a complementary input to capital or as an input in the Cobb-Douglas production function.

The inter-fuel and energy-capital substitution nests have been incorporated in the ORANI application (Industry Commission, 1991) to estimate the costs and benefits of reducing greenhouse gas emissions for Australia. In this application although a multi-level production structure has been defined to allow substitution between energy products, and between energy input and primary factors, all industries have a uniform production structure.

A variety of inter-energy and energy-capital substitution pattern is found in the energy-economy models for developed countries. For example, the MSG-4 model[3] incorporates substitution possibilities between capital, labour, an aggregated energy input, and an aggregated material input. The aggregated energy input is defined as an aggregate of electricity and fuels.

In GE-PAK, we have defined five types of input structures that depict energy-factor and inter-energy substitution patterns which are specific to some groups of industries. Figs. 4.8 to 4.12 show these input structures which correspond to:

1.   agricultural industries;
2.   manufacturing (both large and small-scale), mining, and construction industries;
3.   road transport industry;
4.   combined cycle electricity industry; and
5.   steam electricity industry.

These input structures have been defined in line with the pattern of energy consumption in these industries in Pakistan. Except for inter-energy and factor-energy substitution nests, these five input-structures are similar to the special production structure given in fig. 4.7, and discussed in sections 4.8 to 4.12. For example, in all industries the 'effective labour' input is defined by a two-level nested production function of four types of labour. Similarly, the 'effective commodity' input is also defined as a CES aggregate of a commodity supplies from two sources.

In the following subsections, we derive equations for the input structures shown in figs. 4.8 to 4.12. Since these structures are more elaborated versions of the special structure discussed in the above sections, we define a new equation for each new variable introduced in the following sub-sections. Hence, in the list of variables in table B1 in Appendix B, we have not included all the new variables defined in these subsections. Similarly, equations corresponding to these variables have also not been added in the number of equations reported in table B2 in Appendix B. Furthermore, for the elaborated production structures, the demand equations derived for primary factors and energy products are not the same as defined for the special production structure. Therefore, these equations are replaced by those discussed in the following subsections. All such equations are marked by '‡'.

69

4.13.1 Input structure for the agricultural industries

Two petroleum products and electricity are energy inputs to the agricultural industries in Pakistan, while chemical fertiliser is the major energy-intensive input. Of the two petroleum products, HSD is used to run tractors and accessories whereas LDO is used for underground water pumping. In these industries, the capital stock mainly represents tractors and accessories, and consumption of HSD depends on their usage and their fuel intensities. We, therefore, define a CES composite of HSD and capital (x1caphsd$_j$). As fertiliser consumption is related to the usage of land, a CES composite of land and fertiliser (x1lndfrt$_j$) is defined. The three composite inputs 'motor-fuel-capital', 'fertiliser-land' and 'effective labour' are assumed to form a CES production function at the middle-level (see fig. 4.8). Accordingly, the following equations define the demands for primary factors, fertiliser and energy products in the agricultural industries.

$$x1lnd_j = x1lndfrt_j + a1lnd_j + a1prm_j$$

$$- \sigma AGR1 \left(\{ p1lnd_j + a1lnd_j + a1prm_j \} - p1lndfrt_j \right), \quad j \in IAGR, \tag{4.13.1.1‡}$$

$$x1\_s_{ij} = x1lndfrt_j + a1\_s_{ij} - \sigma AGR1(\{ p1\_s_{ij} + a1\_s_{ij} \} - p1lndfrt_j),$$
$$i = fertiliser, j \in IAGR, \tag{4.13.1.2‡}$$

$$p1lndfrt_j = \frac{1}{PUR1\_s_{ij} + V1LND\_d_j} (PUR1\_s_{ij} \times \{ p1\_s_{ij} + a1\_s_{ij} \}$$

$$+ V1LND\_d_j \times \{ p1lnd_j + a1lnd_j + a1prm_j \}),$$
$$i = fertiliser, j \in IAGR, \tag{4.13.1.3}$$

$$x1cap_j = x1caphsd_j + a1cap_j - + a1prm_j$$

$$- \sigma AGR2(\{ p1ap_j + a1cap_j + a1prm_j \} - p1caphsd_j), \quad j \in IAGR, \tag{4.13.1.4‡}$$

$$x1\_s_{ij} = x1caphsd_j + a1\_s_{ij} - \sigma AGR2(\{ p1\_s_{ij} + a1\_s_{ij} \} - p1caphsd_j),$$
$$i = HSD, j \in IAGR, \tag{4.13.1.5‡}$$

$$p1caphsd_j = \frac{1}{PUR1\_s_{ij} + V1CAP\text{-}c_j} (PUR1\_s_{ij} \times \{ p1\_s_{ij} + a1\_s_{ij} \}$$

$$+ V1CAP\_c_j \times \{ p1cap_j + a1cap_j + a1prm_j \}),$$
$$i = HSD, j \in IAGR, \tag{4.13.1.6}$$

$$x1lndfrt_j = x1prmerg_j - \sigma AGR3 (p1lndfrt_j - p1prmerg_j), \quad j \in IAGR, \tag{4.13.1.7}$$

$$x1caphsd_j = x1prmerg_j - \sigma AGR3(p1caphsd_j - p1prmerg_j), \quad j \in IAGR,$$

$$(4.13.1.8)$$

$$x11ab\_rp_j = x1prmerg_j + a11ab\_rp_j - \sigma AGR3(p11ab\_rp_j - p1prmerg_j),$$

$$j \in IAGR, \quad (4.13.1.9\ddagger)$$

$$p1prmerg_j = \frac{1}{\sum_i PUR1\_si_j + V1PRM_j}(\sum_i PUR1\_si_j \times \{p1\_si_j + a1\_si_j\}$$

$$+ V1PRM_j \times \{p1prm_j + a1prm_j\}),$$

$$i = \text{fertiliser, HSD,} \quad j \in IAGR. \quad (4.13.1.10)$$

These equations are derived from the series of optimisation problems of inputs aggregation defined at various levels in the production function (see fig. 4.8). Hence, the derivation procedures resemble that discussed in the above sections. For example, the demand for land ($x11nd_j$) and fertiliser input ($x1\_si_j$) are derived from the cost minimisation of these inputs subject to a CES function of land-fertiliser composite. $\sigma AGR1$ to $\sigma AGR3$ represent the elasticities of substitution between land and fertiliser, capital and HSD, and between labour, 'fertiliser-land', and 'capital-HSD', respectively.

The composite demand for land and fertiliser, *i.e.* $x11ndfrt_j$, and the relative prices of these two inputs determine their demands in (4.13.1.1) and (4.13.1.2). The price of land-fertiliser composite input, $p11ndfrt_j$, is defined in (4.13.1.3). Similarly, the price for the composite input of capital and HSD capital-HSD ($p1caphsd_j$) is determined by (4.13.1.6). In eq. (4.13.1.7) to (4.13.1.9), the variable $x1prmerg_j$ represents the composite of all primary factors and the two intermediate inputs, and is referred to the 'facto-energy' input. Its price ($p1prmerg_j$) is determined in (4.13.1.10).

Riaz (1984) has estimated price elasticities of coal, oil, natural gas and electricity for the services, manufacturing and agricultural industries[4]. According to these estimates, electricity's substitute in the agricultural and services industries is oil. In his study, Riaz has aggregated all petroleum products. In view of the energy consumption pattern in the agricultural industries, electricity is most likely to be substituted by LDO as both are used for the same operation, i.e. water pumping. Therefore, We define 'pumping energy' ($x1pumerg_j$) as a CES composite of electricity and LDO.

$$x1\_si_j = x1pumerg_j - \sigma AGR4_j(\{p1\_si_j + a1\_si_j\} - p1pumerg_j),$$

$$i = \text{electricity, LDO,} \quad j \in IAGR, \quad (4.13.1.11\ddagger)$$

$$p1pumerg_j = \frac{1}{\sum_i PUR\_si_j}\sum_i (PUR1\_si_j \times \{p1\_si_j + a1\_si_j\}),$$

$$i = \text{electricity, LDO,} \quad j \in IAGR. \quad (4.13.1.12)$$

71

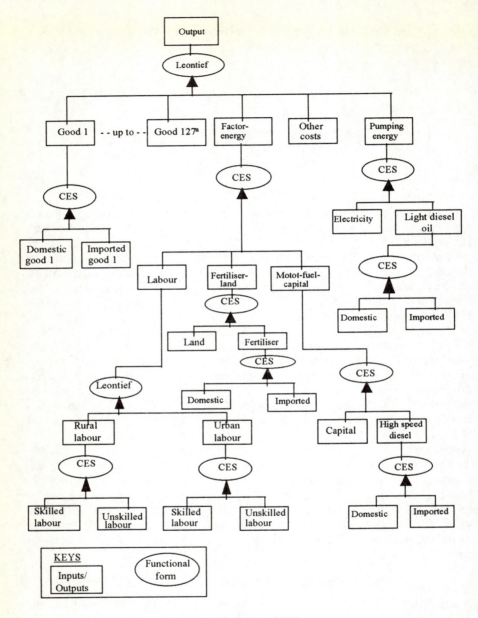

a excluding electricity, fertilizer, LDO and HSD

Figure 4.8   Input structure for the agricultural industries

In eq. (4.13.1.12), the parameter $\sigma AGR4_j$ is elasticity of substitution between these energy products for the agricultural industries and the variable $p1pumerg_j$ represents the price for the 'pumping energy' input. As shown at the top level in fig. 4.8, the Leontief production function combines 'factor-energy' bundle with inputs of 'pumping energy', 'other costs' and all other effective non-energy commodity inputs. Hence, demands for these composite inputs are in direct proportion to the activity level of the agricultural industries as defined in eqs. (4.13.1.13) and (4.13.1.14).

$$x1prmerg_j = atot_j + z_j , \quad j \in IAGR, \qquad (4.13.1.13)$$

$$x1pumerg_j = atot_j + z_j , \quad j \in IAGR. \qquad (4.13.1.14)$$

Eqs. [(4.13.1.1), (4.13.1.4) and (4.13.1.9)] that define demand for land, capital and labour for the agricultural industries in this subsection, replace the factor demand eqs. (2.1 to 2.3) given in Block 2 for these industries. Similarly, equations that define demand for fertiliser (4.13.1.2), electricity and LDO (4.13.1.11), and HSD (4.13.1.5) in this subsection replace demand eq. (4.4) for these intermediate inputs in Block 4 for the agricultural industries.

4.13.2 Input structure for mining, manufacturing and construction industries

Natural gas, furnace oil and electricity are the major commercial energy inputs in the manufacturing, mining and construction industries. According to Riaz's estimates (1984) furnace oil can be substituted only with natural gas in the manufacturing industries. As shown in fig. 4.9, 'fuel' is defined as a CES composite of natural gas and FO, while electricity is assumed to be a substitute of 'fuel'. We have defined the CES production specification for fuel demands as it can be converted into a Leontief one by simply assigning a very low value to the substitution parameter in the CES function.

Equations discussed in this subsection are based on the nests of production functions shown in fig. 4.9. These equations represent substitution amongst energy products, and between energy products and capital. IIND is a subset of industries, and it includes the mining, manufacturing and construction industries. The set ERG contains names of all fuels and electricity, while the subset FUL has only fuel names.

$$x1\_s_{ij} = x1ful_j + a1\_s_{ij} - \sigma IIND1 (\{ p1\_s_{ij} + a1\_s_{ij} \} - p1ful_j) ,$$

$$i \in FUL, j \in IIND, \qquad (4.13.2.1\ddagger)$$

$$\text{plful}_j = \frac{1}{\sum\limits_{i \in FUL} \text{PUR1\_S}_{ij}} (\sum\limits_{i \in FUL} \text{PUR1\_S}_{ij} \times \{\text{pl\_s}_{ij} + \text{al\_s}_{ij}\}), \quad j \in \text{IIND},$$

$$(4.13.2.2)$$

$$\text{xlful}_j = \text{xlerg}_j - \sigma\text{IIND2} (\text{plful}_j - \text{plerg}_j), \quad j \in \text{IIND}, \quad (4.13.2.3)$$

Eq. (4.13.2.1) determines the demand for each fuel, while eq. (4.13.2.3) determines total demand for fuels, (xlful_j). The price of composite of all fuels, plful_j is determined by eq. (4.13.2.2). In these eqs. the parameters σIIND1 to σIIND2 are elasticities of substitution between fuels, and between aggregated fuels and electricity, respectively, for all industries in IIND.

$$\text{xl\_s}_{ij} = \text{xlerg}_j + \text{al\_s}_{ij} - \sigma\text{IIND2}(\{\text{pl\_s}_{ij} + \text{al\_s}_{ij}\} - \text{plerg}_j),$$

$$i = \text{electricity}, \quad j \in \text{IIND}, \quad (4.13.2.4\ddagger)$$

$$\text{plerg}_j = \frac{1}{\sum\limits_{i \in ERG} \text{PUR1\_S}_{ij}} (\sum\limits_{i \in ERG} \text{PUR1\_S}_{ij} \times \{\text{pl\_s}_{ij} + \text{al\_s}_{ij}\}), \quad j \in \text{IIND},$$

$$(4.13.2.5)$$

$$\text{xlerg}_j = \text{xlcaperg}_j - \sigma\text{IIND3} (\{\text{plerg}_j - \text{plcaperg}_j\}), \quad j \in \text{IIND},$$

$$(4.13.2.6)$$

$$\text{xlcap}_j = \text{xlcaperg}_j + \text{alcap}_j + \text{alprm}_j$$

$$- \sigma\text{IIND3}(\text{plcap}_j + \text{alcap}_j + \text{alprm}_j - \text{plcaperg}_j) \quad j \in \text{IIND}, \quad (4.13.2.7\ddagger)$$

$$\text{plcaperg}_j = \frac{1}{\sum\limits_{i \in ERG} \text{PUR1\_S}_{ij} + \text{V1CAP\_c}_j} (\sum\limits_{i \in ERG} \text{PUR1\_S}_{ij} \times \{\text{pl\_s}_{ij}$$

$$+ \text{al\_s}_{ij}\} + \text{V1CAP\_c}_j \times \{\text{plcap}_j + \text{alcap}_j + \text{alprm}_j\}), \quad j \in \text{IIND}.$$

$$(4.13.2.8)$$

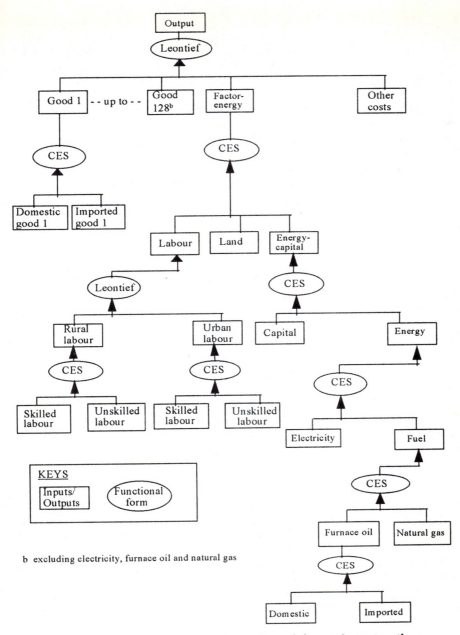

Figure 4.9   Input structure for manufacturing, mining and construction

b excluding electricity, furnace oil and natural gas

75

Eq. (4.13.2.6) determines the demand for composite of fuels and electricity ($x1erg_j$), and its price, $p1erg_j$, is determined in eq. (4.13.2.5). The variable $x1caperg_j$ in eqs. (4.13.2.6) and (4.13.2.7) represents the CES composite of capital and fuel-electricity inputs, while the price of this composite input, ($p1caperg_j$), is defined in eq. (4.13.2.8). The parameter $\sigma IIND3$ represents elasticity of substitution between aggregated energy products and capital.

We have assumed that capital is a substitute for 'energy', while the 'energy-capital' composite is treated as a substitute for labour and land. The parameter $\sigma IIND4$ is the elasticity of substitution between labour, land and the composite 'capital-energy' input.

$$x1caperg_j = x1prmerg_j - \sigma IIND4(p1caperg_j - p1prmerg_j), j \in IIND,$$

$$(4.13.2.9)$$

$$x1lab\_rp_j = x1prmerg_j + a1lab\_rp_j + a1prm_j$$

$$- \sigma IIND4 (p1lab\_rp_j + a1lab\_rp_j + a1prm_j - p1prmerg_j), j \in IIND,$$

$$(4.13.2.10\ddagger)$$

$$x1lnd_j = x1prmerg_j + a1lnd_j + a1prm_j$$

$$- \sigma IIND4(p1lnd_j + a1lnd_j + a1prm_j - p1prmerg_j) , j \in IIND,$$

$$(4.13.2.11\ddagger)$$

$$p1prmerg_j = \frac{1}{\sum_{i \in ERG} PUR1\_s_{ij} + V1PRM_j} (\sum_{i \in ERG} PUR1\_s_{ij} \times \{p1\_s_{ij} + a1\_s_{ij} \}$$

$$+V1PRRM_j \times \{p1prm_j + a1prm_j\}), j \in IIND. \quad (4.13.2.12)$$

The variable $x1prmerg_j$ in eqs. (4.13.2.9) to (4.13.2.11) represents the composite of all primary factors and energy products. The price of this composite input, $p1prmerg_j$, is determined in eq. (4.13.2.12).

As shown in fig. 4.9, output in industry j is a Leontief composite of non-energy goods, 'other costs' input, and 'energy-factor' input (see the top level nest). Consequently the 'energy-factor' input demand is in direct proportion to the output or activity level of an industry.

$$x1prmerg_j = atot_j + z_j , \quad j \in IIND. \quad (4.13.2.13)$$

76

Eqs. (4.13.2.7), (4.13.2.10) and (4.13.2.11) define demand for capital, labour and land, respectively, for the industries in the set IIND. These equations replace demand eqs. (2.1) to (2.3) in Block 2, for capital, labour and land for these industries. Eqs. (4.13.2.1) and (4.13.2.4) replace intermediate input demand eqs. (4.3) for energy products in Block 4 for the industries in the set IIND.

4.13.3 Input structure for the road transport industry

Gasoline and HSD are the two fuels used in road transport. We define a CES production function to make 'motor fuel' input by combining gasoline and HSD. The composite input of 'fuel-capital' is then defined as the CES composite of 'motor fuel' and capital stock (see the bottom of fig. 4.10). The rest of the production structure resembles that for the manufacturing industries.

$$x1\_s_{ij} = x1ful_j + a1\_s_{ij} - \sigma IRDT1(\{p1\_s_{ij} + a1\_s_{ij}\} - p1ful_j),$$

$$i = gasoline, HSD, j \in IRDT, \qquad (4.13.3.1\ddagger)$$

$$p1ful_j = \frac{1}{\sum_i PUR1\_s_{ij}} (\sum_i PUR1\_s_{ij} \times p1\_s_{ij} + a1\_s_{ij}\}),$$

$$i = gasoline, HSD, j \in IRDT, \qquad (4.13.3.2)$$

$$x1ful_j = x1capful_j - \sigma IRDT2 (\{p1ful_j - p1capful_j), \qquad j \in IRDT \qquad (4.13.3.3)$$

$$x1cap_j = x1capful_j + a1cap_j + a1prm_j$$

$$- \sigma IRDT2(p1cap_j + a1cap_j + a1prm_j - p1capful_j), \quad j \in IRDT,$$

$$(4.13.3.4\ddagger)$$

$$p1capful_j = \frac{1}{\sum_i PUR1\_s_{ij} + V1CAP\_c_j} (\sum_i PUR1\_s_{ij} \times \{p1\_s_{ij} + a1\_s_{ij}\}$$

$$+ V1CAP\_c_j \times \{p1cap_j + a1cap_j + a1prm_j\}),$$

$$i = gasoline, HSD, j \in IRDT, \qquad (4.13.3.5)$$

$$x1capful_j = x1prmful_j - \sigma IRDT3(p1capful_j - p1prmful_j) \quad j \in IRDT,$$

$$(4.13.3.6)$$

77

$$x1lab\_rp_j = x1prmful_j + a1lab\_rp_j + a1prm_j$$

$$- \sigma IRDT3\ (p1lab\_rp_j + a1lab\_rp_j + a1prm_j - p1prmful_j)\,,\ j \in IRDT,$$

$$(4.13.3.7\ddagger)$$

$$x1lnd_j = x1prmful_j + a1lnd_j + a1prm_j$$

$$- \sigma IRDT3\ (p1lnd_j + a1lnd_j + a1prm_j - p1prmful_j)\,,$$

$$j \in IRDT, \qquad (4.13.3.8\ddagger)$$

$$p1prmful_j = \frac{1}{\sum_i PUR1\_s_{ij} + V1PRRM_j} \left(\sum_i PUR1\_s_{ij} \times \{p1\_s_{ij} + a1\_s_{ij}\} \right.$$

$$\left. + V1PRRM_j \times \{p1prm_j + a1prm_j\} \right),$$

$$i = gasoline,\ HSD,\ j \in IRDT, \qquad (4.13.3.9)$$

$$x1prmful_j = atot_j + z_j\,, \qquad j \in IRDT. \qquad (4.13.3.10)$$

In the above equations the parameters $\sigma IRDT1$ to $\sigma IRDT3$ are elasticities of substitution between gasoline and HSD, between motor fuels and capital, and between land, labour and 'capital-fuel' inputs. Since these parameters are specific to the road transport industry, we have labelled them with the industry subset. The derivation procedure for these equations is similar to that defined for the nested production function of other industries in the previous sections.

In eqs. (4.13.3.1) and (4.13.3.3), the variable $x1ful_j$ represents the composite demand for gasoline and HSD, while the price for this composite input ($p1ful_j$) is determined in (4.13.3.2). Similarly, the variable $x1capful_j$ represents the composite of capital and the two fuels inputs. The price of this composite input, $p1capful_j$, is defined in eq. (4.13.3.5). The CES composite of all primary factors and the two fuels is defined in eq. (4.13.3.10) and its price, $p1prmful_j$, is determined in eq. (4.13.3.9).

In this subsection, eqs. (4.13.3.4), (4.13.3.7) and (4.13.3.8) define demand for capital, labour and land for the road transport industry according to the production structure given in fig. 4.10. These equations replace demand eqs. of these factors for this industry in Block 2. Similarly, eq. (4.13.3.1), that defines demand for gasoline and HSD, replaces intermediate-input demand eq. (4.3) in Block 4 for these fuels for the road transport industry.

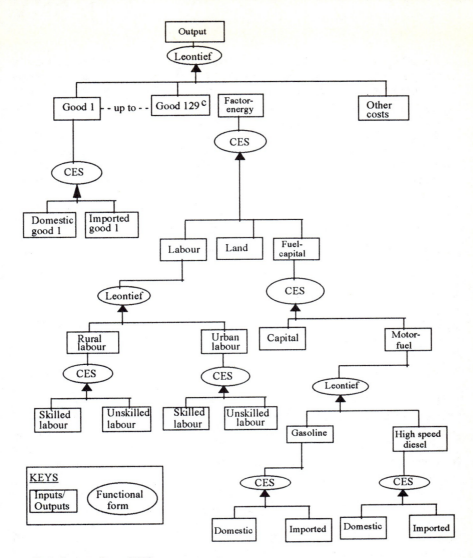

c Excluding gasoline and HSD

Figure 4.10 Input structure for the road transport industry

79

4.13.4 Input structure for the steam electricity industry

In GE-PAK there are four electricity industries. This disaggregation is discussed in detail in section 4.15. In this section, we discuss the input structure for the combined cycle electricity and steam electricity industries which have specific patterns of energy inputs. The input structure of the other two electricity industries resembles that of the special input-structure given in fig. 4.7.

FO and natural gas are two fuels used in the steam electricity industry. In Pakistan, most of the steam plants have a dual-firing system. Therefore, the two fuels are substitutes in steam electricity generation. In the steam electricity industry we assume that the composite input 'fuel' is a CES composition of natural gas and furnace oil (see fig. 4.11).

$$x1\_s_{ij} = x1ful_j + a1\_s_{ij} - \sigma STM(\{p1\_s_{ij} + a1\_s_{ij}\} - p1ful_j),$$

$$i = \text{natural gas, FO}, j \in \text{ISTM}, \qquad (4.13.4.1\ddagger)$$

$$p1ful_j = \frac{1}{\sum\limits_i PUR1\_s_{ij}} (\sum_i PUR1\_s_{ij} \times \{p1\_s_{ij} + a1\_s_{ij}\}),$$

$$i = \text{natural gas, FO}, j \in \text{ISTM}, \qquad (4.13.4.2)$$

$$x1ful_j = atot_j + z_j, \quad j \in \text{ISTM}. \qquad (4.13.4.3)$$

Eqs. (4.13.4.1) define demand for natural gas and furnace oil for the steam electricity industry. These equations replace the demand equations for these two fuels in Block 4 for the steam electricity industry. The parameter σSTM is the elasticity of substitution between these fuels in steam electricity generation. The demands for the composite 'fuel' input ($x1ful_j$) and its price ($p1ful_j$) are defined in eqs. (4.13.4.2) and (4.13.4.3).

4.13.5 Input structure for the combined cycle electricity industry

Fig. 4.13 shows the pattern of energy substitutions for the combined cycle electricity industry. In this industry, natural gas and HSD are the major energy inputs. A combined cycle plant consists of one steam plant and two gas turbine plants. Since steam plants can be operated on FO and natural gas, we assume that 'steam fuel' is a CES composite of natural gas and furnace oil, while HSD which is used by the gas turbine plant is used in a fixed proportion to the output level (see fig. 4.12). A Leontief production function aggregates 'steam fuel' with all other inputs.

The fuel demand equations for natural gas and FO for the combined cycle electricity industry are defined in (4.13.5.1). The parameter $\sigma ICCY$ is the elasticity of substitution between these fuels.

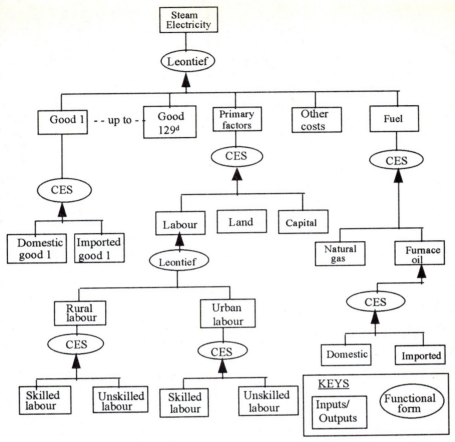

d   excluding natural gas and furnace oil

Figure 4.11   Input structure for the steam electricity industry

The composite fuel demand $(x1stmful_j)$ is in direct proportion to electricity production in the industry as defined in eq. (4.13.5.3), while its price is $(p1stmful_j)$ given in eq. (4.13.4.2).

$$x1\_s_{ij} = x1stmful_j + a1\_s_{ij} - \sigma ICCY(\{p1\_s_{ij} + a1\_s_{ij}\} - p1stmful_j),$$

$$i = \text{natural gas, FO, } j \in ICCY, \qquad (4.13.5.1‡)$$

$$p1stmful_j = \frac{1}{\sum_i PUR1\_s_{ij}} \left(\sum_i PUR1\_s_{ij} \times \{p1\_s_{ij} + a1\_s_{ij}\} \right),$$

$$i = \text{natural gas, FO}, \quad j \in \text{ICCY}, \qquad (4.13.5.2)$$

$$x1stmful_j = atot_j + z_j, \qquad j \in \text{ICCY}, \qquad (4.13.5.3)$$

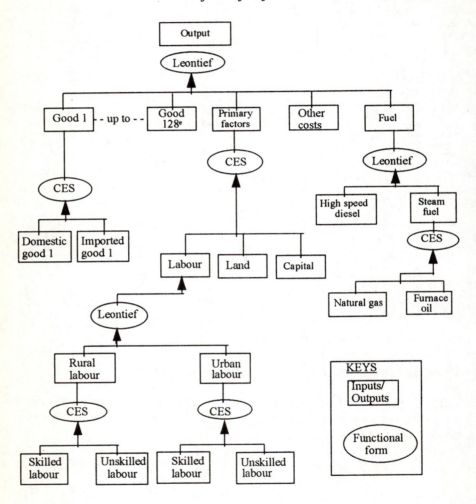

e   excluding natural gas, HSD and furnace oil

Figure 4.12   Input structure for the combined cycle electricity industry

4.14 Output structure of industries

Fig. 4.13 gives a schematic representation of the three categories of industries in GE-PAK.

Industries	Single Output	Multiple Outputs
Single Industry	All industries other than the oil and gas, refinery and electricity industries.	Oil and gas industry, refinery industry.
Multiple Industries	Electricity industries.	

Figure 4.13   Three categories of industries with respect to output structure

In the first category, every industry produces a single commodity which is not produced by other industries. For example, 'Large-farm wheat' commodity is produced only by the 'large-farm wheat' industry.

In the second category, each industry produces more than one commodity but no other industry produces these commodities. For example the oil and gas industry produces two commodities which are not produced by any other industry. The CET specification in these industries allows to choose the degree of substitution in the composition of multiple products. Alternatively, we can assume a Leontief aggregation of these products by setting the CET parameter equal to zero.

In the third category, each industry produces a single commodity but that commodity is also produced by some other industries. The electricity industries in GE-PAK fall in this category. Section 4.15 discusses how output level in each electricity industry is determined.

In this section, we discuss equations that determine output levels in industries from the second categories. These equations correspond to the top level nest given in fig. 4.7.

Block 5 Equations for output-mix in multiple-output industries:

$$x0_{ij} = z_j + \sigma OUT_j \, (p0dom_i - p0ind_j), \quad i \in NONCELE,$$
$$j \in NONIELE, \tag{5.1}$$

$$p0ind_j = \frac{1}{MAKE\_ij} \sum_{i \, \in \, COM} MAKE_{ij} \times p0dom_i,$$
$$j \in NONIELE, \tag{5.2}$$

83

$$x0dom_i = \frac{1}{MAKE\_ji} \sum_{j \in NONIELE} MAKE_{ij} \times x0_{ij},$$

$$i \in NONCELE \qquad\qquad (5.3)$$

The above equations are derived from the following optimisation problem.

Industry j maximises its total revenue from all outputs subject to the transformation frontier given below:

$$Z_j = \underset{i \in COM}{CET} (X0_{ij}) \qquad\qquad j \in IND. \qquad (4.15.1)$$

The CET aggregation function is identical to CES, except that the transformation parameter in the CET function has the opposite sign to the substitution parameter in the CES function. Here, an increase in the price of a commodity, relative to the average price, induces transformation in favour of that output. The variable $p0ind_j$ is the average unit-revenue of industry j, and is defined by eq. (5.2) as the weighted-average of prices of commodities produced by industry j. Elements in the data matrix $MAKE_{ij}$ give the output values of commodities produced by industry j. Eqs. (5.1) state that commodity i in industry j is produced in proportion to the activity level, Z_j, and to a price term. The price term consists of an elasticity of transformation, σOUT_j, multiplied by the price of commodity i relative to the average price received by the industry. It is worth noting that the symbol for the average unit-revenue, $p0ind_j$, is the same as that used in the equation defining the effective price of a unit of activity (see Block 4). This confirms our interpretation of equation (5.4) as a zero pure-profit condition.

Although only two industries have multiple outputs, we have defined these equations for all industries for the sake of uniformity and algebraic convenience. For single-output industries, $p0dom_i$ is equal to the corresponding $p0ind_j$. Hence, the output of commodity i is produced in direct proportion to the activity level z_j.

Eq. (5.3) defines the total supply of domestically produced commodity i as the weighted-sum of its supplies from all industries.

Eqs. (5.1) to (5.3) are active for all industries other than the four electricity industries because the production levels in those four industries are determined according to a supply structure. NONIELE is the subset of industries that contains all non-electricity industries, and NONCELE includes all commodities except electricity.

4.15 Electricity supply structure

Block 6 contains the equations determining electricity supply from the four industries, according to a supply structure given in fig. 4.15. In Pakistan, two major sources of electricity generation are hydro and thermal. Thermal electricity is generated by three types of plants: (1) combined cycle; (2) steam generator; and (3) gas turbine. Each type of electricity plant has a different composition of capital cost, fuel costs, and types of fuel used. The four types of plants also differ in their engineering characteristics, as follows:

1. Capacity factor—this indicates the generating mode for which a plant is designed, *i.e,* base load, intermediate load, or peak load.
2. Starting time; time required to start generation from a plant.
3. Fast-spinning-surge capability, which refers to the time required to increase generation in the event of a sudden increase in electricity demand or failure of another plant.
4. Percent of the plant capacity that can be used for fast-spinning reserve.
5. Instant on-off capability.

GE-PAK distinguishes between the four types of electricity plants by identifying four industries which are operated as an integrated system by an electricity utility. The contribution of each industry in total electricity supply is determined by its economic cost of production and by operational constraints in electricity generation. Thus, two assumptions have been made:

1. Each electricity industry minimises the cost of producing a given level of output which is supplied to the electricity utility.
2. The job of the electricity utility is to supply electricity to all consumers. As consumers have a certain pattern of electricity demand, the utility apportioned total electricity need to generated to four industries in such a way that the generation mix matches the demand pattern.

In the following subsections, we discuss:

1. The nature and pattern of electricity demand in general.
2. The operational characteristics of four types of electricity plants, and the constraints in combining electricity generated by these plants.
3. A two-level electricity supply function that allows substitution between electricity generated by the four types of plants under their operational constraints.

4.15.1 Nature and pattern of electricity demand

At a point in time, electricity demand is for electricity power measured in units of Megawatt (MW), which is called 'Load' demand. As the consumer demand for power (MW) varies with time say—from one hour to another—the total electricity demand in a day (24 hours) is defined as:

$$\text{ELEC} = \int_0^{24} \text{LOAD}(t) \, dt \qquad (4.15.1)$$

85

where ELEC is Megawatt-hours (MWh) of electricity demand, and LOAD is demand for electric power in megawatt (MW) units of electricity. A hypothetical daily load curve with a sharp afternoon peak load is shown in fig. 4.14. The area under the curve is the total electricity requirement, in units of megawatt-hours. The shape of the curve shows the pattern of power demand.

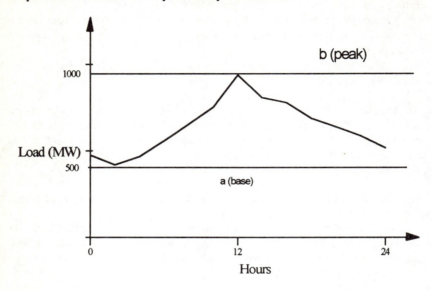

Figure 4.14 Hypothetical daily load curve

4.15.2 Operational constraints in electricity generation and operational characteristics of electricity plants

To meet both daily and seasonal variations in load demand, electricity is supplied by combining output from different types of plants. The electricity plants are brought into production line in a certain order, referred to as the 'loading order'. Electricity plants are ranked according to the average cost per MWh (least cost plants are placed first), and the 'operational constraints' of the electricity system which requires smooth supply of electricity at the minimum cost.

Two of the operational constraints on the electricity supply are as follows:

1. As the demand for load varies, the electricity system should be able to adjust production without any losses.
2. If there is a sudden increase in the load demand or failure in a plant there should be some units that have the capability to start production in a short time.

86

Table 4.3
Typical characteristics of electricity plants

Types of Plant	Fast spinning reserve capability		3 Maximum rate of sustained load change[a]	4 Start-up time
	1 Available per cent of rating	2 Time required (second)		
Steam (gas or oil)	30	30	2-5% per minute	Hours
Steam (coal)	15-20	10-30	2-5% per minute	Hours
Nuclear	8-20	10-30	1.5-3% per minute	Hours
Gas turbine	100	5	20% per second	1-10 minute[a]
Hydro	0-100[a]	10	1%-10% per second	1-5 minute[a]

a for various types of plants within the category

Source: International Atomic Energy Agency, Vienna, (1984), Table 7.IV.

Table 4.3 shows the operational characteristics of five types of electricity plants. The fast spinning reserve capability of an electricity plant refers to the time required to increase electricity generation from a plant if there is a sudden increase in electricity demand, or another unit fails. Column 2 shows the fast spinning reserve capability of various types of plants, while column 1 shows the percentage of their capacity that has this fast spinning capability. It appears that hydro plants and gas turbines have about the same level of fast spinning reserve capability and about the same percentage of capacity available to utilise it. Fossil steam and nuclear plants are comparable in their fast spinning reserve capability. Turning to start up time, the gas turbine and hydro plants are fast while the other two types of plants are slow. Column 3 of table 4.3 shows that for sustained load changes, the response of the hydro and gas turbine plants are similar, and are much faster than the other plants.

The combined cycle plants consist of steam plants and gas turbines. Hence, their operational characteristics are overlapping. These plants can be grouped with gas turbine plants or steam plants depending on their cost of production and the duties assigned to them in the generation system.

On the demand side, the model computes the percentage change in total electricity demand (MWh). We assume that the pattern of electricity use changes with the change in total electricity demand. Hence, we need to allow substitution between electricity generated by the four types of plants for two reasons:

1.   Changes in electricity generation apportioned to various plants, which is required to meet the change in total electricity demand.
2.   Changes in the relative production costs of the four types of plants.

   GE-PAK incorporates the four electricity industries, each representing a plant type. On the basis of the operational characteristics of the plant types, these industries have been grouped into two categories.

1.   IMFLEX; more flexible technology group which consists of the hydro and gas turbine electricity industries; and
2.   ILFLEX; less-flexible technology group which consists of steam and combined cycle electricity industries. We have included combined cycle plants in this category as the production cost of electricity from these plants is closer to that of steam plants.

   We have defined a two-level nested function that apportions units of electricity demanded to the four industries, categorised by two types of technologies. Fig. 4.15 shows the structure of this function.
   The supply equations in Block 6 are derived from the solution to the two-part cost-minimisation problem of the electricity utility. The total cost of supply from less-flexible technologies is minimised subject to the following CES supply function:

$$\text{X0ELEC\_LFLEX} = \text{CES}(\text{X0}_j), \qquad j \in \text{ILFLX}, \quad (4.15.2)$$

where X0 is electricity generated (in MWh) by j industry and ILFLX is the set of less-flexible electricity industries, X0ELEC_LFLEX is total electricity generated by such industries. Similarly, the total cost of supply from more-flexible technologies is minimised subject to the following CES supply function:

$$\text{X0ELEC\_MFLEX} = \text{CES}(\text{X0}_j), \qquad j \in \text{IMFLX}, \quad (4.15.3)$$

where IMFLX is a set of more-flexible electricity industries, and X0ELEC_MFLEX is electricity generated by them. The solutions to the two optimisation problems in percentage-change form are given in Block 6.

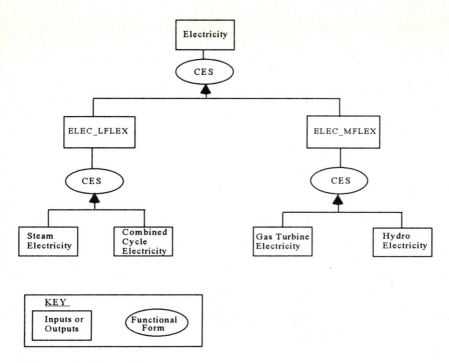

Figure 4.15 Electricity supply structure

Block 6 Equations of electricity supply structure:

$$x0_{ij} = x0elec\_lflex - \sigma ILFLX \, (p0ind_j - p0elec\_lflex),$$

$$i = electricity, j \in ILFLX, \qquad (6.1)$$

$$p0elec = lflex = \frac{1}{\sum\limits_{j \,\in ILFLX} MAKE_{ij}} \, (\sum\limits_{j \,\in ILFLX} MAKE_{ij} \times p0ind_j \,),$$

$$i = electricity, \qquad (6.2)$$

$$x0_{ij} = x0elec\_mflex - \sigma IMFLX \, (p0ind_j - p0elec\_mflex),$$

$$i = electricity, j \in IMFLX, \qquad (6.3)$$

$$p0elec\_mflex = \frac{1}{\sum\limits_{j \,\in\, IMFLX} MAKE_{ij}} \, (\sum\limits_{j \,\in\, IMFLX} MAKE_{ij} \times p0ind_j \,),$$

$$i = electricity, \qquad (6.4)$$

89

$$x0elec\_lflex = x0dom_i - \sigma IELE \,(p0elec\_lflex - p0dom_i),$$

$$i = electricity, \tag{6.5}$$

$$x0elec\_mflex = x0dom_i - \sigma IELE \,(p0elec\_mflex - p0dom_i),$$

$$i = electricity, \tag{6.6}$$

$$p0dom_i = \frac{1}{\sum\limits_{j\,\in\,IELE} MAKE_{ij}} \,(\sum\limits_{j\,\in\,IELE} MAKE_{ij} \times p0ind_j).$$

$$i = electricity. \tag{6.7}$$

Eq. (6.1) states that electricity generation in steam and combined cycle electricity industries are in proportion to the total electricity supply from the less-flexible electricity industries (x0elec_lflex), and a price term. In all the equations, variables beginning with 'p0' are the basic prices of electricity and, hence, represent the production costs. As shown in eq. (6.2), poelec_lflex is a weighted-average cost of electricity generation using the less flexible technologies. A change in the relative production costs in the two electricity industries induces substitution in favour of the industry which experiences the lower production cost. The parameter $\sigma ILFLX$ represents this substitution elasticity.

The total cost of electricity supply from the two types of technologies is minimised subject to the following production function:

$$X0ELEC = CES\,(\,X0ELEC\_LFLEX, \;X0ELEC\_MFLEX\,). \tag{4.15.3}$$

The solution to this problem in percentage-change form is given in eqs. (6.5) and (6.6). Electricity generation is determined in proportion to the total supply of electricity and a price term. The elasticity parameter $\sigma IELE$ represents substitution possibility in electricity generation from two types of technologies. However, $\sigma IELE$ is governed by the consumers' ability to change the pattern of electricity demand. A high value of $\sigma IELE$ indicates flexibility in the demand pattern.

4.16   Demands for commodities for capital formation

The production structure of new units of capital is similar to the structure which governs intermediate input use in current production (see fig. 4.7). The demand equations for commodities in Block 7 are derived from the solutions to the investors' two-part cost minimisation problem. In the first part, the total cost of input i, from the two sources, is minimised subject to the following CES production function:

$$X2\_s_{ij} = \underset{s\,\in\,SRC}{CES}\,(\frac{X2_{isj}}{A2_{isj}}), \quad i \in COM, j \in IND, \tag{4.16.1}$$

90

where $X2_{isj}$ is the intermediate input demand for capital formation in industry j. In the second part, total cost of inputs (all composite commodities) is minimised subject to the Leontief production function:

$$Y_j = \underset{i \in COM}{MIN} \frac{1}{A2\_isj} \left(\frac{X2\_sij}{A2\_sij} \right), \quad j \in IND. \qquad (4.16.2)$$

Total value of investment in each industry, Y_j, is exogenous to the cost-minimisation problem, and is determined by eqs. given in Block 20.

Eqs. (7.1) to (7.3) determine the demands for source-specific inputs and for composite inputs to capital formation. The parameter $\sigma SRC2_i$ is elasticity of substitution between domestic and imported intermediate inputs for capital formation. Eq. (7.4) determines the price of a new unit of capital as the average cost of its production — a zero pure-profit condition.

Block 7 Equations of demand for commodities for capital formation:

$$x2_{isj} = x2\_sij + a2_{isj} - \sigma SRC2_i \left[\{ p2_{isj} + a2_{isj} \} - p2\_sij \right],$$

$$i \in COM, s \in SRC, j \in IND, \qquad (7.1)$$

$$p2\_sij = \frac{1}{PUR2\_sij} \left(\underset{s \in SRC}{\Sigma} PUR2_{isj} \{ p2_{isj} + a2_{isj} \} \right),$$

$$i \in COM, j \in IND, \qquad (7.2)$$

$$x2\_sij = y_j + a2\_isj + a2\_sij, \quad i \in COM, j \in IND, \qquad (7.3)$$

$$p2\_isj = a2\_isj + \frac{1}{PUR2\_isj} \left(\underset{i \in COM}{\Sigma} PUR2\_sij \{ p2\_sij + a2\_sij \} \right),$$

$$j \in IND. \qquad (7.4)$$

4.17 Household demands for items

Horridge *et al.*, (1993) have given a very simple and systematic procedure to derive demand equations (in percentage-change form) for households with the LES demand system. We have adopted that procedure to derive equations of household demand for consumption items. As shown in fig. 4.16, it has been assumed that the households in each category derive utility from consumption of items, which are aggregated by the Stone-Geary function leading to the LES demand functions.

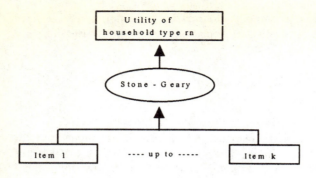

Figure 4.16 Structure of household demand

To analyse the Stone-Geary utility function, it is helpful to divide consumption of each item (XITEM) by a household type into two components: a luxury or supernumerary part, XITEMLUX; and a subsistence or minimum part, XITEMSUB. By definition then:

$$XITEM_{krn} = XITEMSUB_{krn} + XITEMLUX_{krn} ,$$

$$k \in ITM, r \in REG, n \in INC. \qquad (4.17.1)$$

In percentage-change form, eq. (4.17.1) is defined as:

$$xitem_{krn} = (1-ALPHA\_I_{krn}) \times xitemsub_{krn} + ALPHAI_{krn} \times xitemlux_{krn} ,$$

$$k \in ITM, r \in REG, n \in INC, \qquad (4.17.2)$$

where $ALPHA\_I_{krn}$, is the share of supernumerary expenditure on item k in total expenditure on k, by household type n in region r (Appendix D shows the formulae used to arrive at percentage-change forms). As shown in Block 8, $ALPHA\_I_{krn}$ are computed using econometric estimates of the Frisch parameters ($FRISCH_{rn}$) and expenditure elasticities of items (EPS_{krn}) for 14 types of households. $FRISCH_{rn}$ represents the reciprocal of share of luxury expenditure in total expenditure of household type rn.

Block 8 Coefficients in household demand equations:

$$ALPHA\_I_{krn} = ALPHARN\_EPS_{krn}, \quad k \in ITM, r \in REG, n \in INC, \quad (8.1)$$

$$ALPHA_{rn} = (-1/FRISCH_{rn}), \qquad r \in REG, n \in INC, \qquad (8.2)$$

92

$$\text{DELTA}_{krn} = \text{EPS}_{krn} \times \frac{\text{VITEM}_{krn}}{\text{VITEM\_}_{krn}},$$

$$k \in \text{ITM}, r \in \text{REG}, n \in \text{INC}. \quad (8.3)$$

The demand for an item from a household group, has a subsistence component which is proportional to the number of households (Q_p_{rn}) in that group and a taste-change variable AITEMSUB_{krn}. Hence, in the percentage-change form xitemsub_{krn} can be defined as:

$$\text{xitemsub}_{krn} = q\_p_{rn} + \text{aitemsub}_{krn},$$

$$k \in \text{ITM}, r \in \text{REG}, n \in \text{INC}. \quad (4.17.3)$$

Only the luxury components enter into a household utility function which is assumed to be maximised by the household. The utility function has the well-known Cobb-douglas form:

$$\text{UTILITY}_{rn} = \frac{1}{Q\_p_{rn}} \prod_k \text{XITEMLUX}_{kr}^{\text{DELTA}_{krn}},$$

$$r \in \text{REG}, n \in \text{INC}, \quad (4.17.4)$$

where $\sum_k \text{DELTA}_{krn} = 1$.

The demand equations derived from the solution to this problem in percentage-change form are as follows:

$$\text{xitemlux}_{krn} = \text{luxexp}_{rn} + \text{aitemlux}_{krn} - \text{pitem}_k,$$

$$k \in \text{ITM}, r \in \text{REG}, n \in \text{INC}, \quad (4.17.5)$$

$$\text{utility}_{rn} + q\text{-}p_{rn} = \sum_k (\text{DELTA}_{krn} \times \text{xitemlux}_{krn}),$$

$$r \in \text{REG}, n \in \text{INC}. \quad (4.17.6)$$

The coefficient DELTA_{krn} in eq. (4.17.6) is the marginal share of item k in the budget of household type rn [see eq. (9.3) in Block 9]. Note that the Cobb-Douglas form gives rise to exogenous budget shares for spending on luxuries:

$$\text{XITEMLUX}_{krn} \times \text{PITEM}_k = \text{DELTA}_{krn} \times \text{LUXEXP}_{rn},$$

$$k \in \text{ITM}, r \in \text{REG}, n \in \text{INC}, \quad (4.17.7)$$

where LUXEXP_{rn} is the household's total expenditure on luxuries. DELTA_{krn}, therefore, may be interpreted as the marginal budget share of item k in total spending on luxuries.

93

We arrived at eq. (9.1) in Block 9 by replacing xitemsub_{krn} and xitemlux_{krn} in (4.17.2) using (4.17.3) and (4.17.5). Similarly, we replace xitemlux_{krn} in (4.17.6) to arrive at eq. (9.4) in Block 9.

Equation (9.1) states that the demand for an item for household type rn is determined by the number of households in that category, shift in the taste for subsistence and luxury consumption of that item, total luxury expenditure of that household type, and price of that item. It is noteworthy that the price of an item affects its demand for luxury consumption only.

Block 9 Equations for household demand:

$$\text{xitem}_{krn} = [1 - \text{ALPHA\_I}_{krn}]\,[\text{q\_p}_{rn} + \text{aitemsub}_{krn}]$$
$$+ \text{ALPHA\_I}_{krn} \times [\text{luxexp}_{rn} + \text{aitemlux}_{krn} - \text{pitem}_k],$$
$$k \in \text{ITM, } r \in \text{REG, } n \in \text{INC,} \qquad (9.1)$$

$$\text{aitemlux}_{krn} = \text{aitemsub}_{krn} - \sum_{l \in \text{ITM}}(\text{DELTA}_{lrn} \times \text{aitemsub}_{lrn}),$$
$$k \in \text{ITM, } r \in \text{REG, } n \in \text{INC,} \qquad (9.2)$$

$$\text{aitemsub}_{krn} = \text{aitem}_{krn} - \sum_{l \in \text{ITM}}(\text{VTEM}_{lrn} \times \text{aitem}_{lrn}),$$
$$k \in \text{ITM, } r \in \text{REG, } n \in \text{INC,} \qquad (9.3)$$

$$\text{utility}_{rn} = \text{luxexp}_{rn} - \text{q\_p}_{rn} - \sum_{k \in \text{ITM}}(\text{DELTA}_{krn} \times \text{pitem}_k),$$
$$r \in \text{REG, } n \in \text{INC,} \qquad (9.4)$$

$$\text{chou}_{rn} = \frac{1}{\text{VITEM\_k}_{rn}} \sum_{k \in \text{ITM}}(\text{VITEM}_{krn} \times \{\text{xitem}_{krn} + \text{pitem}_k\}),$$
$$r \in \text{REG, } n \in \text{INC.} \qquad (9.5)$$

In eq. (9.3), aitem is a taste-change variable represented by a change in the average budget share of the item. Eqs. (9.2) and (9.3) give default settings for the taste-change variables specific to luxury and subsistence components of the household consumption, *i.e.* aitemlux_{krn} and aitemsub_{krn}, respectively. These equations allow the average budget shares to be shocked *via* aitem in a way that preserves the pattern of expenditure elasticities (see Horridge, 1993 for further details).

4.18 Demands for commodities for item formation

It has been assumed that items are produced by domestic and imported commodities, and no primary factor is used as input to item formation. The input demand equations in Block 10 are derived from the solution to the two-part cost-minimisation problem which is similar to that defined for capital formation. Hence, input demand equations for item formation in Block 10 are similar to those in Block 7.

Eq. (10.1) determines demand for commodity i, from two sources, to produce item k ($x3item_{kis}$). Total demand for item k, from all households is an aggregate of its demand. In these equations, $\sigma SRC3_i$ represents elasticity of substitution for commodity i from the two sources, and $\sigma COMITM_i$ represents elasticity of substitution between commodities in formation of item k.

Block 10 Demand equations for formation of items:

$$x3item_{kis} = x3item\_s_{ki} - \sigma SRC3_i \, [p3_{is} - p3item\_s_{ki}],$$
$$k \in ITM, \; i \in COM, \; s \in SRC, \qquad (10.1)$$

$$p3item\_s_{ki} = \frac{1}{COMITEM\_s_{ki}} (\sum_{s \in SRC} COMITEM_{kis} \times p3_{is}),$$
$$k \in ITM, \; i \in COM, \qquad (10.2)$$

$$x3item\_s_{ki} = xitem\_rn_k - \sigma COMITM_i \, [p3item\_s_{ki} - p3item_k],$$
$$k \in ITM, \; i \in COM, \qquad (10.3)$$

$$pitem_k = \frac{1}{COMITEM\_is_k} (\sum_{i \in COM} COMITEM\_s_{ki} \times p3item\_s_{ki}),$$
$$k \in ITM, \qquad (10.4)$$

$$x3_{is} = \frac{1}{COMITEM\_k_{is}} (\sum_{k \in ITM} COMITEM_{kis} \times x3item_{kis}),$$
$$i \in COM, \; s \in SRC. \qquad (10.5)$$

$$xitem\_rn_k = \frac{1}{VITEM\_k_{rn}} (\sum_{r \in REG} \sum_{n \in INC} VITEM_{krn} \times xitem_{krn}),$$
$$k \in ITM, \qquad (10.6)$$

Block 10 contains two equations to determine prices. Eq. (10.4) states the price of item k equal to the average cost of its production — a zero pure profit condition, while the price of composite commodity i for item k formation (p3item_s$_{chi}$) is the weighted-average of the prices of imported and domestic commodities used in item formation (p3$_{is}$). The matrix, COMITEM$_{kis}$, contains base-year data on consumption of commodity i, by source, for item k formation.

Total demand for a commodity (x3$_{is}$) to produce all items is arrived at by aggregating x3item$_{kis}$ in eq.(10.5).

4.19   Exports and government consumption

Eq. (11.1) in Block 11 specifies downward-sloping foreign demand schedules for commodities. In levels, the equations is defined as:

$$X4_i = FEQ_i \left[\frac{PE_i}{FEP_i}\right]^{EXP\_ELAST_i}, \qquad i \in COM, \quad (4.19.1)$$

where EXP_ELAST$_i$ is a negative parameter — the constant elasticity of demand. Eq. (11.1) states that export volume (x4$_i$) of commodity i is a declining function of its price in foreign currency (PE$_i$). The variables FEQ$_i$ and FEP$_i$ allow for horizontal (quantity) and vertical (price) shifts in the demand schedule, respectively.

The export-price equation states that the export-price of commodity i is equal to the average cost of its supply in terms of foreign currency. The variable phi in (11.2) represents the exchange rate.

Block 11 Equations for export demands and government consumption:

$$x4_i - feq_i = EXP\_ELAST_i \, [pe_i - fep_i], \qquad i \in COM, \qquad (11.1)$$

$$pe_i + phi = \frac{1}{PUR4_i}((V4BAS_i + V4TAX_i) \times (p0dom_i + t4_i)$$

$$+ \sum_{m \in MAR} V4MAR_{im}[p0dom_i + a4mar_{im}]),$$

$$i \in COM, \qquad (11.2)$$

$$x5_{is} = chour\_rn + f5_{is} + f5tot, \qquad i \in COM, \, s \in SRC. \qquad (11.3)$$

Eq. (11.1) can be used flexibly. For example, we might assume that the export elasticity is zero for commodities that have export volumes and prices fixed by the government agreement, and then set x4$_i$ exogenously. Similarly, we can set export elasticities to zero for all non-exported commodities, and then exogenously set their export quantities to zero. For these commodities, the export quantity-shift variables are determined endogenously.

For some of the commodities, for which we want to set a target of export-volume, we might assume that x4$_i$ are given exogenously, while the export tax will be determined endogenously. Hence, by swapping exogenously given tax rates on exports with endogenously defined export quantities, we can compute the changes in tax rates on exports which are required to meet the targets of export volumes in the presence of some other policy shocks.

Eq. (11.3) in Block 11 determine demands for commodities for government consumption by source. In these equations, there are two shift variables: f5tot and $f5_{is}$, f5tot allows an exogenous change in the demand for all commodities, and $f5_{is}$, allows shift in the demand for a commodity from a source. It is assumed that government consumption is in direct proportion to real private consumption in the absence of any exogenous shift in the government demand (*i.e.* f5tot and $f5_{is}$ are all exogenously set to zero).

4.20   Demand for margin goods

Margins goods are required to transport commodities from their production point (or port in the case of imports) to their consumption point.

Block 12 Equations of demands for margin goods:

$$x1mar_{isjm} = x1_{isj} + a1mar_{isjm},$$
$$i \in COM, s \in SRC, j \in IND, m \in MAR, \quad (12.1)$$

$$x2mar_{isjm} = x2_{isj} + a2mar_{isjm},$$
$$i \in COM, s \in SRC, j \in IND, m \in MAR, \quad (12.2)$$

$$x3mar_{ism} = x3_{is} + a3mar_{ism}, \quad i \in COM, s \in SRC, m \in MAR, \quad (12.3)$$

$$x4mar_{im} = x4_i + a4mar_{im}, \quad i \in COM, m \in MAR, \quad (12.4)$$

$$x5mar_{ism} = x5_{is} + a5mar_{ism}, \quad i \in COM, s \in SRC, m \in MAR. \quad (12.5)$$

Equations in Block 12 specify the demand for margin-goods on flows of commodities to: producers ($x1mar_{isjm}$), investors ($x2mar_{isjm}$), item producer ($x3mar_{ism}$), government ($x5mar_{ism}$); and for exports (from production point to the ports, $x4mar_{im}$). It has been assumed that, in the absence of technical change, the demands for margins goods are in direct proportion to the commodities flows with which the margins are associated. For households, it has been assumed that margins are on commodities flows that are used to produce items rather than on flows of items. In eqs. (12.1) to (12.5) the variables a1mar to a5mar represent technical changes in the usage of margin-goods.

97

4.21   Purchasers' prices

Equations in Block 13 define purchasers' prices for the four groups of users; producers; investors; item producer; and government. Purchasers' prices are defined as the weighted-sum of basic prices (average production cost), sales taxes and the costs of margin-goods. We refer to the sum of the basic price of a commodity and the sales tax on it as the sale price of the commodity. The sales tax variable, t, in the linearised model represents percentage change in the power of tax rate.

The equation for the power of tax, in levels, is defined as:

$$T3_i = (1 + TAXRATE3_i), \qquad\qquad i \in COM, \qquad (4.21.1)$$

where TAXRAT is the *ad valorem* tax rate on the use of commodity i for item formation. We derive the equations of purchasers prices from the following procedure. The purchasers' cost of commodity i from source s — say for item formation — is:

$$P3_{is} \times X3_{is} = X3_{is} \times P0_{is} \times T3_{is} + \sum_{m \in MAR} X3MAR_{ism} \times P0DOM_{ism},$$

$$i \in COM, s \in SRC, \qquad (4.21.2)$$

where $X3_{is}$ is the quantity of commodity i purchased from source s for item formation, and $P3_{is}$ is its purchasers' price.
In the percentage-change form this is:

$$(p3_{is} + x3_{is}) = \frac{1}{PUR3_{is}} (\sum_i (V3BAS_{is} + V3TAX_{is}) [p0_{is} + t3_{is} + x3_{is}]$$

$$+ \sum_{m \in MAR} (V3MAR_{i\,sm} [p0dom_m + x3mar_{ism}]),$$

$$i \in COM, s \in SRC, \qquad (4.21.3)$$

where the coefficients are shares of sales values (basic value plus sales taxes) of commodity i, and the share of the cost of margin-goods m in purchasers' prices. Using eq. (13.3) from Block 13 to substitute x3mar$_{ism}$. we can cancel out the term $x3_{is}$ to obtain:

$$p3_{is} = \frac{1}{PUR3_{is}} \sum_{i \in COM} ([V3BAS_{is} + V3TAX_{is}] \times \{t3_{is} + p0_{is}\}$$

$$+ \sum_{m \in MAR} V3MAR_{ism} \{p0dom_m + a3mar_{ism}\}),$$

$$i \in COM, s \in SRC, j \in IND. \qquad (4.21.4)$$

Using the above discussed procedure we can derive the purchasers' prices equations for producers, investors and the government which are stated in Block 13.

The matrices PUR1 to PUR5 and V1BAS to V5BAS contain base-year data on costs of commodity sales to five consumer categories in purchasers' prices and basic prices, respectively. V1TAX to V5TAX matrices contain taxes on the sales, and V1MAR to V5MAR contain margins costs, on the sales of the commodities, paid by these five groups (see Section 4.4 on the input-output data base).

Block 13 Equations for purchasers' prices:

$$p0_{is} = p0dom_i, \quad s = \text{domestic}, \ i \in \text{COM}, \tag{13.1}$$

$$p0_{is} = p0imp_i, \quad s = \text{imported}, \ i \in \text{COM}, \tag{13.2}$$

$$p1_{isj} = \frac{1}{PUR1_{isj}} \left([V1BAS_{isj} + V1TAX_{isj}] \times \{p0_{is} + t1_{isj}\} \right.$$
$$\left. + \sum_{m \ \in \ MAR} (V1MAR_{isj\,m}\{p0dom_m + a1mar_{isjm}\}) \right),$$
$$i \in \text{COM}, \ s \in \text{SRC}, \ j \in \text{IND}, \tag{13.3}$$

$$p2_{isj} = \frac{1}{PUR2_{isj}} \left([V2BAS_{isj} + V2TAX_{isj}]\{p0_{is} + t2_{isj}\} \right.$$
$$\left. + \sum_{m \ \in \ MAR} (V2MAR_{isjm}\{p0dom_m + a2mar_{isj\,m}\}) \right),$$
$$i \in \text{COM}, \ s \in \text{SRC}, \ j \in \text{IND}, \tag{13.4}$$

$$p3_{is} = \frac{1}{PUR3_{is}} \left([V3BAS_{is} + V3TAX_{is}] \times \{\ p0_{is} + t3_{is}\} \right.$$
$$\left. + \sum_{m \ \in \ MAR} V3MAR_{ism}\{p0dom_m + a3mar_{ism}\} \right),$$
$$i \in \text{COM}, \ s \in \text{SRC}, \tag{13.5}$$

$$p5_{is} = \frac{1}{PUR5_{is}} \left([V5BAS_{is} + V5TAX_{is}] \times \{p0_{is} + t5_{is}\} \right.$$
$$\left. + \sum_{m \ \in \ MAR} V5MAR_{ism}\{p0dom_m + a5mar_{ism}\} \right),$$
$$i \in \text{COM}, \ s \in \text{SRC}, \tag{13.6}$$

$$p0imp_i = pm_i + phi + tm_i, \qquad i \in \text{COM}. \tag{13.7}$$

99

Eq. (13.7) defines the basic price of imported commodity i, as the local currency value of its import cost, plus the import tax on it. In levels it is:

$$POIMP_i = PM_i \times PHI_i \times TM_i ,\qquad\qquad (4.21.5)$$

where PM_i is the CIF value of imported commodity i in foreign currency; PHI is the nominal exchange rate; and TM_i is the power of the import tax on commodity i (see Appendix D for converting this equation into the percentage change form).

4.22 Indirect taxes

In Pakistan, there are three types of indirect taxes: excise or import duty, sales taxes, and surcharges. There is no difference between these categories in economic terms. The administrative distinction is that excise duty is levied on domestic production, and import duty is levied on imports. In both categories some commodities are taxed at specific rates and the remaining at *ad valorem* rates. In the original data on taxes [see Jetha, Akhtar and Rao (1984)] some of the commodities had both excise duty and sales tax: excise duty at specific rates and sales tax at *ad valorem* rates. In GE-PAK, we simply assume that there are two types of indirect taxes: domestic (sales tax) and import tax (tariff). Moreover, due to the lack of detailed data and for the sake of simplicity, we also assume that all taxes are charged at *ad valorem* rates.

This simplification will not greatly affect our analysis. The tax collection from excise duties in 1983-84 at specific rates was about 40 per cent of the total indirect tax revenues from domestic commodities. There were four commodities that made major contributions. Three of them, (cement, edible oil and petroleum products) contributed 25 per cent; the remaining 15 per cent was from all other commodities. The prices of cement, edible oil and petroleum products are fixed by the government. So the issue is not whether taxes on them are levied at specific rate or *ad valorem* rates. Jetha *et al.* (1984, p. 48), in their analysis of Pakistan's tax system, made a similar comment:

> In Pakistan, specific rates and the Government's pricing policy are closely related, and the conversion of specific rates into *ad valorem* rates may not help much unless accompanied by a modification of the pricing policy.

Block 14 Equations for indirect taxes:

$$t1_{isj} = t_{is} + t1\_isj + t0 + t1\_e_{ij}, \qquad i \in COM, s \in SRC, j \in IND, \qquad (14.1)$$

$$t2_{isj} = t_{is} + t2\_isj + t0 + t2\_e_{ij}, \qquad i \in COM, s \in SRC, j \in IND, \qquad (14.2)$$

$$t3_{is} = t_{is} + t3\_is + t0 + t3\_e_i, \qquad i \in COM, s \in SRC, \qquad (14.3)$$

$$t5_{is} = t_{is} + t5\_is + t0, \qquad i \in COM, s \in SRC. \qquad (14.4)$$

In Block 14, eqs. (14.1) to (14.4) define indices of the powers of sale taxes for producers, investors, item producers, and the government, respectively.

An index of the power of sale tax for each user category is defined using the following 4 types of sale taxes:

1. Commodity-and-source specific sale taxes, t_{is}.
2. User-specific sale-taxes such as t1 for producers and t2 for investors.
3. Uniform tax rate on all users and all commodities, t0.
4. User-and-commodity specific taxes such as, t1_e_{ij}.

The default rule for the power of sale tax for a user category in levels is:

$$TU_{is} = T_{is} \times TU\_is \times T0 \times TU\_E_{ij}, \qquad\qquad i \in COM, s \in SRC, (4.22.2)$$

while U stands for the user category (1, 2, 3 or 5). Eqs. (14.1) to (14.4) are the percentage-change forms of the above equation (see Appendix D for the conversion rules). Of the four types of tax variables, the user-and-commodity-specific tax rate variables (TU_E_{ij}) need some explanation.

The variables t1_e_{ij}, t2_e_{ij}, and t3_e_i represent commodity-and-user-specific sales taxes. In Chapter 2, we have discussed user-discriminating sale taxes on natural gas and electricity. For example, tax rate on electricity sales to the agricultural industries differ from the tax rate on the sales to the manufacturing industries.. The variables t3_e_{ij} represent commodity-and-user-specific taxes for households. These commodity-and-user-specific tax variables are introduced to simulate the impact of removing the user-discriminating taxes on energy products. Though these commodity-and-user-specific taxes are levied only on some selected commodities in Pakistan, we have introduced them for all commodities for the sake of uniformity.

4.23   Modelling of regulated prices

In section 4.21, we have discussed the equations determining purchasers' prices. We assume that the purchasers' price of commodity i is the sum of its sales price (basic price plus the exogenously given taxes on it) and the costs of margins on its supply. The tax rates are normally given exogenously, while the other two components of purchasers' prices are determined endogenously. As discussed in Chapter 2, however, the basic prices of the three major energy commodities are set by the government, and are revised occasionally. Hence, changes in the production costs of these commodities do not immediately pass on to purchasers. We interpret the difference between the production costs of a commodity and its regulated basic price, as an implicit tax. The rate of this implicit tax changes whenever there is a change in the basic price of a commodity.

In the application of GE-PAK to analyse energy pricing policy in Pakistan in this book, we have assumed that all prices are determined by the market to compute the full impact of reforming this policy. That is, we have held implicit tax rates (rather than purchasers' prices) exogenous in our reported simulations. However, in the model we have introduced an equation that can be switched on to make the regulated prices exogenous[5]. The equation, then, determines the changes in the powers of tax rates for these commodities. In the set of equations for indirect taxes, we include the following equations which give a default rule to determine the power of source-specific sales tax on commodities that have regulated prices.

Block 15 Tax rate equations for commodities with regulated prices:

$$fp0pub_{as} = p0_{as} + t_{as}, \qquad a \in ADM, s \in SRC, \qquad (15.1)$$

where ADM is a subset of commodities that have regulated prices. Eq. (15.1) states that a shift in the sale price of commodity 'a', from source s, is the sum of its basic price plus the commodity-and-source-specific sales-tax on it. For any change in the production costs of the commodity, when $fp0pub_{as}$ is exogenous, there is an off-setting change in the power of commodity-and-source-specific sales tax ($t0_{as}$) on this commodity.

Eq. (15.1) can be used flexibly. If we assume that there is no regulation on the prices of commodities in the subset ADM, we can set commodity-source-specific sales taxes on them exogenously. In this case, endogenously determined shift variables fp0pub will show the necessary changes in the sale prices of all commodities in the set ADM. These shift variables, however, will not affect any other variable in the model as the former variables do not appear in any other equation.

4.24   Market clearing equations for commodities

Block 16 below reports market-clearing equations for domestic commodities, and equations which compute the aggregate demand for imports. Eqs. (16.1) set total production of margin-goods equal to the aggregate demands for them. Margin-goods are supplied only from domestic sources. They are used both as intermediate inputs by industries, and as a margin on the supply of imported and domestic commodities to five types of consumers. Eqs. (16.2) set the production level equal to aggregate demand for commodities other than margin commodities. Eq. (16.3) gives the aggregate demand for imported commodities from all users. The matrix V0IMP contains the base-year data on import costs of commodities (see section 4.4). We have assumed that the prices of imports are given exogenously, and import supplies are infinite, *i.e.* an increase in the consumption of an imported commodity will not increase its price.

Block 16 Market clearing equations for commodities:

$$x0dom_m = \frac{1}{SALES_j} [\sum_{j \in IND} V1BAS_{mlj} \times x1_{mlj} + \sum_{j \in IND} V2BAS_{mlj}$$

$$\times x2_{mlj} + V3BAS_{ml} \times x3_{ml} + V4BAS_m \times x4_m + V5BAS_{ml} \times x5_{ml}$$

$$+ \sum_{i \in COM} [V4MAR_{im} \times x4mar_{im} + \sum_{s \in SRC} V3MAR_{ism} \times x3mar_{ism}$$

$$+ \sum_{s \in SRC} V5MAR_{ism} \times x5mar_{ism} + \sum_{s \in SRC} \sum_{j \in IND} V1MAR_{ismj}$$

$$\times x1mar_{ismj} + \sum_{s \in SRC} \sum_{j \in IND} V2MAR_{ismj} \times x2mar_{ismj}]],$$

$$l = \text{domestic}, \ m \in MAR, \quad\quad (16.1)$$

$$x0dom_i = \frac{1}{SALES_j} [\sum_{j \in IND} V1BAS_{ilj} \times x1_{ilj} + \sum_{j \in IND} V2BAS_{ilj} \times x2_{ilj}$$

$$+ V3BAS_{il} \times x3_{il} + 4BAS_i \times x4_i + V5BAS_{il} \times x5_{il}],$$

$$l = \text{domestic}, \ i \in NONMAR, \quad\quad (16.2)$$

$$x0imp_i = \frac{1}{V0IMP_j} [\sum_{j \in IND} V1BAS_{ilj} \times x1_{ilj} + \sum_{j \in IND} V2BAS_{ilj}$$

$$\times x2_{ilj} + V3BAS_{il} \times x3_{il} + V5BAS_{il} \times x5_{il}],$$

$$l = \text{imported}, \ i \in COM. \quad\quad (16.3)$$

4.25 Demands for primary factors by type

Equations in Block 17 aggregate demands for primary factors from industries. Eq. (17.1) determines aggregate labour demands, of a skill type from a region, in industries (lambda$_{rp}$). Total usage of capital (x1cap_j$_c$) and land (x1lnd_j$_d$) by all industries for each type of capital and land are given in eqs. (17.2) and (17.3), respectively. The coefficients V1LAB, V1CAP and V1LND are data matrices containing wage bills and rental values of capital and land, respectively. Eq. (17.4) gives total labour demand by region (lambda_p$_r$), and eq. (17.5) determines total labour demand by profession (lambda_r$_p$). In section 4.33, we have discussed market clearing conditions for primary factors by setting these demands equal to their aggregate supplies from institutions. We have also discussed there the factor market closure in the short-run.

Block 17 Demand equations for aggregate primary factors:

$$\text{lambda}_{rp} = \frac{1}{\text{V1LAB\_jrp}} \sum_{j \in \text{IND}} \text{V1LAB}_{rpj} \times \text{x1lab}_{rpj},$$

$$r \in \text{REG}, \ p \in \text{PRF}, \qquad (17.1)$$

$$\text{x1cap\_jc} = \frac{1}{\text{V1CAP\_jc}} \sum_{j \in \text{IND}} \text{V1CAP}_{cj} \times \text{x1cap}_j, \quad c \in \text{CAP}, \qquad (17.2)$$

$$\text{x1lnd\_jd} = \frac{1}{\text{V1LND\_jd}} \sum_{j \in \text{IND}} \text{V1LND}_{dj} \times \text{x1lnd}_j, \quad d \in \text{LND}, \qquad (17.3)$$

$$\text{lambda\_p}_r = \frac{1}{\text{V1LAB\_pjr}} \sum_{p \in \text{PRF}} \text{V1LAB\_rjp} \times \text{lambda}_{rp},$$

$$r \in \text{REG}, \qquad (17.4)$$

$$\text{lambda\_r}_p = \frac{1}{\text{V1LAB\_rjp}} \sum_{r \in \text{REG}} \text{V1LAB\_pjr} \times \text{lambda}_{rp},$$

$$p \in \text{PRF}. \qquad (17.5)$$

4.26 Aggregate demand for final consumption, exports, imports and indirect tax revenues

Equations in Block 18 determine macroeconomic variables which are used to define GDP from income- and expenditure-side Eqs. (18.1) and (18.3) determine aggregate export earnings and export volume (see Annexure D for the aggregation procedure). Similarly, eqs. (18.2) and (18.4) give aggregate import volume and import bill, respectively. The variables xik3, xi4, xim and xi5 are the price indices defined for the four consumer categories. These indices are discussed in section 4.29. Eq. (18.5) give real consumption by households category (chour_{rn}); deflating the nominal consumption of each group by its price index (xiitem_{rn}).

Eq. (18.6) computes real *per capita* consumption for household categories. In levels, the *per capita* consumption for each category is defined as:

$$\text{PERCON}_{rn} = \frac{\text{CHOUR}_{rn}}{\text{Q\_p}_{rn} \times \text{HSIZE}_{rn}}$$

where HSIZE$_{rn}$ is number of persons per household, and Q_p$_{rn}$ is number of households in each category. Eq. (18.6) is the linear form of the above equation. Since GE-PAK determines private consumption by household group, eq. (18.7) computes total real private consumption by adding up real consumption for all household categories. Similarly, eq. (18.8) computes total nominal private consumption.

Block 18 Equations of aggregate demand for final consumption, exports, imports and indirect tax revenues:

$$\text{exp} = \frac{1}{\text{PUR4\_i}} \sum_{i \in \text{COM}} \text{PUR4}_i \times [\text{pe}_i + \text{x4}_i], \tag{18.1}$$

$$\text{imp} = \frac{1}{\text{V0IMP\_i}} \sum_{i \in \text{COM}} \text{V0IMP}_i \times [\text{pm}_i + \text{x0imp}_i], \tag{18.2}$$

$$\text{expvol} = \text{exp} + \text{phi} - \text{xi4}, \tag{18.3}$$

$$\text{impvol} = \text{imp} + \text{phi} - \text{xim}, \tag{18.4}$$

$$\text{chour}_{rn} = \text{chou}_{rn} - \text{xiitem}_{rn}, \quad r \in \text{REG}, n \in \text{INC}, \tag{18.5}$$

$$\text{perconr}_{rn} = \text{chour}_{rn} - \text{q\_p}_{rn} - \text{hsize}_{rn}, \quad r \in \text{REG}, n \in \text{INC}, \tag{18.6}$$

$$\text{chour\_rn} = \frac{1}{\text{VITEM\_krn}} \sum_{r \in \text{REG}} \sum_{n \in \text{INC}} \text{VITEM\_k}_{rn} \times \text{chour}_{rn}, \tag{18.7}$$

$$\text{chou\_rn} = \frac{1}{\text{VITEM\_krn}} \sum_{r \in \text{REG}} \sum_{n \in \text{INC}} \text{VITEM\_k}_{rn} \times \text{chou}_{rn}, \tag{18.8}$$

$$\text{inv} = \text{invr} + \text{xi2}, \tag{18.9}$$

$$\text{invr} = \frac{1}{\text{PUR2\_isj}} \sum_{j \in \text{IND}} \text{PUR2\_is}_j \times \text{y}_j, \tag{18.10}$$

$$\text{oth} = \text{othr} + \text{xi5}, \tag{18.11}$$

$$\text{oth} = \frac{1}{\text{PUR5\_is}} \sum_{i \in \text{COM}} \sum_{s \in \text{SRC}} \text{PUR5}_{is} \times [\text{x5}_{is} + \text{p5}_{is}], \tag{18.12}$$

105

$$labrev = \frac{1}{V1LAB\_rpj} \sum_{j \in IND} \sum_{r \in REG} \sum_{p \in PRF} V1LAB_{rpj}$$

$$\times (p1lab_{rpj} + x1lab_{rpj}), \qquad (18.13)$$

$$caprev = \frac{1}{V1CAP\_cj} \sum_{j \in IND} V1CAP\_cj \times (p1cap_j + x1cap_j), \qquad (18.14)$$

$$lndrev = \frac{1}{V1LND\_dj} \sum_{j \in IND} V1LND\_dj \times (p1lnd_j + x1lnd_j), \qquad (18.15)$$

$$octrev = \frac{1}{V1OCT\_j} \sum_{j \in IND} V1OCT_j \times (p1loct_j + x1oct_j), \qquad (18.16)$$

$$t1rev\_isj = \frac{1}{V1TAX\_isj} \sum_{i \in COM} \sum_{s \in SRC} \sum_{j \in IND} (V1TAX_{isj}$$

$$\times \{ p0_{is} + x1_{isj} \} + [V1TAX_{isj} + V1BAS_{isj}] \times t1_{isj}), \qquad (18.17)$$

$$t2rev\_isj = \frac{1}{V2TAX\_isj} \sum_{i \in COM} \sum_{s \in SRC} \sum_{j \in IND} (V2TAX_{isj}$$

$$\times \{ p0_{is} + x2_{isj} \} + [V2TAX_{isj} + V2BAS_{isj}] \times t2_{isj}), \qquad (18.18)$$

$$t3rev\_is = \frac{1}{V3TAX\_is} \sum_{i \in COM} \sum_{s \in SRC} (V3TAX_{is} \times \{ p0_{is} + x3_{is} \}$$

$$+ [V3TAX_{is} + V3BAS_{is}] \times t3_{is}), \qquad (18.19)$$

$$t4rev\_i = \frac{12H}{V4TAX\_i} \frac{1}{} \sum_{i \in COM} (V4TAX_i \times \{ p0dom_i + x4_i \}$$

$$+ [V4TAX_i + V1BAS_i] \times t4_i), \qquad (18.20)$$

$$t5rev\_is = \frac{1}{V5TAX\_is} \sum_{i \in COM} \sum_{s \in SRC} (V5TAX_{is} \times \{ p0_{is} + x5_{is} \}$$

$$+ [V5TAX_{is} + V5BAS_{is}] \times t5_{is}), \qquad (18.21)$$

106

$$tmrev\_i = \frac{1}{VOTAR\_i} \sum_{i \in COM} VOTAR_i \{pm_i + phi + x0imp_i\}$$

$$+ \sum_{i \in COM} IMPORTS_i \times tm_i, \qquad (18.22)$$

$$t0rev = \frac{1}{VOTAX} (V1TAX\_isj \times t1rev\_isj + V2TAX\_isj \times t2rev\_isj$$

$$+ V3TAX\_is \times t3rev\_is + V4TAX\_i \times t4rev\_i + V5TAX\text{-}i \times t5rev\_is$$

$$+ VOTAR \times tmrev\_i + V1OCT\_j \times octrev. \qquad (18.23)$$

Eq. (18.10) computes total real investment which is a sum of real investments in all industries, while eq. (18.9) gives total investment in nominal terms. Eq. (18.12) adds up all nominal values of commodities consumed by government, while eq. (18.11) computes this aggregate government expenditure in real term.

Eqs. (18.13) to (18.15) compute total wage bill of labour, and rental values of capital and land. These aggregates are computed using prices of, and demand for, these factors. Eq. (18.16) computes total 'other costs'. We treat this cost as a production tax or subsidy. Hence total 'other costs' is treated as revenue for government which is then added to the total indirect tax revenues given in eq. (18.23). Eqs. (18.17) to (18.21) compute indirect sales tax revenues paid by four consumer categories: producers; investors; item producer; and government, while eq. (18.22) computes import tax revenues. The total indirect tax revenue is computed in eq. (18.23).

4.27 GDP and the balance of trade

In Block 19, eq. (19.1) computes the trade balance in nominal term (*i.e.*, billion Rs). We define the trade balance as the difference between aggregate exports and imports. The percentage change in exports (imports), when multiplied by the base-year export (import) level, gives the change in the balance of trade in nominal term. We divide this value by 1000 to arrive at billions of Rs.

Eq. (19.2) computes GDP from the expenditure-side which is sum of: private consumption, investment expenditure, government consumption, and exports less imports. In this equation, the coefficients are the base-year values of these components, while GDPEXP is their sum. For example, the coefficient VITEM_krn is total private consumption, and PUR4_i is total exports in the base year. Eq. (19.4) computes real GDP using the GDP deflator xigdp. Eqs. (19.5) to (19.7) compute total labour, capital and land stock.

Block 19 Equations for GDP and other macro-economic indicators:

$$delB = (PUR4\_i \times exp - V0IMP\_i \times imp) \times 100.0 / 1000.0, \tag{19.1}$$

$$gdpexp = \frac{1}{GDPEXP} (VITEM\_krn \times chou\_rn + PUR2\_isj \times inv$$

$$+ PUR5\_is \times oth + PUR4\_i \times (exp + phi) - V0IMP\_i \times (imp + phi)), \tag{19.2}$$

$$gdpinc = \frac{1}{GDPINC} (V1LND\_dj \times lndrev + V1CAP\_cj \times caprev$$

$$+ V1LAB\_rpj \times labrev + V0TAX \times t0rev), \tag{19.3}$$

$$gdpreal = gdpexp - xigdp, \tag{19.4}$$

$$x1cap\_cj = \frac{1}{V1CAP\_cj} \sum_{j \in IND} V1CAP\_cj \times x1capj, \tag{19.5}$$

$$x1lab\_rpj = \frac{1}{V1LAB\_rpj} \sum_{j \in IND} V1LAB\_rpj \times x1lab\_rpj, \tag{19.6}$$

$$x1lnd\_dj = \frac{1}{V1LND\_dj} \sum_{j \in IND} V1LND\_dj \times x1lndj. \tag{19.7}$$

4.28   Investment allocation by industry and rate of return

Block 20 Equations for investment allocation:

$$r0j = QCOEF_j \times [p1capj - p2\_isj], j \in IND, \tag{20.1}$$

$$r0j - rtot = BETA\_R_j \times [x1capj - x1cap\_cj] + fr0j, \quad j \in IND, \tag{20.2}$$

$$x1capj = INV\_ELAST_j \times yj + fx1capj, \quad j \in IND. \tag{20.3}$$

Dixon *et al.* (1982) has defined a theory of investment allocation across industry for ORANI. We have adopted their investment equations in our model. Eq. (20.1) defines the rate of return ($r0_j$) on capital (net of depreciation in industry). In levels,

108

this is the ratio of the rental price of capital $(P1CAP_j)$ to its supply price $(P2\_is_j)$ minus the rate of depreciation. Hence, the coefficient $QCOEF_j$ is the ratio of the gross to the net rate of return. The total capital stock, $X1CAP_j$ is allocated across industries by a function given in equation (20.2). The function states that the change in the net rate of return in an industry (relative to the economy-wide rate) is a positive function of the change in the industry's capital stock (relative to the economy-wide stock). According to Horridge *et al.* (1993), this function can be interpreted as a risk-related relationship with relatively fast- (slow-) growing industries requiring premium (accepting discounts) on their rates of return. The parameter $BETA\_R_j$ specifies the strength of this relationship. Further, the variable $fr0_j$ allows an exogenous shift in the rate of return in an industry. Eq. (20.3) translates the demand for capital in industry j $(x1cap_j)$ into investment funds required by industry j (y_j). The elasticity of capital demand in industry j with respect to its investment is represented by the coefficient INV_ELAST_j. The variable $fx1cap_j$ allows an exogenous shift in the capital stock of industry j. The model allows us to set investment by industries exogenously. In such simulations the shift variables $fx1cap_j$, are determined endogenously to match the demand for capital stock in industries with their exogenously given investments (see section 19 in Dixon *et al.*, 1982 for details or Horridge *et al.*, 1993).

4.29 Price indices

Price indices are defined as the weighted-average of commodity prices for consumers categories. The weights are the shares of commodities in total expenditure incurred by these categories (see conversion rule in table D1 in Appendix D). For example, eq. (21.1) states that investment price index $(xi2)$ is the weighted-sum of prices of commodities used for capital formation. The weights are the shares of commodities in total investment. Eqs. (21.2) to (21.4) compute the price indices for: aggregate private consumption $(xi3)$, consumption by households group $(xiitem_{rn})$ and government consumption $(xi5)$, respectively.

Block 21 Equations of price indices:

$$xi2 = \frac{1}{PUR2\_is_j} \sum_{i \,\in COM} \sum_{s \,\in SRC} \sum_{j \,\in IND} PUR2_{isj} \times p2_{isj}, \qquad (21.1)$$

$$xi3 = \frac{1}{PUR3\_is} \sum_{i \,\in COM} \sum_{s \,\in SRC} PUR3_{is} \times p3_{is}, \qquad (21.2)$$

$$xiitem_{rn} = \frac{1}{VITEM\_k_{rn}} \sum_{k \,\in ITM} VITEM_{krn} \times pitem_k,$$

$$r \in REG, \ n \in INC, \qquad (21.3)$$

109

$$xi5 = \frac{1}{PUR5\_is} \underset{i \in COM}{\Sigma} \underset{s \in SRC}{\Sigma} PUR5_{is} \times p5_{is}, \tag{21.4}$$

$$xi4 - phi = \frac{1}{PUR4\_i} \underset{i \in COM}{\Sigma} PUR4_i \times pe_i, \tag{21.5}$$

$$xim - phi = \frac{1}{V0IMP\_i} \underset{i \in COM}{\Sigma} V0IMP_i \times pm_i, \tag{21.6}$$

$$ximp0 = \frac{1}{IMPORTS\_i} \underset{i \in COM}{\Sigma} IMPORTS_i \times p0imp_i, \tag{21.7}$$

$$xigdp = \frac{1}{GDPEXP} (PUR2\_isj \times xi2 + PUR3\_is \times xi3 + PUR4\_i \times xi4$$

$$+ PUR5\_is \times xi5 - V0IMP\_i \times xim), \tag{21.8}$$

$$xifac = \frac{1}{V1PRM\_j} \underset{j \in IND}{\Sigma} V1PRM_j \times p1prm_j. \tag{21.9}$$

Item price indices are computed for 14 types of household groups because the consumption patterns of these groups are not uniform. The prices of items in eq. (21.3) are weighted by the shares of items in total consumption for a household group. Eqs. (21.5) and (21.6) compute indices of foreign currency prices of exports and imports. Eq. (21.7) computes the price index of imports inclusive of taxes on them. Using these price indices, we compute an index for the GDP (expenditure) deflator in eq. (21.8). Eq. (21.9) defines the factor price index (xifac), which is a weighted-average of price indices for primary-factors ($p1prm_j$); the weights are the shares of industries in total value added.

4.30   Data base on institutions' incomes

Fig. 4.17 shows the structure of data base for incomes of institutions as defined for GE-PAK. The rows show four types of institutions:(1) households, (2) corporations, (3) government, (4) ROW, and the columns show seven sources of income, as follows:

1.   Labour is owned by households, and wages are received by them.
2.   Capital is owned by, and its rents accrue to, all institutions.
3.   Land is owned by, and its rent accrue to, all institutions.
4.   Households make transfer-payments to other households and, pay direct taxes to government. Hence, households are sources of income.
5.   Corporations pay dividends to their shareholders (households and the government), and pay corporate tax to the government.

110

6. Government makes transfer payments such as pensions to households.
7. Remittances from the ROW are received by households only.

In fig. 4.17, the first row shows the names of the data matrices containing household income (VYHOU) from seven sources in the base-year. The matrices VYCORCAP and VYCORLND are matrices of corporation income from two sources (see the second row). The government receives income from four sources, its income matrices are listed in the third row. The ROW owns some capital and land in Pakistan. Its base-year income from the two sources is given in VYROWCAP and VYROWLND matrices.

		1	2	3	4	5	6	7
		Sources of Income						
		Labour	Capital	Land	Households	Corporations	Government	Rest of the World
Institutions	Size	PRF	CAP	LND	REG ×INC	COR	GOV	ROW
Households	REG × INC × PRF ↑↓	VYHOU LAB (r,n,p)	VYHOU CAP (r,n,c)	VYHOU LND (r,n,d)	VYHOU HOU (r,n,r,n)	VYHOU COR (r,n,o)	VYHOU GOV (r,n)	VYHOU ROW (r,n)
Corporations	COR ↑↓		VYCOR CAP (o, c)	VYCOR LND (o, d)				
Government	1		VYGOV CAP (c)	VYGOV LND (d)	VYGOV OU (r,n)	VYGOVC OR (o)		
Rest of the World	1		VYROW CAP (c)	VYROW LND (d)				

		V1LAB (r,p)	V1CAP (c)	V1LND (d)				

Note: Characters in parentheses represent the subscripts of these matrices.

Figure 4.17 Structure of the data base on incomes of institutions

111

4.31 Price indices of primary factors by type

Block 22 (below) contains equations determining price indices for labour, capital and land. Eqs. (22.1) compute labour wage indices for 4 types of labour. Each wage index is defined as the weighted-average unit-cost of labour in industries for a labour category. The weights are the wage-bill shares of industries in the total wage-bill for a labour type in all industries.

Block 22 Equations for factor prices indices:

$$p1lab\_jrp = \frac{1}{V1LAB\_j} \sum_{j \,\in IND} V1LAB_{rpj} \times p1lab_{rpj},$$

$$r \in REG, \, p \in PRF, \qquad (22.1)$$

$$p1cap\_jc = \frac{1}{V1CAP\_jc} \sum_{j \,\in IND} V1CAP_{cj} \times p1cap_j, \qquad c \in CAP, \qquad (22.2)$$

$$p1lnd\_jd = \frac{1}{V1LND\_jd} \sum_{j \,\in IND} V1LND_{dj} \times p1lnd_j, \qquad d \in LND. \qquad (22.3)$$

The model determines rental prices of capital ($p1cap_j$) and land ($p1lnd_j$) at the industry level. As discussed, the data base contains ownership of capital and land by institution at the industry level. To allocate returns on capital (land) to the institutions, we define capital price index for each institution as follows:

$$p1cap\_jc = \frac{1}{V1CAP\_jc} \sum_{j \,\in IND} V1CAP_{cj} \times p1cap_j, \qquad c \in CAP.$$

where $V1CAP_{cj}$ is the matrix of rental value of capital stock in industry j in the base year for C type of capital. The variable $p1cap_j$ represents rental price of capital in industry j, while $p1cap\_jc$ is the rental price index which is the weighted-average price of a capital type - say corporate capital - in all industries. Similarly, a land price index is defined for all institutions.

4.32 Segmentation of labour market into urban and rural

In the literature and statistics, the labour market in Pakistan is divided into two regions; urban and rural. In this section, we first discuss the main features of the labour markets in Pakistan, and then define a rural-urban migration function.

In 1989-90 rural labour accounted for 73 per cent of the total labour force (GOP, 1990). Some recent works on labour markets in Pakistan show that real wage rates are flexible and responsive to the changes in labour supply and demand in the two markets.

Chaudhry and Chaudhry (1992) have analysed trends in the employment and real wage rates in Pakistan's rural-labour market for the period 1966-85. According to them, the rural labour market is highly segmented and variations in employment and wage rates of labour occur in various segments. Villages, being physically separated, represent independent segments and each of them has its own distinct market conditions. Nevertheless, the trends of rural employment and average wages in the rural labour market, as a whole, show that both employment levels and wages are determined by the free interplay of market forces. This empirical evidence on flexibility in wage rates in the rural-labour markets of Pakistan is in line with that for other Asian countries. Binswanger and Rosenweig (1986) and Bardhan (1984) have shown that the wage rates are flexible in rural Asia in the face of changes in relative scarcity, as are individual labour supplies and demands in the face of changes in wage rates. According to Bell (1991)[6] such propositions about rural labour markets now command wide assent, and form an important element in the 'neo-classical resurgence' in development economics. As discussed by Bell (1991) two quite different interpretations may be made about this empirical evidence of wage and demand flexibility in the rural-labour markets. A group of development economists including Binswanger and Rosenweig asserts that the rural labour market is perfectly or nearly perfectly competitive, while Bardhan and some others assert that flexibility in wage rates and labour demand are compatible with various forms of imperfection in these markets. Dreze and Mukherjee (1989) argue that though the 'competitive' version is untenable as an exact description of how the labour market actually functions, it may nevertheless prove to be a good approximation. Considering the structure of rural activities in Pakistan, particularly agricultural production activities, we agree with the conclusion of Dreze and Mukherjee (1989). In the presence of various types of contracts for agricultural activities such as tenancy, share-cropping and leasing of land in Pakistan, we consider that labour and other markets in rural areas are flexible in the sense that the terms of contracts respond to changes in scarcity. Hence, in our modelling of labour market and agricultural industries, we implicitly assume perfectly competitive markets. Furthermore, as stated by Chaudhry and Chaudhry (1992), the consistent increases in real wages observed for rural workers suggest that Pakistan may no longer be considered a labour surplus economy. Khan and Lee (1984) has found that real wages of the agricultural workers in Pakistan witnessed continuous increases between 1960-61 and 1979-80; against the negligible increases in real wages in India, and falling real wages in Bangladesh during the same period. Chaudhry and Chaudhry (1992), and Bilquees (1992) also found consistent increase in real wages of the agricultural workers during 1980s. In this period, return of workers from the middle-east had started and net-return migration had become evident. In fact, some studies indicate that Pakistan's agriculture sector might be facing labour shortages, especially during the peak-demand period (Chaudhry, 1982; Guisinger, 1978).

For the urban-labour market, Guisinger (1978), Irfan (1982), and Irfan and Ahmad (1985) show that over the period from 1970-84, real wages of workers in the large-scale manufacturing and construction industries increased while that for government employees declined. Bilquees (1992) analysed this trend on an annual

113

basis, and found that it continued in the late 1980s. Thus, real wages in Pakistan were found to be flexible even in the short run. Another issue related to the urban labour market is the role of trade unions in wage setting, or the implementation of minimum wage rates set by the government. No recent evidence is found on the role of trade unions in wage setting in Pakistan [7]. A survey of trade unions in Asia (Far Eastern Economic Review, 1986) shows that the trade union activities in Pakistan were undermined by the 1977's martial law restrictions, and since then they have been facing factional and ideological divisions.

Considering this empirical evidence, we assume that wage rates in both urban and rural labour markets are flexible and responsive to changes in the labour supply and demand. The labour markets are cleared at the margin within the given structure of these markets.

4.32.1 Rural-urban migration

Harris and Todaro (1970) developed an analytical model incorporating rural-urban migration to explain the urban unemployment in developing countries. Since then, various versions of their model have been developed [8]. In all these models, the basic assumption is the rigidity of urban wages. Some of these models assume that urban wages are given exogenously, while other assume a minimum urban wage rate. Either way, the difference in the wage rates for urban and rural labour determines migration of labour between the two markets.

Besides these analytical models, rural-urban migration has been incorporated in some applied general equilibrium models. In these models, real urban wages are assumed to be given exogenously [9].

GE-PAK incorporates a set of equations that links the two rural and urban labour markets. Similar to the migration model of Harris and Todaro, or Blitzer, the difference in the wage rates in the two labour markets determines rural-urban migration. However, our migration function differs from that of others in four respects.

1. The model does not presume any rigidity in wage rate or labour supply for any type of labour. It incorporates an interaction of labour supplies and demands in a regional labour market which either determines wage rate or employment depending on the closure of the model.
2. Inter-region migration occurs through migration of households.
3. Each migration function has been defined on real wage rate for a household group which incorporates the differences in the consumption patterns across income groups and regions.
4. The inter-region migration functions have been defined by professional groups in each income category.

114

In levels the household migration function is defined as:

$$\left(\frac{Q\text{"urban"}np}{Q\text{"rural"}np}\right) = f\left(\frac{P1LABR\_j\text{"urban"}np}{P1LABR\_j\text{"rural"}np}\right), \qquad n \in INC, p \in PRF,$$

where Q_{rnp} is the number of households in region r in the professional group p and income group n, while $P1LABR\_j_{rnp}$ is the real wage rate for this household group. A change in the real wage of urban labour relative to that of rural labour of the profession type p, changes the ratio of urban to rural households of that type, within each income group. Fig. 4.18 shows the schematic representation of this migration function for an income group for the CET functional form. Households owning skilled labour in income group n are the CET composite of urban and rural households owning skilled labour in that income group. Eq. 23.1 in Block 23 gives this behavioural assumption in percentage change form.

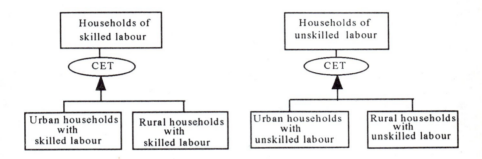

Figure 4.18   Structure of household migration functions

Block 23 Rural-urban migration and real wages:

$$q_{rnp} = q\_r_{np} + \sigma REG_p \, (p1labr\_j_{rnp} - p1labr\_rj_{np}),$$

$$r \in REG, n \in INC, p \in PRF, \qquad (23.1)$$

$$p1labr\_rj_{np} = \frac{1}{VYHOULAB\_r_{np}} \sum_{r \,\in REG} VYHOULAB_{rnp} \times p1labr\_j_{rnp},$$

$$n \in INC, p \in PRF, \qquad (23.2)$$

$$q\_P_{rn} = \frac{1}{VYHOULAB\_P_{rn}} \sum_{p \,\in PRF} (VYHOULAB_{rnp}) \times q_{rnp},$$

$$r \in REG, n \in INC, \qquad (23.3)$$

115

$$p11abr\_j_{rnp} = p11ab\_j_{rp} + xiitem_{rn}, \quad r \in REG, n \in INC, p \in PRF, \quad (23.4)$$

$$p11ab_{rpj} = xi3 + f1wag\_j_{rp}, \qquad r \in REG, p \in PRF, j \in IND. \quad (23.5)$$

Our assumption is that the number of households by profession in an income group (q_r_{np}) is given exogenously. Any change in the real wage rate ($p11abr\_j_{rp}$), for profession p in region r, relative to the average wage rate ($p11abr\_j_{rnp}$), determines the number of households of type n, possessing labour type p, in region r. For example, an increase in the real wage of urban-skilled labour relative to the average increase in the wage rate for skilled labour will increase the number of urban-skilled households in that group of households. The average wage rate is the weighted-average of real wages in the two regions for a profession (see eq. 23.2). The parameter, σREG_p, is the elasticity of inter-region migration for profession p; which measures the responsiveness of households to changes in the relative real wage rates in the two regions.

Eq. (23.1) states that households in each group make migration decisions on the basis of real wages received by them. Therefore in eq. (23.4), we have defined real wage for each income group ($p11abr\_j_{rnp}$) separately by deflating industry-aggregated wage rate for each profession in a region ($p11ab\_j_{rp}$) with the price index specific to the group of households ($xiitem_{rn}$). The weights in equation (23.2) are shares of wage-earnings of household type n, from region r, in the total wage bill of households with profession p. Eq. (23.3) aggregates households by profession, as the expenditure accounts of households are not given separately by profession type. We use shares of labour income by profession as the weights to aggregate the households by profession.

Eqs. (23.5) define real wages for labour by region and profession at the industry level, and $f1wag\_j_{rp}$ represent shifts in these wages. In a closure of inelastic supply of labour, when changes in labour supply by profession and region ($ulab\_j_{rp}$) are given exogenously, these shift variables are determined endogenously, and represent changes in real wages at which the labour markets are cleared.

4.33 Endowment of primary factors by institution

Eqs. in Block 24 set default rules to determine the supply of primary factors from the four types of institutions. Eq. (24.1) states that the labour supply of profession p, from the household group n in region r, is determined by the number of households, and the shifts in their labour supplies. The variable $ulab_{rp}$ indicates a shift in the labour supply of profession p in region r which are assumed to occur in all types of households uniformly. For example, if we assume an increase in the supply of urban-skilled labours then urban-skilled labours increase in all income groups at a uniform rate. The number of households of type np in a region (q_{rnp}) is determined by the inter-region migration function discussed in section 4.32.

Block 24 Equations determining factor supplies from institutions:

$$ehoulab_{rnp} = ulab\_j_{rp} + q_{rnp}, \quad r \in REG, n \in INC, p \in PRF, \quad (24.1)$$

$$ehoucap_{rnc} = ucap\_j_c + q\_p_{rn}, \quad r \in REG, n \in INC, c \in CAP, \quad (24.2)$$

$$ehoulnd_{rnd} = ulnd\_j_d + q\_p_{rn}, \quad r \in REG, n \in INC, d \in LND, \quad (24.3)$$

$$ecorcap_{oc} = ucap\_j_c, \quad o \in COR, c \in CAP, \quad (24.4)$$

$$ecorlnd_{od} = ulnd\_j_d, \quad o \in COR, d \in LND, \quad (24.5)$$

$$egovcap_c = ucap\_j_c, \quad c \in CAP, \quad (24.6)$$

$$egovlnd_d = ulnd\_j_d, \quad d \in LND, \quad (24.7)$$

$$erowcap_c = ucap\_j_c, \quad c \in CAP, \quad (24.8)$$

$$erowlnd_d = ulnd\_j_d, \quad d \in LND. \quad (24.9)$$

The model recognises ownership of land and capital by households, which are categorised by region and income groups. The land and capital ownership of a household group changes when households migrate from a region. The underlying assumption is that when households migrate from a region, they keep on drawing returns on assets they own in the region they migrate from. For example, if some rural low-income households migrate to urban region, then income of these households from returns to capital and land is now counted in the income of the urban low-income group.

4.34   Market clearing equations for primary factors

Up till now, we have discussed the supply and demand functions for three types of primary factors. In this section, we discuss their market clearing equations. Fig. 19 shows interaction of demand for and supply of four types of labour. The labour demand for skill type p from region r is a sum of labour demands from all industries

117

for that type of labour. The supply of labour, of skill type p, from region r is a sum of labour supplies from all income groups in that region. According to the market clearing condition, total labour demand is set equal to the total supply in eq. (25.1).

Two alternative closures of the labour market are as follows: (1) Labour supply is perfectly elastic of skill type p from a region. To clear the labour market, labour employment is determined endogenously for a given fixed real wage rate. (2) Alternatively, the labour supply is assumed to be perfectly inelastic. The real wage rate is determined endogenously for the given labour supplies.

Block 25 Market clearing equations for primary factors:

$$lambda_{rp} = \frac{1}{VYHOULAB\_n_{rp}} \sum_{n \in INC} VYHOULAB_{rnp} \times ehoulab_{rnp}$$

$$r \in REG, \; p \in PRF, \qquad (25.1)$$

$$x1cap\_j_c = \frac{1}{V1CAP\_j_c} (\sum_{r \in REG} \sum_{n \in INC} VYHOUCAP_{rnc}$$

$$\times ehoucap_{rnc} + \sum_{o \in COR} VYCORCAP_{oc} \times ecorcap_{oc}$$

$$+ \; YGOVCAP_c \times egovcap_c + VYROWCAP_c \times crowcap_c),$$

$$c \in CAP, \qquad (25.2)$$

$$x1lnd\_j_d = \frac{1}{V1LND\_j_d} (\sum_{r \in REG} \sum_{n \in INC} VYHOULND_{rnd} \times ehoulnd_{rnd}$$

$$+ \sum_{o \in COR} VYCORLND_{od} \times ecorlnd_{od} + VYGOVLND_d \times egovlnd_d$$

$$+ \; VYROWLND_d \times erowlnd_d), \qquad d \in LND. \qquad (25.3)$$

The coefficients in the equations are computed from the income matrices given in fig. 4.17.

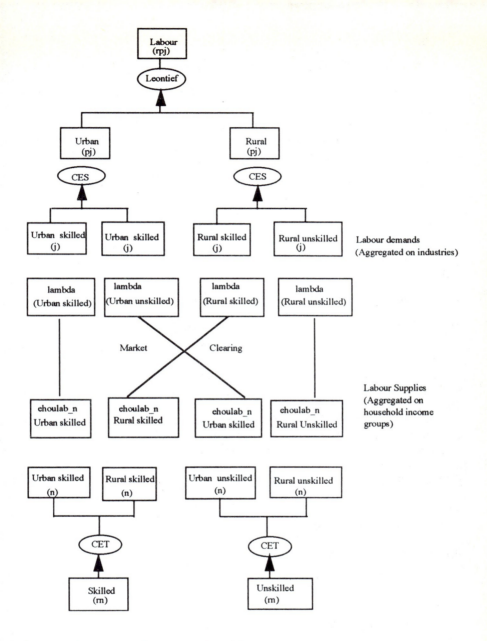

Figure 4.19 Labour demand and supply structure

119

In levels, eq. (25.1) can be written as:

$$P1LAB_{rp} \times EHOULAB\_n_{rp} = \sum_{n \in INC} EHOULAB_{rnp} \times P1LAB_{rp},$$

$$r \in REG, p \in PRF, \qquad (4.34.1)$$

where $EHOULAB_{rnp}$ represents supply of p type labour from household type n in region r in the base year, while $EHOULAB\_n_{rp}$ is sum of these supplies over all 14 types of households. In the percentage-change form, this is:

$$p1lab_{rp} + ehoulab\_n_{rp} = \sum_{n} [\frac{EHOULAB_{rnp} \times P1LAB_{rp}}{P1LAB_{rp} \times EHOULAB\text{-}n_{rp}}$$

$$(ehoulab_{rnp} + p1lab_{rp})],$$

$$r \in REG, p \in PRF. \qquad (4.34.2)$$

We cancel out $p1lab_{rp}$ from both sides to obtain the supply equation:

$$lambda_{rp} = \frac{1}{VYHOULAB\_n_{rp}} \sum_{n} VYHOULAB_{rnp} \times ehoulab_{rnp},$$

$$r \in REG, p \in PRF. \qquad (4.34.3)$$

Eqs. (17.1) and (17.2), given in Block 17, compute total demands for labour by types from all industries. According to the market clearing assumption, we equate total demand for labour by type, $lambda_{rp}$, to their supplies defined in eq. (4.34.3) to arrive at eq. (25.1).

Similarly equations (25.2) and (25.3) define the market clearing conditions for capital and land. The coefficients in these equations are institutions' shares in total rental value of a factor type because these two factors are owned by all the institutions. Total earning of all institutions from a factor is equal to the total rental value of that factor in all industries.

4.35   Income of institutions by source

Block 26 Equations determining institutions' income by source:

$$yhoulab_{rnp} = ehoulab_{rnp} + p1lab\_j_{rp}. \quad r \in REG, n \in INC, p \in PRF, (26.1)$$

$$yhoucap_{rnc} = ehoucap_{rnc} + p1cap\_j_{c}. \quad r \in REG, n \in INC, c \in CAP, (26.2)$$

$$yhoulnd_{rnd} = ehoulnd_{rnd} + p1lnd\_j_{d}. \quad r \in REG, n \in INC, d \in LND, (26.3)$$

120

$$ycorcap_{oc} = ecorcap_{oc} + p1cap\_j_c, \quad o \in COR, c \in CAP, \tag{26.4}$$

$$ycorlnd_{od} = ecorlnd_{od} + p1lnd\_j_d, \quad o \in COR, d \in LND, \tag{26.5}$$

$$ygovcap_c = egovcap_c + p1cap\_j_c, \quad c \in CAP, \tag{26.6}$$

$$ygovlnd_d = egovlnd_d + p1lnd\_j_d, \quad d \in LND, \tag{26.7}$$

$$yrowcap_c = erowcap_c + p1cap\_j_c, \quad c \in CAP, \tag{26.8}$$

$$yrowlnd_d = erowlnd_d + p1lnd\_j_d, \quad d \in LND, \tag{26.9}$$

$$yhouhou_{rnuv} = fyhouhou_{rnuv} + yh_h,$$
$$r \in REG, n \in INC, u \in REG, v \in INC, \tag{26.10}$$

$$yhoucor_{rno} = drate_o + ycor_o, \quad r \in REG, n \in INC, o \in COR, \tag{26.11}$$

$$yhougov_{rn} = fyhougov_{rn} + ygov, \quad r \in REG, n \in INC, \tag{26.12}$$

$$yhourow_{rn} = fyhourow_{rn} + phi, \quad r \in REG, n \in INC, \tag{26.13}$$

$$ygovhou_{rn} = yhou_{rn} + tyhou_n, \quad r \in REG, n \in INC, \tag{26.14}$$

$$ygovcor_o = ycor_o + tycor_o, \quad o \in COR. \tag{26.15}$$

As discussed, each institution has various sources of income. The institutions' incomes from rental values of primary factors are determined by their endowment of primary factors and prices of these factors. In levels, an institutions' income from a source—say private corporation's income from capital ($YCORCAP_c$)— is defined as:

$$YCORCAP_c = E0CORCAP_c \times P1CAP\_j_c,$$
$$o = \text{private corporations}, c \in CAP, \tag{4.35.1}$$

where $E0CORCAP_c$ and $P1CAP\_j_c$ represent private corporations' endowment of capital type c and its price index, respectively.

In the percentage-change form this is defined as:

$$ycorcap_c = ecorcap_c + plcap\_j_c, \quad c \in CAP. \tag{26.4}$$

The above procedure is applied to arrive at eqs. (26.1) to (26.9) which compute institutions' income from primary factors.

In Block 26, eqs. (26.10) to (26.15) set the default rules to determine the households' income from the payments received from:

1. other households;
2. corporations;
3. government; and
4. ROW.

The payments received by a household group are in proportion to the incomes of the above mentioned donor institutions. For example, in eq. (26.11), the income of household type rn from private corporations is determined by the private corporations' income ($yprc_o$) and the average dividend rate ($drate_o$).

It is noteworthy that for households, the average rate of transfer payments from other household group ($fyhouhou_{rnuv}$), from the government ($fyhougov_{rn}$), and from the ROW ($fyhourow_{rn}$) are specific to the household type, while the dividend rate from the two types of corporations ($drate_o$) are uniform for all 14 types of households. Eqs. (26.14) to (26.15) give total transfer payments received by the government from households and the two types of corporations.

4.36   Incomes of institutions

Block 27 Equations determining institution's income:

$$
\begin{aligned}
yhou_{rn} = \frac{1}{VYHOU_{rn}} \Bigl(&\sum_{p \in PRF} VYHOULAB_{rnp} \times yhoulab_{rnp} \\
&+ \sum_{c \in CAP} VYHOUCAP_{rnc} \times yhoucap_{rnc} \\
&+ \sum_{d \in LND} VYHOULND_{rnd} \times yhoulnd_{rnd} \\
&+ \sum_{o \in COR} VYHOUCOR_{rno} \times yhoucor_{rno} \\
&+ \sum_{u \in REG} \sum_{v \in PINC} VYHOUHOU_{rnuv} \times yhouhou_{rnuv} \\
&+ YHOUGOV_{rn} \times yhougov_{rn} + VYHOUROW_{rn} \times yhourow_{rn} \Bigr),
\end{aligned}
$$

$$r \in REG, n \in INC, \tag{27.1}$$

$$ycor_o = \frac{1}{VYCOR_0} (\underset{c \ \in CAP}{\Sigma} VYCORCAP_{oc} \times ycorcap_{oc}$$

$$+ \underset{d \ \in LND}{\Sigma} VYCORLND_{od} \times ycorlnd_{od}), \quad o \in COR, \quad (27.2)$$

$$ygov = \frac{1}{VYGOV} (\underset{c \ \in CAP}{\Sigma} VYGOVCAP_c \times ygovcap_c$$

$$+ \underset{d \ \in LND}{\Sigma} VYGOVLND_d \times ygovlnd_d$$

$$+ \underset{o \ \in COR}{\Sigma} VYGOVCOR_o \times ygovcor_o$$

$$+ \underset{r \ \in REG}{\Sigma} \ \underset{n \ \in INC}{\Sigma} VYGOVHOU_{rn} \times ygovhou_{rn}$$

$$+ VYGOVTAX \times t0rev + V1OCT\_j \times octrev). \quad (27.3)$$

Total income of an institution is the weighted-sum of its income from various sources. For example, total income of private corporations in eq. (27.2) is the weighted sum of its income from rental values of capital and land. See fig. 4.17 for the names of the data matrices used as coefficients in these equations.

It is noteworthy that in aggregating total income of government, we have included income from indirect tax revenues. The equations determining indirect tax revenues is discussed in section 4.26.

4.37 Aggregate expenditure and disposable income of households by household types

Block 28 Equations of the household expenditure and disposable income:

$$yhoud_{rn} = \frac{1}{VYHOUD_{rn}} (VYHOU_{rn} \times yhou_{rn} - VYGOVHOU_{rn}$$

$$\times ygovhou_{rn} - \underset{u \ \in REG}{\Sigma} \ \underset{v \ \in INC}{\Sigma} VYHOUHOU_{rnuv} \times yhou_{rnuv}),$$

$$r \in REG, n \in INC. \quad (28.1)$$

$$yhoudr_{rn} = yhoud_{rn} - xiitem_{rn}, \quad r \in REG, n \in INC, \quad (28.2)$$

$$chou_{rn} = yhoud_{rn} + apc_{rn}, \quad r \in REG, n \in INC. \quad (28.3)$$

Disposable income of the household type rn, (yhoud$_{rn}$), is defined as total household's income (yhou$_{rn}$) net of payments made to government (ygovhou$_{rn}$) and other households (yhouhou$_{rn}$). Eq. (28.1) gives this default rule in the percentage-change form. The real disposable income of household type rn is obtained by deflating its disposable income by its CPI (see section 4.29 for computation of consumer price indices for 14 types of households). Eq. (28.3) determines household expenditures. It is assumed that the nominal expenditure of the household type rn is a linear function of its disposable income. The variable apc$_{rn}$ represents the average propensity to consume for the household groups.

4.38 GNP and the balance of payments

Eq. (29.1) states that the gross national expenditure of the economy is the weighted-sum of current expenditures of the private and the public sectors and the domestic savings. Eq. (29.2) defines aggregate domestic savings as the weighted-sum of savings from households, private corporations, public corporations and the government.

Block 29 Equations for GNP and balance of payments:

$$gnpexp = \frac{1}{GNPEXP} (VITEM\_krn \times chou\_rn + PUR5\_is \times oth$$

$$+ VSAV \times sav), \tag{29.1}$$

$$sav = \frac{1}{VSAV} (\sum_{o \in COR} VSAVCOR_o \times savcor_o + VSAVGOV \times savgov$$

$$+ \sum_{r \in REG} \sum_{n \in INC} VSAVHOU_{rn} \times savhou_{rn}), \tag{29.2}$$

$$gnpinc = \frac{1}{GNPINC} (GDPIN \times gdpinc + VNFI \times nfi), \tag{29.3}$$

$$nfi = \frac{1}{VNFI} (\sum_{r \in REG} \sum_{n \in INC} VYHOUROW_{rn} \times hourow_{rn}$$

$$- \sum_{c \in CAP} VYROWCAP_c \times yrowcap_c$$

$$- \sum_{d \in LND} VYROWLND_d \times yrowlnd_d), \tag{29.4}$$

$$1000 \times 100 \times delLON = PUR2\_isj \times inv - VSAV \times sav. \tag{29.5}$$

In eq. (29.3), we define the gross national income (gnpinc) as the weighted-sum of GDP and net factor income from abroad. Eq. (29.4) states that the net factor income from abroad (nfi) is the difference between the income received in Pakistan for factors' services supplied from the ROW and the payments made by Pakistan for employing foreign-owned factors.

Eq. (29.5) computes the ordinary change in the transfer of resources from the ROW to Pakistan; this is defined as the difference between the national savings and investment.

4.39   Savings of domestic institutions

Block 30 Equations of domestic savings by institutions:

$$yhoud_{rn} = \frac{1}{VHOUD_{rn}} (VSAVHOU_{rn} \times savhou_{rn} + VITEM\_k_{rn} \times chou_{rn}),$$

$$r \in REG, n \in INC, \tag{30.1}$$

$$ygov = \frac{1}{VYGOV} (VSAVGOV \times savgov + PUR5\_is \times oth$$

$$+ VYHOUGOV_{rn} \times yhougov_{rn}), \tag{30.2}$$

$$ycor_o = \frac{1}{VYCOR_o} (VSAVCOR_o \times savcor_o + VYGOVCOR_o \times ygovcor_o$$

$$+ \sum_{r \in REG} \sum_{n \in INC} \Sigma YHOUCOR_{rno} \times yhoucor_{rno}),$$

$$o \in COR. \tag{30.3}$$

Eqs. (30.1) to (30.3) compute savings of the domestic institutions. Households' savings are their disposable incomes net of their expenditures. Eq. (30.2) defines government savings. The government's expenditure consists of its current expenditure and the transfer payments to households. Expenditures for corporations are the sum of dividends and corporate taxes.

4.40   Closing the model

Table 4.4 gives the number of equations and variables defined for each set. Column 1 gives the total number of variables which have same dimensions, and column 2 gives the number of equations with these dimensions. In our model, total number of variables (m) is greater than the number of equations (n). The third column gives the number of unexplained variables (m-n). To close the model, we treat (m-n) variables exogenous to the model. The last column in table 4.4 contains our selected exogenous variables. This selection represents one plausible closure of the model which is suitable for a short-run simulation. One can select another set of exogenous variables, as the model allows us to swap exogenous variables with endogenous variables, but the total number of exogenous variables should remain the same.

We have used the closure given in table 4.5 for the simulation results reported in Chapter 6 (section 6.2 explains this closure in detail). As discussed by Dixon *et al.* (1982, p.148), no theory can be made to formulate a closure. Nevertheless, two general rules should be observed. Firstly, if the quantity of a factor or commodity is given exogenously then its price is determined endogenously. If both the quantity and the price variables are given exogenously then a slack variable should be determined endogenously to meet the market clearing condition. In GE-PAK, there are various shift variables that may be used as slack variables. Secondly, because the model determines prices only in relative terms, at least, one monetary variable should be included in the exogenous list to determine the absolute price level.

Table 4.4
Tally of variables and equations for a short-run closure

Set name	(1) Variable count	(2) Equation count	(3) Exogenous count	(4) Unexplained variables
Macros	52	44	8	$f5tot$, phi, $t0$, $t1\_isj$, $t2\_isj$, $t3\_is$, $t5\_is$, $rtot$.
ADM $\times$SRC	1	1	0	
CAP	7	7	0	
COM	12	6	6	fep_i, feq_i, pmi_i, $t4_i$, tm_i, $t3\_e_i$.
COM $\times$IND	8	4	4	$a1\_s_{ij}$, $a2\_s_{ij}$, $t1\_e_{ij}$, $t2\_e_{ij}$.
COM $\times$MAR	2	1	1	$a4mar_{im}$.
COM $\times$SRC	9	7	2	$f5_{is}$, t_{is}.
COM $\times$SRC $\times$IND	8	6	2	$a1_{isj}$, $a2_{sj}$.
COM $\times$SRC $\times$IND $\times$MAR	4	2	2	$a1mar_{isjm}$, $a2mar_{isjm}$.
COM $\times$SRC $\times$MAR	4	2	2	$a3mar_{ism}$, $a5mar_{ism}$.
COR	5	3	2	$tycor_o$, $drate_o$.
COR $\times$CAP	2	2	0	
COR $\times$LND	2	2	0	
IND	27	16	11	$atot_j$, $a1cap_j$, $a1lab\_rp_j$, $a1lnd_j$, $a1oct_j$, $a2\_is_j$, $floct_j$, $a1prm_j$, $x1lnd_j$, $x1cap_j$, y_j.
INC $\times$PRF	2	1	1	q_r_{np}.

.....*continued*

Table 4.4 (continued)

Set name	(1) Variable count	(2) Equation count	(3) Exogenous count	(4) Unexplained variables
ITM	2	2	0	
ITM ×COM ×SRC	1	1	0	
ITM ×COM	2	2	0	
ITM ×REG ×INC	4	3	1	$aitem_{krn}$.
LND	7	7	0	
PRF	1	1	0	
REG	1	1	0	
REG ×INC	19	14	5	$fyhou\_gov_{rn}$, $fyhou\_row_{rn}$, $thou_{rn}$, apc_{rn}. $hsize_{rn}$.
REG ×INC ×CAP	2	2	0	
REG ×INC ×COR	1	1	0	
REG ×INC ×PRF	4	4	0	
REG ×INC ×LND	2	2	0	
REG ×IND	2	1	1	$allab\_p_{rj}$.
REG ×PRF	4	3	1	$unemp_{rp}$.
REG ×PRF ×IND	3	2	1	$allab_{rpj}$.
REG ×INC ×REG × INC	2	1	1	$fyhouhou_{rnrn}$.

4.41   A comparative-static interpretation of the model's results

GE-PAK has been designed for comparative-static simulations. Its equations and variables all refer implicitly to the economy at a future time-period.

Our interpretation of the results is illustrated by fig. 4.20 which graphs the value of some variable, say GDP, against time. 'A' is the level of GDP in the base year, and 'B' is the level which it would attain in T years time, if some policy change say — a tariff change—was not implemented. With the tariff change, GDP would reach C, all other things being same. The model generates the percentage change in GDP,

127

100(C-B)/B, showing how GDP in period T would be affected by the tariff change alone.

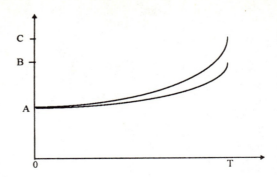

Figure 4.20 Comparative-static interpretation of results

The model can be used to carry out comparative static simulations of a policy change to analyse the short-run or long-run effects. For the short-run simulations, capital stocks are held at their pre-shock levels. This implies that the short-run period is long enough for the prices and quantities of all commodities and factors to adjust the given shock, but sufficiently short that we can ignore changes in industry capital stock available for use in production. This period could be two years, *i.e*, T = 2. In long-run simulations, it is assumed that capital stock will have adjusted to restore (exogenous) rates of return—this might take 10 or 20 years.

In either case the choice of closure and the interpretation of results depend on the timing of changes: the model itself is atemporal. Consequently it tells us nothing of adjustment paths (the shape of curves between 0 and T in fig. 4.20).

4.42   The percentage change approach to solve the model

GE-PAK is solved as series of linear equations relating percentage changes in the model's variables. In this section, we first explain how the linearised form can be used to generate exact solutions of the underlying non-linear equations, as well as to compute linear approximations to those solutions. This section is based on the explanation for solving ORANI-F contained in Horridge *et al.*, (1993). Subsection 4.42.1 explains the role of the initial solution in solving the model by this method.

A typical AGE model can be represented in levels as:

$$F(Y,X) = 0 \qquad\qquad (4.42.1)$$

128

where **Y** is a vector of endogenous variables, **X** is a vector of exogenous variables, and **F** is a system of non-linear functions. The problem is to compute **Y**, given **X**. Normally we can not write **Y** as an explicit function of **X**.

Several techniques have been devised for computing **Y**. The linearised approach starts by assuming that we already possess some solution to the system, $\{Y^0, X^0\}$ *i.e*:

$$F(Y^0, X^0) = 0 \qquad (4.42.2)$$

Normally, the initial solution $\{Y^0, X^0\}$ is drawn from historical data: we assume that our system of equations was true for a point in the past. With conventional assumptions about the form of the F function, it will be true that for small changes; **dy** and **dx**:

$$F_Y(Y,X)dY + F_X(Y,X) \, dX = 0, \qquad (4.42.3)$$

where F_Y and F_X are matrices of the derivatives of **F** with respect to **Y** and **X**, evaluated at $\{Y^0, X^0\}$. For reasons explained below, we find it more convenient to express **dy** and **dx** as small percentage changes, *i.e.*, y and x. Thus y and x are some typical elements of **Y** and **X** vectors, and are given by:

$$y = 100dY/Y, \text{ and } x = 100dX/X. \qquad (4.42.4)$$

Correspondingly we define:

$$G_Y(Y,X) = F_Y(Y,X)\hat{Y} \text{ and } G_X(Y,X) = F_X(Y,X)\hat{X} , \qquad (4.42.5)$$

where $\hat{Y}$ and $\hat{X}$ are diagonal matrices. Hence, the linearised system becomes:

$$G_Y(Y,X)y + G_X(Y,X)x = 0 \qquad (4.42.6)$$

Such systems are easy for computers to solve, using standard techniques of linear algebra. But they are accurate only for small changes in **Y** and **X**. Otherwise, linearisation error may occur. The error is illustrated by fig. 4.21 which shows how some endogenous variable, *i.e.* elements of Y, change as an exogenous variable, *i.e.* an element of X, moves from X^0 to X^F. The true, non-linear relation between X and Y is shown as a curve labelled as 'exact'. The linear, or first-order, approximation:

$$y = - G_Y(Y,X)^{-1} G_X(Y,X)x \qquad (4.42.7)$$

leads to the Johansen estimate Y^J— an approximation to the true answer, Y^{exact} .

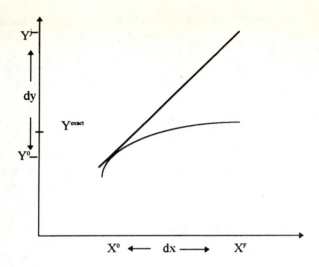

Figure 4.21   Linearisation error

Fig. 4.21 suggests that, the larger is x, the greater is the proportional error in y. This observation leads to the idea of breaking large changes in $\mathbf{X}$ into a number of steps, as shown in fig. 4.22. For each sub-change in $\mathbf{X}$, we use the linear approximation to derive the consequent sub-change in $\mathbf{Y}$. Then using the new values of $\mathbf{X}$ and $\mathbf{Y}$, we recompute the coefficient matrices $\mathbf{G_Y}$ and $\mathbf{G_X}$. The process is repeated for each step. If we use 3 steps (see fig. 4.22), $\mathbf{Y}^3$, *i.e.* the final value of $\mathbf{Y}$, is closer to $\mathbf{Y}^{\text{exact}}$ than was the Johansen estimate $\mathbf{Y}^J$. We can show, in fact, that given sensible restrictions on the derivatives of $\mathbf{F(Y, X)}$, we can obtain a solution as accurate as we like by dividing the process into a sufficient number of steps.

The technique illustrated in fig. 4.22, known as the Euler method, is the simplest of several related techniques of numerical integration—the process of using differential equations (change formulae) to move from one solution to another. GEMPACK, the computer software used to solve the model, offers the choice of several such techniques. Each requires the user to supply an initial solution ($\mathbf{Y}^0$, $\mathbf{X}^0$); formulae for the derivative matrices $\mathbf{G_Y}$ and $\mathbf{G_X}$, and the total percentage change in the exogenous variables, x. The levels functional form, $\mathbf{F(Y, X)}$, need not to be specified, although it underlies $\mathbf{G_Y}$ and $\mathbf{G_X}$.

The accuracy of multi-step solution techniques can be improved by extrapolation. Suppose the same experiment was repeated using 4-step, 8-step and 16-step Euler computations, yielding the following estimates for the total percentage change in some endogenous variable $\mathbf{Y}$:

$$y(\text{4-step}) = 4.5\%,$$
$$y(\text{8-step}) = 4.3\% \ (0.2\% \text{ less), and}$$

130

$$y(16\text{-step}) = 4.2\% \ (0.1 \ \% \ \text{less}).$$

Extrapolation suggests that the 32-step solution would be:

$$y(32\text{-step}) = 4.15 \ \% \ (0.05 \ \% \ \text{less}),$$

and that the exact solution would be:

$$y(\infty\text{-step}) = 4.1\%.$$

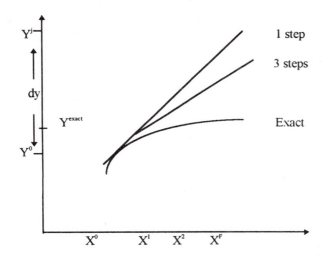

Figure 4.22   Multi-step process to reduce linearisation error

The extrapolated result requires 28 (= 4 + 8 + 16) steps to compute but would normally be more accurate than the results given by a single 28-step computation. Alternatively, extrapolation enables us to obtain given accuracy with fewer steps [see Dixon et al. (1982) and Horridge et al. (1993) for further details].

As we noted above, each step of a multi-step solution requires: computation of the percentage-change derivative matrices $\mathbf{G_Y}$ and $\mathbf{G_X}$ from historical data; solution of the linear system (4.42.6); and the use of that solution to update the data $(\mathbf{Y}, \mathbf{X})$. To update the data base, we need to define a set of data coefficients $\mathbf{V}$, which is a function of $\mathbf{X}$ and $\mathbf{Y}$, *i.e*, $\mathbf{V} = \mathbf{H(X,Y)}$. Most elements of $\mathbf{V}$ are simple costs or expenditure flows from the input-output table. $\mathbf{G_Y}$ and $\mathbf{G_X}$ turn out to be simple functions of $\mathbf{V}$, often indeed identical to elements of $\mathbf{V}$. After each small change, $\mathbf{V}$ is updated using the formula $\mathbf{v} = \mathbf{H_Y(X,Y)}y + \mathbf{H_x(X,Y)}x$. Hence the basic flows in the base year are updated for every small change. The updated data base contains

131

the basic flows for the shock in the next step (see Horridge et al., (1993) for application of the updating method).

4.42.1 The role of the initial solution and its appropriate explanation

In our explanation of the model's simulation results in percentage change form, it is assumed that we posses an initial solution of the model—$\{Y^0, X^0\}$ or the equivalent V^0—and that results are deviations from this initial state. However, this assumption raises one difficulty. Our data base does not, like B in fig. 4.20, show the expected state of the economy at a future date. Instead the most recently available historical data, represented by A in fig. 4.20, is used. In our study this point is represented by 1983-84 data. At best this data base refers to the present-day economy. Note that for an atemporal static model, 'A' provides a solution to the model for period T. In the static model, setting all exogenous variables at their base-period levels would leave all the endogenous variables at their base-period level. Nevertheless, 'A' may not be an empirically plausible control state for the economy at period T, and the question, therefore, arises: do estimates of the percentage-change effects of B-to-C of a cut in the import tax in 1988 differ much from the cut in 1993? Probably not. Firstly, a balanced growth, or a proportional enlargement of the model data base, just scales equation coefficients equally: it does not affect our results. Second, compositional changes, which do alter percentage-change effects, happen quite slowly. So for short- and medium-run simulations, 'A' is a reasonable proxy for B.

4.43 Computational aspects of the model

We have used GEMPACK for the computer implementation of our model. It is a suite of general-purpose economic modelling software especially suitable for general and partial equilibrium models. It has been developed to automate the solution of large economic models by Johansen's method. It can handle a wide range of economic behaviour, and contains capabilities for solving inter-temporal models. The objective of this section is to briefly introduce GEMPACK and its solution strategy. We also describe the steps involved in implementation of a model using GEMPACK. First, we discuss the solution strategy of GEMPACK, and then outline the procedure to implement GE-PAK using GEMPACK. See *GPD-1* to *GPD-4* (*IMPACT Project, 1993*) for further details on the implementation.

4.43.1 The solution strategy

In GEMPACK, Johansen solutions are calculated by solving the linearised equations of the model. As discussed in section 4.42, a typical AGE model can be represented by a system of linear equations:

$$F(Y,X) = 0, \qquad (4.43.1)$$

and the solution to this equation system is:

$$y = - G_Y(Y, X)^{-1} G_X(Y, X)x, \qquad (4.43.2)$$

or alternatively:

$$y = - A_Y^{-1} A_X x, \qquad (4.43.3)$$

where A_Y is the matrix of coefficients of endogenous variables, and A_X is the matrix of coefficients of exogenous variables. y and x the vectors of percentage changes in the model's endogenous and exogenous variables, respectively. If there are n equations in a model containing m variables (m should always be greater than n) then to solve the system of equations, the number of endogenously determined variables should be equal to the number of equations. Out of the total m variables, (m-n) variables should be exogenous. Thus the matrix A_Y is a square matrix of n×n and the matrix A_X is of dimension n×(m-n). The solution vector (y) is of dimension n×1 and the vector of exogenous variables has dimension of (m-n)×1. In eq. (4.43.3), $A_Y^{-1} A_X$ can be interpreted as a matrix of elasticities (E) of the endogenous variables with respect to the exogenous variables. The ijth element of E is the elasticity of the ith endogenous variable with respect to the jth exogenous variable.

One way of solving (4.43.3) is the traditional matrix inversion method. However, this approach uses significant computer processing time for big models when the size of matrix A_Y is large. To solve the linear equation system (4.43.3), GEMPACK uses an 'LU method[10] ' together with the sparse matrix method for solving the GE models from Johensen class. In this method, a *'Doolittle decomposition'* or *'Crout decomposition'* is performed on the matrix A_Y and the equation system is solved in two steps. The following paragraphs describe the application of the 'LU method' to solve the linear equation system (4.43.3).

To compute E, the square matrix A_Y is decomposed using the LU method.

$$A_Y = LU, \qquad (4.43.4)$$

where L is a lower triangular matrix and U is an upper triangular matrix.

Following this, we first solve the problem:

$$L Z = A_X, \qquad (4.43.5)$$

where Z is a vector containing intermediary values. Second, with Z computed, we solve:

$$U E = Z. \qquad (4.43.6)$$

Eqs. in (4.43.5) and (4.43.6) can be solved directly. By performing 'forward substitution' in (4.43.5) and 'backward substitution' in (4.43.6), there is only one unknown variable in each equation[11] . Although for a given A_Y the LU method is scarcely more efficient than simpler methods such as Gaussian elimination, it facilitates the re-computation of y for a new shock vector x. If the coefficient matrices A_Y and A_X are unchanged, the same LU decomposition may be used to compute the effects of a series of shocks [see Pearson and Rimmer (1983) for a simple numerical example of this approach].

4.43.2 Steps to implement the model on computer using GEMPACK

GEMPACK provides a computer-assisted method of converting an algebraic representation of the equations of a GE model into a tailor-made computer program which produces accurate solutions of the model. The programs included in GEMPACK are as follows:

1. For implementing and carrying out simulations:
TABLO	for processing the description of the model.
SAGEM	for carrying out Johansen simulations.
GEMPIE	for printing simulation results.
MODHAR	for translating text data files to binary files.
2. Utility programs:
SUMEQ	for information about the numerical equations.
SUMHAR	for data management.
SEEHAR	for data management.
CMPHAR	for data management.
SLTOHT	for post-solution processing of simulation results.

Apart from these programs, there are a number of other programs for transferring a model between different machines (*i.e.*, different operating systems). Further, a computer language is designed that allows us to write equations in an algebraic form. The TABLO program is then used to transfer this algebraic form of the model into FORTRAN programme.

Fig. 4.23 shows the steps in computer implementation of GE-PAK using GEMPACK software. In the first step the equations of GE-PAK are written in an algebraic form; this text file is referred to as GE-PAK.TAB. This is given as an input to the TABLO program which produces a FORTRAN program implementing the model's equations (GE-PAK.FOR). The FORTRAN program is then compiled and linked to generate an executable program (GE-PAK.EXE).

In step 3 (which may be done before step 1 and 2) the Pakistan Data Base (PDB), which is discussed in Chapter 5, is processed by MODHAR to generate a data base which is used by GE-PAK.EXE. In step 4 this program is executed to solve the model. In this step, the closure of the model is defined by choosing the exogenous variables and some of these variables are given exogenous values to define a policy shock. The solution of the model for exogenous changes in some of the variables is stored in GE-PAK.SL4. Since this output file is a binary file, in step 5, we run GEMPIE to generate simulation results in a print file.

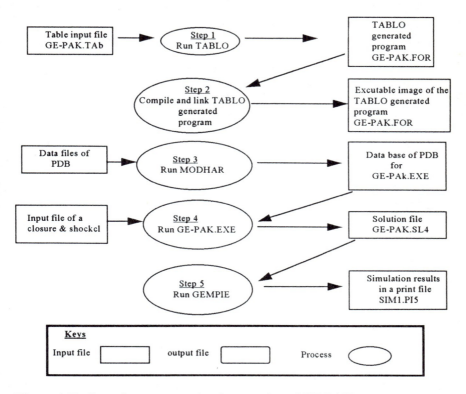

Figure 4.23   Steps for computer implementation of GE-PAK

Notes

[1]   If no digit is given then user distinction is irrelevant.
[2]   Constant Elasticity of Substitution (CES) functions.
[3]   A complete description of MSG-4 is given in Longva, Lorentsen, and Olsen (1985).
[4]   These price elasticities are used in the study by ENERPLAN discussed in Chapter 3. In that study, Riaz's estimates were modified to meet the two restrictions of symmetry and homogeneity.

5   An example of such experiment can be seen in the study by Sarkar and Kadekodi (1988) on energy pricing issues in India.

6   Bell (1991) made a comprehensive review of the recent work on the issues of markets, power and productivity in rural Asia.

7   A study by Irfan (1982) found an interdepedence between real wage gain and unionization in the large-scale manufacturing industries during 1947-1969 period.

8   Some recent versions of Harris and Todaro model can be found in Chao and Yu (1992), Hazari and Sgro (1991), Margit (1991), Batra and Naqvi (1987), Beladi (1988), Beladi and Naqvi (1988), Khan and Naqvi (1983) *etc*.

9   With reference to energy-economy interaction models, Blitzer (1986) has defined two sectors, urban and rural; and two types of labour in the applied general equilibrium model for developing countries. Changes in the rural and urban labour forces depend on population growth rate in the two sectors and the rate of rural-urban migration. The latter is a positive function of the ratio of expected urban labour income to the average rural labour income.

10 Pearson and Rimmer (1983) discussed this more efficient alternative technique of 'LU methods' which was first suggested by Duff (1977, 1981).

11 The order of the rows and/or columns of Ay may be changed before (4.43.3) is solved; this causes no problem as it only corresponds to a change in the order of the equations and/or variables.

5 The data base for GE-PAK

5.1 Introduction

This chapter discusses the data base of Pakistan (from now on called PDB) for GE-PAK, and presents the parameter values of the model. We used the 1983-84 SAM for Pakistan (Dhanani, 1986a, 1986b) to construct PDB. The matrix in its original form was not fully suitable for the model. Therefore, we expanded and modified it according to the model's specifications using supplementary data.

In section 5.2, we give a brief introduction to the original SAM. Dhanani (1986a, 1986b) has discussed, at great length, the development of the SAM and sources of data. We, therefore, discuss in section 5.3 only the expansions and modifications made in the original SAM. Section 5.4 presents the parameters of the model which were assigned externally estimated values. Various micro-level studies have been carried out for Pakistan to estimate production and consumption functions in a partial equilibrium framework. We selected values for some of the parameters from these econometric studies. For the remaining parameters, where econometric estimates were not available for Pakistan, we used parameter values from other CGE models for developing countries.

5.2 Social accounting matrix of Pakistan 1983-84

The SAM of Pakistan comprises of the following twelve accounts:
1. Wants.
2. Factors.
3. Domestic current account of households.
4. Domestic current account of private corporations.
5. Domestic current account of public corporations.
6. Domestic current account of government.

| | | | | Domestic Institutions (current) | | | | | Rest of the World | | | | | |
| | | 1 | 2 | 3 | 4 | 5 | 6 | 7 | 8 | 9 | 10 | 11 | 12 | |
	Account	Wants	Factors	House-holds	Private Corp.	Public Corp.	Govt.	Consolidated Capital Account for Domestic Institutions	Current	Capital	Domestic Commodities	Imported Commodities	Indirect Taxes	Total
1	Wants			XX										
2	Factors								XX		XX			
3	Domestic Institutions — Households		XX	XX	XX	XX	XX		XX					
4	Current Account — Private Corp.		XX											
5	Public Corp.		XX											
6	Government		XX	XX	XX	XX							XX	
7	Domestic Institutions — Consolidated Capital Account			XX	XX				XX	XX				
8	ROW — Current		XX									XX		
9	Capital								XX					
10	Domestic Commodities	XX					XX	XX	XX		XX			
11	Imported Commodities	XX					XX	XX			XX			
12	Indirect Taxes										XX	XX		
	Total													

Note: 'xx' indicates a submatrix of data

Figure 5.1   Layout of the aggregate social accounting matrix for Pakistan

7. Consolidated capital account.
8. Current account of the ROW.
9. Capital account of the ROW.
10. Production account of domestic commodities.
11. Supply account of imported commodities.
12. Indirect taxes.

A schematic diagram of the SAM is given in fig. 5.1. According to the standard notion, a SAM is a square matrix in which each column-sum is equal to its corresponding row-sum. A column gives expenditure entities in an account, while a row shows receipts in that account. In fig. 5.1, we have used the names of the income and expenditure matrices from the data base discussed in Chapter 4. The following paragraphs give a brief description of the twelve accounts at an aggregated level (see Dhanani, 1986b, pp. 18-32 for further details).

1. The Wants account represents income and expenditure accounts for item formation. In this account, income is derived from the sales of consumption items to households (row 1). These items are produced by using domestic and imported commodities. Expenditure in this account is on purchase of these commodities (column 1).

2. In the Factors account, factors of production render their services to domestic producers and the ROW. The second row shows payments made for these services. These primary factors are owned by the four institutions: households, corporations, government, and the ROW. In the second column, rentals of primary factors are paid to these institutions.

3. In the Household account, income comprises of the factor earnings, dividends from corporations, and transfer payments from other households and the government. The third row represents this income account. The third column shows household expenditure on consumption items, transfer payments, direct taxes paid to government, and household savings.

4. In the private corporations account, income comprises of the rental value of primary factors (row 4). Expenditures are: payments of dividends to households; payments of direct taxes to government; and residual income retained by these corporations as savings (column 4).

5. In the public corporations account, income flows in from the rental value of primary factors (row 5). Expenditure comprises of payments of dividends to households and to the government, and savings in the form of retained income (column 5).

6. In the government account, income comprises of: the rental values of primary factors; direct taxes paid by households, private and public corporations; dividends from public corporations; and all indirect tax revenues (row 6). The government expenditure account (column 6) consists of transfer payments to households, purchase of commodities for government consumption, and savings.

139

7.	There is one capital account consolidated for the four domestic institutions. Income in this account comprises of savings of the four institutions (row 7) and loans from the ROW. This loan is equal to the deficit in the balance of payments. The expenditure in the consolidated capital account is on purchase of investment goods and services (column 7).

8.	There are two accounts for the ROW: current, and capital. The current account receives payments made for primary factors' services and import of commodities (row 8). The expenditure in the ROW's current account comprises of payments made for employing primary factors from Pakistan; purchase of commodities from Pakistan, and the loans given to Pakistan to meet the deficit in the balance of payments (column 8).

9.	Income in the Capital account of the ROW is defined as the difference between its current income and expenditure which is equivalent to the deficit in the balance of payments of Pakistan (row 9). Expenditure in this account is transfer of this money to the consolidated capital account of the domestic institutions (column 9).

10.	Income in the Production account for domestic commodities is from sales of these commodities to five accounts: wants, government, the ROW and current goods producers (row 10). Expenditure in this account is costs of primary factors and intermediate inputs to produce domestic commodities (column 10). Since, the SAM is in purchasers' prices, indirect taxes are part of production costs.

11.	The income account for imported commodities receives payments for selling imported goods and services to various accounts (row 11). The expenditure account shows purchase of imported goods and services from the ROW and indirect taxes paid on them (column 11).

12.	There are two Indirect-tax accounts: (i) for taxes on domestic commodities, and (ii) for taxes on imported commodities. Income in this account is from indirect tax revenues (row 12). The corresponding expenditure is the transfer of indirect taxes to government.

5.3   Development of PDB

We incorporated nine changes in the SAM to develop PDB. Subsections 5.3.1 to 5.3.9 discuss these changes, while subsection 5.3.10 discusses a procedure which was adopted to incorporate the changes in the SAM.

5.3.1   Disaggregation of mining sector

We disaggregated the mining sector of the SAM into three industries: oil and gas, coal and other minerals. The *Census of Mining Industries of Pakistan* (GOP, 1988) gives 1983-84 statistics on output of and inputs in the six types of mining industries including oil, gas, and coal industries. The total output value of the mining industries in the Census is not equal to that in the SAM. Therefore, the distribution pattern of inputs among the industries reported in the Census is used to disaggregate the input flows in the mining sector of the SAM. The sum of all inputs consumed in each new industry was used to get the first estimate of its output.

On the demand side, output of the mining sector given in the SAM was disaggregated into crude oil, raw natural gas, coal and Other minerals. We made the following assumptions about the mining industry's output:

1. Supplies to the refinery and the gas processing industries were solely oil and raw natural gas, respectively.

2. Supplies to produce the consumption item 'coal' was all coal.

3. Supplies to all other industries were coal and Other minerals. The ratio of coal to Other minerals was set equal to the ratio of estimated total output of coal and Other minerals.

The initial estimates of supplies from the three new mining industries were not equal to the assumed consumption of these commodities. Production of coal and Other minerals was much lower than their estimated consumption. According to one of the studies on the coal industry (See Khan *et al.*, 1986), about 50 per cent of the coal industry's output is not reported. Assuming the same level of under-reporting for the Other minerals industry, the estimated outputs of these two industries were increased by 50 per cent. After subtracting the new estimates of the two products from the total output of the three mining industries, the remaining output was disaggregated into oil and gas according to their ratios in the Census. The average of consumption estimates and the new output levels were used as target values for column-sum and row-sum in the application of the RAS method to balance the SAM. The SAM was scaled using the RAS method (see subsection 5.3.10 for the RAS application).

5.3.2 Disaggregation of electricity sector

We disaggregated the electricity sector of the SAM into four types of electricity industries. The *Power System Statistics* (WAPDA, 1989) gives the break up of cost per kilowatt hour in nine major electricity plants for five cost categories: (a) interest charges, (b) depreciation charges, (c) establishment charges, (d) maintenance charges and (e) fuel charges by type of fuel, *i.e.*, natural gas, FO and HSD (table 1.11 in WAPDA, 1989). Table 1.23 in the *Power System Statistics* (WAPDA, 1989) shows electricity generation in KWh from each plant. This supplementary data on costs and generation were used to disaggregate the electricity sector in the SAM. Since the cost categories in the supplementary data in the SAM were not the same, we made the following assumptions about the cost categories in the supplementary data:

1. Interest payments and depreciation charges represent rental value of capital.
2. Establishment charges represent payments to labour.
3. Maintenance costs represent inputs from services industries. We made this assumption because in the SAM all intermediate inputs (other than fuels) in the electricity sector were supplied by the services industry).
4. Fuel costs are inputs from various fuel-producing industries.

We computed the values of output and inputs for each plant using the production costs per unit of output and units of electricity produced by that plant (WAPDA, 1989). This input-output matrix was used to compute the shares of the four electricity industries in each input (see table 5.1).

Table 5.1
Input distribution matrix used for disaggregation of
electricity sector

Production cost category	(1) Hydro electricity	(2) Combined cycle electricity	(3) Steam electricity	(4) Gas turbine electricity	Total
Labour	0.25	0.09	0.54	0.12	1.0
Capital	0.47	0.30	0.17	0.06	1.0
Petroleum products	0.00	0.54	0.26	0.20	1.0
Gas	0.00	0.14	0.46	0.40	1.0
Maintenance	0.37	0.16	0.36	0.11	1.0

Source: Based on table 1.11 and table 1.23 in WAPDA (1989).

We disaggregated the electricity sector of the SAM (with single industry) into a sector with four industries using the following formula:

$$SAM_{ij} = D_{ij} \times SAMO_{i, \text{electricity}}, \quad \therefore \sum_j D_{ij} = 1, \qquad (5.3.2.1)$$

where SAMO is the SAM before this modification,
j = hydro, combined cycle, steam generator, gas turbine industries,
i = rental value of capital, labour wages, and intermediate inputs of three types of fuel and services, and
D = input-distribution matrix given in table 5.1.

5.3.3 Disaggregation of petroleum products

In the original SAM, the refinery industry was treated as a single-output industry. The *Energy Year Book* (GOP, 1989) gives statistics on production, import and export values of six types of petroleum products. We used this supplementary data source to disaggregate the output of the refinery industry and its exports into six products. Similarly, aggregated imports of petroleum products was also disaggregated into six products. From the statistics given in the *Energy Year Book* (GOP, 1989), we calculated shares of the six products in the total value of production, import and export given in the SAM.

On the consumption side, the SAM had already contained usage of petroleum products in households by product type. We applied shares of petroleum products in their aggregated export values from the *Energy Year Book* (GOP, 1989) to disaggregate export values of petroleum products. The reliable data on intermediate and government usage of petroleum products by type were not available. In a research study on energy demand forecasting, Khan *et al.* (1986) have estimated fuel use by the agricultural, manufacturing, service and construction industries. In their study, estimates of fuel usage were also made for four modes of transportation, *i.e.,* rail, road, water and air. In line with these estimated shares, we prepared a distribution pattern to disaggregate consumption of aggregated petroleum products given in the SAM into six types of petroleum products (see table 5.2).

We assumed this disaggregation pattern for consumption of petroleum products supplied from both domestic and foreign sources. The resulting pattern of consumption was then mapped to the computed production and imports of these products. Since the estimated demand pattern did not match with the computed supply pattern, the two were reconciled by using the RAS iterative process.

In the SAM, indirect taxes on domestically produced commodities were included in the production costs. Thus, there was a single tax-revenue entry for the refinery industry showing aggregated indirect taxes on the six petroleum products. In the *Energy Year Book* (GOP, 1989) the structure of the retail prices is given for five petroleum products. This structure reports all components of these prices. As discussed in Chapter 2, there are two types of taxes on petroleum products: customs or excise duty, and the 'development surcharge' which is calculated as the difference between the cost of supply (including trade and transport margins) and the regulated sale price of a product. Using these two types of tax rates and production volumes, we estimated indirect tax revenues on each product. Total tax revenues generated by applying the computed tax rates from the supplementary data did not match with the total sales tax revenues given in the SAM. We first computed a ratio of the two sums and then scaled the set of computed tax rates by that ratio to adjust our estimated indirect taxes on six types of petroleum products.

5.3.4 Splitting of value added into returns to labour and fixed primary factor in small-scale manufacturing industries

In the SAM, it was assumed that returns to fixed factors (capital and land) are zero in all the small-scale manufacturing industries. Dhanani faced a problem in distributing the value added between fixed factor and labour in these industries. His computed total wage bill in these industries was much higher than the total value added of these industries (see Dhanani, 1986a p. 71).

143

Table 5.2
Consumption pattern of petroleum products

Users	Kerosene	High speed diesel	Light diesel oil	Gasoline	Furnace oil	Others
Households (kerosene)	1.0	0.0	0.0	0.0	0.0	0.0
Households (Non-durable transport)	0.0	0.1	0.0	0.9	0.0	0.0
Exports	0.0	0.0	0.0	0.0	0.4	0.6
Agriculture	0.0	0.8	0.2	0.0	0.0	0.0
Mining and manufacturing	0.0	0.3	0.1	0.0	0.6	0.0
Construction	0.0	1.0	0.0	0.0	0.0	0.0
Hydro electricity	0.0	1.0	0.0	0.0	0.0	0.0
Combined cycle electricity	0.0	1.0	0.0	0.0	0.0[a]	0.0
Steam electricity	0.0	0.0	0.0	0.0	1.0	0.0
Gas turbine electricity	0.0	1.0	0.0	0.0	0.0	0.0
Gas processing	0.0	0.5	0.0	0.0	0.5	0.0
Whole sales and retail	0.0	1.0	0.0	0.0	0.0	0.0
Road transport	0.0	0.8	0.0	0.2	0.0	0.0
Rail transport	0.0	0.5	0.0	0.0	0.5	0.0
Air transport	0.0	0.0	0.0	0.0	0.0	1.0
Water transport	0.0	1.0	0.0	0.0	0.0	0.0
All other users	0.0	0.5	0.0	0.0	0.5	0.0

a In the combined cycle power plants, FO can be used in place of natural gas but in our base-year data consumption of FO in the combined cycle power plants is zero

We disaggregated value added in these industries between labour and fixed factor using the *Survey of Small and Household Manufacturing Industries of 1983-84* (GOP, 1987). This survey gives value added, number of workers, and employment cost for the major industries. Except for a few industries, the grouping of the industries in the survey was identical to that used in the SAM. One distinguishing feature of these small-scale industries is their employment structure. In the employment statistics reported by the Survey, two types of labourers are given: unpaid workers (self-employed), and paid workers. Since the small-scale manufacturing activities are mainly carried out by self-employed persons, a small fraction of the labour is hired. According to the Survey, on the aggregate, about 35 per cent of the labourers were paid workers in these industries. Statistics also given on the number of paid and unpaid workers for each industry along with the wage bill of the paid workers.

Table 5.3
Shares of wage-bill in value added
of small-scale industries in the PDB 1983-84

Industry	Share of wage-bill in value added
Small scale grain milling	0.49
Small scale rice husking	0.49
Small scale gur and raw sugar	0.49
Small scale edible oils	0.49
Small scale other food industries	0.49
Small scale beverages	0.49
Small scale tobacco	0.63
Small scale cotton textile	0.65
Small scale silk and art-silk textiles	0.65
Small scale carpets	0.65
Small scale other textiles	0.76
Small scale shoe making	0.64
Small scale wood	0.65
Small scale furniture	0.66
Small scale steel furniture	0.61
Small scale printing and publishing	0.62
Small scale leather products	0.49
Small scale rubber goods	0.55
Small scale-chemicals	0.60
Small scale-plastic products	0.44
Small scale-non-metallic minerals products	0.49
Small scale-iron and steel remoulding	0.48
Small scale metal products	0.61
Small scale agricultural machinery	0.61
Small scale non-electrical machinery	0.75
Small scale electrical machinery	0.60
Small scale transport equipment	0.46
Small scale sports goods	0.58
Small scale surgical instruments	0.53

Source: Based on the Survey of Small and Household Manufacturing Industries, GOP(1987).

First, we computed an average wage rate for paid workers in each industry. Then, labour costs were imputed for paid and unpaid labour in each industry assuming that wages to the unpaid workers were the same as those for paid workers. The total value-added of these industries in the survey (Rs 11.1 billion) was not equal to the value added (Rs 15.1 billion) reported in the SAM. Therefore, we computed the shares of imputed labour costs (including imputed cost of unpaid labour) in total value-added for these industries in the Survey. Table 5.3 shows these shares for major industries. We applied these shares to disaggregate the value-added of each industry in the SAM.

This procedure of disaggregating value-added is in line with the procedure adopted by Dhanani to compute household income by source. In Dhanani's estimation, the wage earnings of a self-employed person are purely returns to his labour, and the rest of his earnings is return to capital that he owns. As stated by Dhanani (1986a, pp. 58-59),

> Finally, the distinction between wages and unincorporated business income highlighted the fact that a proportion of self-employed people received payments for factor services other than labour as well as an implicit wage component. Their income as recorded in the *Household Income and Expenditure Survey* (GOP, 1983) did not make such a distinction, and it was, therefore, necessary to impute a wage for such workers, and to interpret the difference between this imputed wages and their total factor income as a payment of 'unincorporated business capital'.

5.3.5 Formulation of tax matrices

Our model needs production and consumption accounts to be in producers' prices, with indirect tax components recorded separately. We transformed all flows in the SAM from purchasers' prices into producers' prices, and incorporated a set of indirect tax matrices. Dhanani aggregated various types of indirect tax revenues collected on a domestic commodity and showed the sum as a cost of production of that commodity. Similarly, for imported commodities, indirect taxes were included in the cost of supply. Our model distinguishes only two types of indirect taxes: (i) sales taxes which are levied at an *ad valorem* rate on a commodity irrespective of its source of supply (domestic or foreign); (ii) import taxes which are levied only on imported commodities.

To compute tax revenue matrices from the SAM, we first computed a vector of tax rates on domestic commodities from the SAM. The tax rate on output of industry j was defined as:

$$\text{Tax rate}_j = \frac{\text{Tax revenues}_j}{\text{Gross Value of Output}_j - \text{Exports}_j}, \ j \in \text{IND}, \qquad (5.3.5.1)$$

since all exports and the inputs used to produce them are exempted from tax. This tax rate was then used to compute the tax matrices by user groups. For example, the matrix of intermediate inputs PUR1 from fig. 5.1 given in purchasers' prices, is disaggregated into two matrices. One matrix (V1BAS) contains basic values of intermediate goods, and the second matrix (V1TAX) contains indirect taxes paid on these intermediate inputs using the following equations:

$$V1TAX_{isj} = PUR1_{isj} \times TAXRATE_j, \text{ and} \qquad (5.3.5.2)$$

$$V1BAS_{isj} = PUR1_{isj} - V1TAX_{isj}, \quad s = \text{domestic}, i \in COM, j \in IND. \qquad (5.3.5.3)$$

The above procedure was also applied to compute taxes on commodities used in capital formation, item formation, and government consumption assuming that tax rates were the same for all user groups.

The tax formulae given in equation (5.3.5.1) were applied to the single product industries. For multiple-product industries, *i.e.*, the refinery and oil and gas industries, we used the tax revenues collected on each product which was given in the supplementary data. For petroleum products, first total tax revenues from the refinery industry was computed using the supply quantity of and tax rate on each product given in the *Energy Year Book* (GOP, 1989). The shares of petroleum products in the total tax revenues were then applied to disaggregate the tax revenues given in the SAM for the refinery industry.

Similar computations were made for the three mining industries, using the tax revenues from crude oil, raw natural gas, coal, and Other minerals given in the *Census of Mining Industries* (GOP, 1988). In the above discussion on disaggregation of the mining and the refinery industries we mentioned that the imbalances between the estimated production and consumption of the new commodities were removed by using the RAS method. Consequently, the composition of the resulting supplies of new commodities was not exactly equal to that given in the supplementary data. The computed taxes on output of the four mining products and the six petroleum products were, therefore, adjusted to produce the tax rates given in the supplementary data. We first computed tax revenues on sales of these commodities using the tax rate given in the supplementary data. These revenues were then scaled to match the tax revenues computed from the SAM.

We applied similar methods for imported commodities. To begin with, we assumed that there was only one type of tax on imports and computed a tax rate vector for imported goods. We applied these tax rates to compute tax revenues paid by each user group on the purchase of imported goods. These tax revenues were then subtracted from the purchaser's values of the imports for each user group. Once, we had derived the indirect tax revenues for imported commodities, we then disaggregated them into sales tax revenues and import tax revenues. The method of this splitting is discussed in the next paragraph.

5.3.6 *Splitting the taxes on imported commodities into sales and import taxes*

The tax revenues from imports in the SAM were the sum of sales tax and import tax revenues. We computed revenues for these two categories by disaggregating the total tax revenues on imports using the following equations:

$$V1TAX_{isj} = V1BAS_{isj} \times T0_{ij}, \quad i \in COM, s=imported, j \in IND. \qquad (5.3.6.1)$$

$V1TAX_{isj}$ is the imputed sales tax revenue from the imported good i, $V1BAS_{isj}$ is the basic value of imported good i, and $T0_{ij}$ is the sales tax rate for good i. We computed sales tax matrices for all consumers groups using the above equation, and then calculated the import tax revenue vector $V0TAR_i$ according to the following formula:

$$V0TAR_i = IMPORTS\_TAX_i - V1TAX\_j_{is} - V2TAX\_j_{is} - V3TAX_{is}$$

$$- V5TAX_{is}, \qquad\qquad s = 2, i \in COM, \qquad (5.3.6.2)$$

where $IMPORTS\_TAX_i$ is the vector of total indirect tax revenues from imports given in the SAM.

Thus, if the imputed sales tax revenue on an imported good was equal to total import tax revenue on it then there was no import tax on this imported commodity implying that commodity supply from both sources were equally taxed. There were import taxes on commodities for which total import tax revenues were bigger than the imputed sales tax revenues from their imports. With this method, the resulting import tax rate became negative only if there was a tax on a domestic good but no equivalent tax on import of that good.

5.3.7 *Matrices of trade and transport margins*

The rates of trade and transport margins on domestic supplies were given by Dhanani (1986a, table 2.5, p.19) only for the large-scale manufacturing industries. We estimated trade and transport margin on each commodity by assuming that all sales from the wholesale & trade, road transport, and rail transport industries to other industries were margin costs which were paid by the latter industries. We assumed uniform rates of margins on the supply of a commodity for final/intermediate usage.

We first estimated average rates of margin costs as:

$$MARGIN\_RATE_{ij} = \frac{VIBAS_{isj}}{COSTS_j}, \quad i \in MAR, s=domestic, j \in IND, (5.3.7.1)$$

where $COSTS_j$ is the production cost in industry j (inclusive of the costs of margin goods) given in the SAM, and X_{ij} is the cost of margin good i used in industry j.

This margin rate, MARGIN_RATE$_{ij}$, was applied to compute matrices of margins on sales of commodities to all user groups using the following equations:

$$V1MAR_{isj} = (PUR1_{isj} - V1TAX_{isj}) \times MARGIN\_RATE_{ij} ,$$

$$i \in MAR, s = domestic, j \in IND. \qquad (5.3.7.2)$$

$$V1BAS_{isj} = PUR1_{isj} - V1TAX_{isj} - V1MAR_{isj},$$

$$i \in MAR, s = domestic, j \in IND. \qquad (5.3.7.3)$$

Here, PUR1$_{isj}$ is the purchasers' price matrix given in the SAM for current goods producers. Similarly, matrices of margins and basic values were computed for all other user groups.

The SAM contained sales of the three margin goods to the services industries. We assumed that these margin goods are directly used by these industries.

The average margin rates on imports are given by Dhanani (1986a). Dhanani used these rates to add margins into the value of imported goods at domestic currency prices. We used these rates to first compute a vector of aggregate margin costs on imported commodities. These aggregate margins were then divided into three parts: wholesale and trade, rail transport, and road transport. We assumed that the shares of the three types of margin goods were similar to those for domestically produced goods.

5.3.8   Development of capital formation matrix

As shown in fig. 5.1, sales of investment commodities were not distinguished by user-industries in the SAM. There, the matrix of fixed-capital formation, PUR2_j$_{is}$, shows consumption of investment good i, from source s, for overall fixed capital formation in the economy. We constructed a three-dimensional matrix, PUR2$_{isj}$, that gives flows of investment goods by commodities and user-industries. The *Economic Survey* (GOP, 1985, p. 31) contains data on fixed-capital formation in fifteen groups of industries for 1983-84. Dhanani took values of aggregate capital formation from the same data set (Dhanani, 1986b, table 4.1, p. 55) to form the matrix of fixed capital formation while constructing the SAM. Initially, we grouped all industries into 15 groups. The set GRP contains names of these industry groups.

We divided total investment among these groups of industries using the following equation:

$$PUR2_{isj} = PUR2\_j_{is} \frac{A_{isj}}{\sum\limits_{j \in GRP} A_{isj}} \cdot i \in INVCOM,$$

$$s \in SRC, j \in GRP. \qquad (5.3.8.1)$$

149

In the SAM, out of 236 commodities (domestic and imported), only 30 commodities were used for investment purposes. INVCOM is a set of these investment commodities. Thus, from a vector containing demands for 30 investment goods from the SAM (A_k_i) and a vector of investments in 15 industry groups (A_i_k), we prepared a three-dimensional input-output matrix of investment.

As shown in fig. 5.2, our task was to fill in the matrix A in such a way that the row-sums were equal to the investment by industry groups given in the vector A_i, and the column sums were equal to the investments by commodities given in the vector A_k.

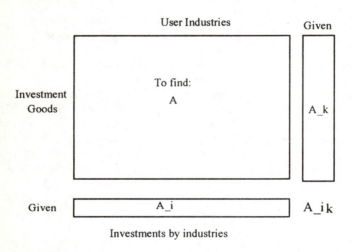

Investments by industries

Figure 5.2   Schematic diagram of vectors of investment goods and investments by industries

In fig. 5.2, A_ik represents total investment in 1983-84. To construct the matrix A, we made a set of rules to allocate investment good demands across industries. These rules were made because there were some investment goods that form capital in specific industries, such as agricultural machinery, and could be mapped to industries on a one to one basis. Similarly, there were some investment goods which, apparently, could not be used to form capital in some of the industries, e.g., use of auto-assembly parts for capital formation in the wholesale and trade industry. Finally, there were some investment goods which could be used to form capital only in some groups of industries. For example, rural buildings could be used to form capital in the agriculture, ownership of dwelling, government services, services-not-elsewhere-specified, wholesale and trade, and infrastructure industries. The use of the rural buildings in the agricultural industries represents all the construction work required for supply of water and storage of agricultural goods. In the ownership of dwelling industry, 'rural buildings' represents construction of residential buildings in the rural region.

150

The government services, services-not-elsewhere-specified, and infrastructure industries provide services of health, education, electricity distribution and community work. Buildings in these industries were treated as rural buildings. In line with these considerations, we made the initial allocations of investment goods between industries, as follows.

1. All sales of 'the agricultural machinery', plus 50 per cent sales of 'rural buildings', and 15 per cent sales of 'infrastructure' were allocated to the agricultural industries.
2. All sales of 'factory building' were assumed to form capital in the manufacturing industries, and were distributed between the small-scale and large-scale manufacturing industries in proportion to their shares in total investments of these industries. In addition, it was assumed that 'public building' was not used to form capital in the manufacturing industries.
3. All 'ship building' and 'road investments' were assumed to form capital in the transport industries. In addition, it was assumed that 70 per cent sales of 'transport equipment' were used for capital formation in the transport industries, while the remaining 30 per cent formed capital in other industries. Furthermore, we assumed that 2 per cent sales of 'public building' were used for capital formation in the transport industries.
4. All sales of 'low-cost residential building' and 'luxury buildings' were assumed to form capital in the ownership of dwelling industry. In addition, 15 per cent sales of 'rural building' was also allocated to this industry. It was assumed that the 'non-electrical machinery' and the 'public building' were not used for capital formation in the ownership of dwelling industry.

Sales of all other investment goods were distributed between industries according to each industry's share in total investment as:

$$A_{ik} = \frac{A\_ik}{A\_ik} \times A\_k_i, \qquad i \in INVCOM, \quad k \in GRP. \qquad (5.3.8.2)$$

These rules were applied for both domestic and imported investment goods. After the initial allocation of investment goods to industries, we applied the RAS procedure to balance the matrix.

To make the full matrix of 131 goods and 128 industries, we distributed purchase of investment goods by a group of industries between its members using the following formula:

$$PUR2_{isj} = PUR2_{isk} \frac{V1CAP_j}{V1CAP_k}, \quad i \in INVCOM, s \in SRC, k \in GRP, \quad (5.3.8.3)$$

where $V1CAP_k$ is the aggregate capital income in industry group k and j refers to industries in this group. We assumed the use of an investment good in an industry was in proportion to its share in total capital in its group. We mapped the investment goods from INVCOM to the set COM of 131 commodities from two sources.

5.3.9   Disaggregation of corporate capital and land

As shown in fig. 5.1, the rental values of capital and land in industries were attributed to three types of capital; non-corporate, corporate and dwelling capital. The non-corporate capital and the dwelling capital are owned by households. The corporate capital is owned by private corporations; public corporations; government; and the ROW, and its rental value is distributed among these institutions which are reported in the income matrices (*i.e.* $VYCORCAP_0$, VYGOVCAP, and VYROWCAP in the SAM) as:

$$VICAP\_COR\_j = \underset{o \in COR}{S} VYCORCAP_0 + VYGOVCAP + VYROWCAP.$$

$$(5.3.9.1)$$

We used this corporate income of each institution to disaggregate rental to corporate capital in industries by ownership. In this way, we transformed the three vectors of value added of capital given in the SAM into a matrix of 128×6. Fig. 5.3 gives this mapping.

We made this disaggregation in four steps.

1. Because no detailed data was available on employment of capital owned by the ROW at the industry level, we distributed the total capital rental paid to the ROW (VYROWCAP) to industries in proportion to the percentage share of each industry in total rental of corporate capital, *i.e.*

$$VICAP5j = VYROWCAP \times \frac{VICAP\_COR_j}{VICAP\_COR\_j}, j \in IND. \qquad (5.3.9.2)$$

2. At the second step, we selected those industries in which corporate capital was solely owned by the government.
    These nine industries are:

    - low-cost residential building.
    - luxurious residential building.
    - rural building.
    - public building.
    - infrastructure.
    - road transportation.
    - rail transportation.
    - roads.
    - government services.

152

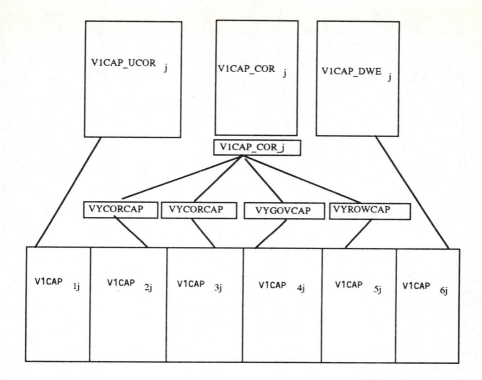

Figure 5.3   Schematic diagram of disaggregation of corporate capital

We assumed government owned all the corporate capital in these industries, except for that part which was assumed to be owned by the ROW. Therefore, rental to corporate capital in these industries fall in the category of govt. corporate capital.

3. The government of Pakistan publishes detailed financial accounts of government sponsored corporations. A summary of the gross profit of these corporations in 1983-84 (GOP, 1985a) for major industries was used as a supplementary data to allocate corporate capital to the following public corporations.

- oil and gas,
- banking and insurance,
- radio,
- television,
- telephone, and
- air transportation.

153

Following the *Government Sponsored Corporation* statistics (GOP, 1985a), we assumed 75 per cent of corporate capital in the electricity industry to be public corporate capital and 25 per cent to be private corporate capital. In the SAM, the ratio of private to public corporate capital on the aggregate was 52:48. We could have used this ratio to allocate corporate capital for all industries. However, according to the statistics given in the *Economic Survey*, (GOP, 1989), the share of public corporate capital was higher than that on the aggregate in some industries such as cement, fertiliser, and electricity. Thus, we distributed corporate capital into private and public ownership in the ratio of 50:50 in all industries except some selected industries for which this ratio was available from the survey (GOP, 1989).

After disaggregation of rental to corporate-capital by industries, we made sure that:

$$V1CAP\_COR_j = V1CAP2_j + V1CAP3_j + V1CAP4_j + V1CAP5_j,$$

$$j \in IND, \tag{5.3.9.3}$$

while:

$$VYCORCAP_o = \sum_{j \in IND} V1CAP2_j, \quad o = \text{private corporations.}$$

$$VYCORCAP_o = \sum_{j \in IND} V1CAP3_j, \quad o = \text{public corporations.}$$

$$VYGOVCAP = \sum_{j \in IND} V1CAP4_j,$$

$$VYROWCAP = \sum_{j \in IND} V1CAP5_j.$$

The above procedure was also applied to split rental to corporate land in industries into four types of rents.

5.3.10 Strategy for development of PDB

During the expansion and modification process, we used the national macroeconomic aggregates as control values to be preserved. The target values of private consumption (C), public consumption (G), imports (M), exports (X), fixed-capital formation (I) and net indirect tax revenues on domestic and imported commodities (TAXREV) for 1983-84 were taken from the *Economic Survey* (GOP, 1985b). Thus, we allowed adjustment in the value added (V1PRM) to satisfy the GDP identity:

$$C + G + INV + EXP - IMP = V1PRM + TAXREV \tag{5.3.10.1}$$

Dhanani also used the same values of macroeconomic aggregates as target values while developing the SAM.

Application of the RAS method After incorporation of every change in the SAM, we used the well-known RAS method to produce a new balanced SAM in which row-sums were equal to column sums. Two sets of FORTRAN programmes[1] were used to keep the SAM balanced. The first program uses a subroutine (RAS_SUB) that updates a square matrix by making column and row sums equal to the given target values using the following equation:

$$BNEW_{ij} = \lambda_i \, B_{ij} \, \beta_j, \text{ s.t. } \sum_i BNEW_{ij} = CT_j, \text{ and } \sum_j BNEW_{ij} = RT_i,$$
$$i \in COM, j \in IND, \qquad\qquad (5.3.10.2)$$

where B_{ij} is the original square matrix, and λ_i and β_j are scaling vectors which produce the new matrix BNEW. The vector CT_j contains the target value of row sum for column j. Similarly, the vector RT_i contains the target value of column sum for row i. In the application of RAS, we made sure that values of the sealing vectors were in a reasonable range.

The SAM did not remain square after disaggregation of the mining and electricity industries and incorporation of multiple products in the refinery industry. The second FORTRAN program (ALTRAS) finds scale vectors l_i and b_j such that:

$$BNEW_{ij} = \lambda_i \, B_{ij} \, \beta_j, \quad i \in COM, j \in IND, \qquad\qquad (5.3.10.3)$$

subject to:

$$\sum_{i \, \in \, COM} BNEW_{ij} = C_j, \qquad\qquad (5.3.10.4)$$

$$\sum_{j \, \in \, IND} BNEW_{ij} = R_i, \qquad\qquad (5.3.10.5)$$

$$\sum_{i \in P(j)} R_i = C_j, \qquad\qquad (5.3.10.6)$$

$$\sum_{j \in Q(i)} C_j = R_i, \qquad\qquad (5.3.10.7)$$

where P(j) is the set of rows associated with column j, and Q(i) is the set of columns associated with row i.

As mentioned, another concern in the development of PDB was to keep the values of selected macroeconomic variables (such as GDP, export earnings) comparable to their values given in the national accounts. In the application of the RAS method the macroeconomic aggregates were computed from the adjusted matrix after every iteration. The relevant parts of the adjusted SAM were then scaled to resolve any discrepancies between the control values and the new values of the macroeconomic variables.

5.4   Sources of the values assigned to the parameters of GE-PAK

The major categories of the model's parameters are two: (i) elasticities of substitutions in production functions, and (ii) expenditure elasticities for multiple household groups. Ideally, these elasticities should be estimated econometrically from cross sectional and time series data. However, given limited time and resources as well as data constraints, this was not possible for this study. One option was to adopt the estimated values of these parameters from the existing literature. A survey of the literature on Pakistan, however, showed that information on most of these elasticities was scant. There were only a few studies on Pakistan that estimated some of the required parameters. This was the case for most of the developing countries (Vincent, 1986, p.11). Therefore, we decided to adopt plausible values of these parameters from CGE models for other developing countries or made some 'educated guess'. But wherever, the estimated values were found, we made use of them.

5.4.1   The elasticities of substitutions between primary factors

Literature on estimates of elasticity of substitution between primary factors for many developed and developing countries is voluminous (Bandara, 1989). This literature suggests that time-series studies in most countries have produced the sectoral estimates centred around 0.5. Almost all such studies for Pakistan have been carried out only for the manufacturing industries[2]. Of these studies, only Khan (1989) has estimated a two-level nested CES function that allows substitution between capital and energy at the bottom level, and between labour and an energy-capital composite at the top level. Khan's estimated substitution elasticity between capital and energy was 0.175, while the elasticity of substitution between the energy-capital composite and labour was 0.48. Considering this information, we assumed a set of values for elasticities of substitution between primary factors or between primary factors and energy products; which is given in table 5.9. We summarise these parameter values below:

1.   Substitution elasticities between primary factors, or between a commodity-factor composite and other factors, were assigned a value of 0.5.
2.   Substitution elasticities between capital and an energy product, or between capital and an energy-products-composite, were assumed to be 0.2. The choice of relatively low elasticity was influenced by this study's interest in short-run simulation.
3.   Substitution elasticities between fuels were assigned relatively higher values than those between primary factors and energy products., even in the short run, as most of them (*e.g.*, natural gas and furnace oil) were close substitutes. We assumed a value of 0.5 for these parameters.
4.   Substitution elasticities between fuels and electricity were assumed to be relatively low (we chose 0.2) because of the short-term simulation period. The

same is true for substitution of gasoline with high speed diesel in the road transport industry.

5.4.2 The elasticities of substitution between domestic and imported commodities

No econometrically estimated values were available for elasticities of substitution between imported and domestic goods for Pakistan. We drew plausible values for these elasticities from the literature on CGE models for other developing countries.

In table 5.4, the import-substitution elasticities reported for Columbia, Turkey and the Philippines were econometrically estimated, the values for other countries were set using 'best guess'. In inferring the 'guesstimates' for Pakistan from table 5.4, we took into account the nature of commodities imported in Pakistan.

In the SAM, agricultural, mining and large-scale manufacturing commodities are supplied from both domestic and imported sources. Major import items are the heavy manufacturing goods such as 'machinery and equipment'. More than 50 per cent of the supplies in this commodity group is imported. Furthermore, the domestic products in this group are not close substitutes for the imported goods. For example, a number of surgical instruments produced in Pakistan are not substitutes for a wide variety of sophisticated surgical apparatus and machinery which are imported in Pakistan. We assumed that the import-substitution elasticities were small and assigned a 0.50 value to these parameters for all imported goods. Further, we assumed that these elasticities are same for all user groups, *i.e.*, current goods producers, investors, government and items producers:

$$\sigma COM1_j = \sigma COM2_j = \sigma COM3_j = \sigma COM5_j$$

Table 5.4
Import-substitution elasticities in
selected CGE models of developing countries

Industry	Sri Lanka	Columbia	Kenya	India	Turkey	Philippines
Agriculture	0.5-2.0	5.0	5.0	5.0	2.00	0.8-3.7
Mining	0.5	0.5	2.0	-	0.50	0.7-1.1
Food	1.0-2.0	3.1	4.0	-	0.65	0.1-4.1
Light-manufacturing	0.5	-	1.5	2.0	-	0.6
Heavy-manufacturin	0.5	-	0.5	0.5	0.50	0.2-5.0
Textiles	1.0	-	2.0	-	0.65	0.2-0.7
Petroleum	0.5	-	0.5	2.0	1.50	0.0
Services	2.0	2.0	3.0	3.0	0.20	0.0

Sources: Vincent (1986), Clarete and Warr (1992), Bandara (1989).

5.4.3 Household expenditure elasticities and the Frisch parameter

Various studies estimated household expenditure and price elasticities in Pakistan[3]. The most recent and comprehensive work was done by Burney and Khan (1991). They estimated marginal expenditure shares and expenditure elasticities for urban and rural households in six income groups. Tables 5.5 and 5.6 give these expenditure elasticities. These estimates were made for twelve groups of consumption items using 1984-85 household level data. These estimates indicate that expenditure elasticities vary across income groups and regions. They exhibit a cyclical pattern across income groups, which is explained in terms of quantitative as well as qualitative changes in the household consumption basket.

Table 5.5
Expenditure elasticities[a] by items and income
groups for rural households

Item groups and item numbers	Income Groups			
	Low	Middle	High	Others
Food and drinks (1-19)	0.85	0.74	0.46	0.79
Clothing and footwear (20-24)	0.75	0.70	0.50	0.68
Fuel and lighting (25-32)	0.57	0.43	0.31	0.63
Housing (33-36)	0.88	0.80	0.80	0.84
Transport and communication (49-50)	0.80	0.86	1.00	1.00
Household effects (37-42)	0.80	0.90	0.63	0.84
Personal effects (43)	0.91	0.92	0.58	0.97
Health care (44)	0.98	0.92	0.74	0.87
Education (45)	0.47	0.69	1.00	0.70
Entertainment (47)	1.00	0.84	1.00	0.98
Durable (46, 48)	0.91	0.75	1.00	0.87
Miscellaneous (51-53)	1.73	1.82	1.64	1.79

a These elasticity values are adjusted for the expenditure shares in PDB

Source: Burney and Khan (1991).

The main characteristics of the two sets of expenditure elasticities are summarised below.

1. For the majority of items, the expenditure elasticities for urban and rural households differ considerably. For example, housing, transport and

communication, education, entertainment and miscellaneous items are technically luxury items for urban households, while only entertainment and miscellaneous items are luxuries for the rural households. The elasticities for food and drinks, household effects, health care, and durables for the rural households are higher than that for the urban households, whereas the opposite is true for clothing and footwear and education.

2. According to the study, the difference between urban and rural expenditure elasticities is statistically significant for most of the items.

3. For the majority of items, the elasticities with respect to total expenditure vary widely across different income groups. Moreover, the pattern of these differences between income groups are not uniform for most of the items.

4. The expenditure elasticities for fuel and lighting are, in general, higher for the urban households than those for the rural households. Expenditure on transport and communication includes gasoline consumption for private transportation. The expenditure elasticities for items in this group are also higher for the urban households compared to those for the rural households. These elasticities are highest for the high income group in both the regions.

Table 5.6
Expenditure elasticities[a] by items and income groups for urban households

Item groups and item numbers	Income Groups			Others
	Low	Middle	High	
Food and drinks (1-19)	0.81	0.67	0.57	0.72
Clothing and footwear (20-24)	0.76	0.57	0.74	0.75
Fuel and lighting (25-32)	0.62	0.36	0.61	0.52
Housing (33-36)	1.0	1.00	1.00	1.19
Transport and communication (49-50)	1.00	1.00	1.68	1.51
Household effects (37-42)	0.73	0.57	0.79	0.76
Personal effects (43)	1.00	1.00	0.83	0.99
Health care (44)	0.83	0.83	0.88	0.77
Education (45)	1.00	1.00	1.00	1.25
Entertainment (47)	1.35	1.00	1.27	1.36
Durable (46,48)	0.50	0.79	1.63	0.87
Miscellaneous (51-53)	1.66	1.75	1.49	1.58

a These elasticity values are adjusted for the expenditure shares in PDB

Source: Burney and Khan (1991).

Our model recognises three income levels (low, middle and high) in each region. We mapped the estimates for income groups I, IV, and VI from the study to the three income groups in our data base. We assumed the same set of elasticities for both employed and self-employed households. The seventh category of household in the two regions is 'others'. Burney and Khan's study gives a set of expenditure elasticities for all households in a region which were used for the 'other' category of households in the PDB.

In GE-PAK, we used average expenditure on items in each household group from the data base and these expenditure elasticities to compute marginal expenditure shares for items by household type (see the equations in Block 8). Since average expenditure shares for employed households were different from that for self-employed, the marginal expenditure shares became different for these two groups.

The estimation of the Frisch parameter is mainly based on the study of Lluch *et al.* (1977). According to this study, the Frisch parameter rises from -7.5 to -2.0 as *per capita* income rises from US $100 to US $3000. Lluch approximates the relationship between *per capita* income in 1970 US dollar (X) and the Frisch parameter ω by:

$$\omega = 36 \, X^{-0.36}. \qquad (5.4.3.1)$$

This relationship was used to estimate the value of the Frisch parameter in several other CGE models[4]. The estimated values for the Frisch parameter for selected developing countries are listed in table 5.7. Bandara (1989) estimated the Frisch parameter for the urban and rural households separately for the CGE model of Sri Lanka. His estimates for the two regions are -4.57 and -5.45, respectively.

Table 5.7
Values for the Frisch parameter in selected CGE models

Country	Value
Chile	-2.525
India	-6.500
Ivory Coast	-3.706
Kenya	-6.000
Turkey	-5.160
South Korea	-3.700

Source: Vincent (1986).

Using (5.4.3.1), we computed a set of Frisch parameters from data on *per capita* income in Pakistan. Ahmad and Ludlow (1988) computed *per capita* income and expenditure series from the *Household Income and Expenditure Survey* (GOP, 1983 and 1986). In this data set, *per capita* income and expenditure of households are given for 20 income groups of urban and rural households in Pakistan. The households are grouped by *per capita* income (expenditure) at 5 per cent interval. The first group represents average *per capita* income (expenditure) of the 5 per cent of households with the lowest income, while the last group represents average income of the 5 per cent of households with the highest income. The same survey data was used by Burney and Khan (1991) to estimate the expenditure elasticities discussed in this section. Burney and Khan distributed households into seven income groups.

Table 5.8
Frisch parameter values assumed for Pakistan

Household category	Frisch-parameter values	
	Rural	Urban
Low-income	-5.90	-5.93
Middle-income	-4.74	-4.54
High-income	-2.82	-2.62
Others	-4.62	-4.07

We selected the *per capita* income values for urban and rural households by mapping the percentage of households covered by our three income-groups; low, middle and high on Ahmad and Ludlow's data. Our computed values for the Frisch parameters are given in table 5.8.

We assumed that the *per capita* income of self-employed and employed groups are the same. For the 'others' categories in the two regions, we computed the Frisch parameters using the average *per capita* income of the regions for all income groups.

5.4.4 Demand elasticities of exports

In most of the CGE models of developing countries, the small country assumption has been made with respect to that country's exports. Accordingly, it has been assumed that, except for a few commodities, the world prices are insensitive to export volumes of a developing country as the market shares of these exports are insignificant. Hence, export demand elasticities are assumed to be high (in absolute term) for most commodities. For example Bandara (1989) assumed a value of -20.0 for all the export commodities except for tea (-1.20). Similarly in a CGE model for India, export elasticities for all the commodities were assumed to be -20.0 except for tea and Jute (see Vincent, 1986). In the absence of any empirical evidence, we assumed that all export commodities of Pakistan have an insignificant share in the world market. Accordingly, we assumed an export elasticity of -20.0 for major exports in line with the values assumed for other developing countries (see the short-run closure in Chapter 6 for treatment of the remaining exports).

5.4.5 Investment parameters

For the investment theory in GE-PAK, it is necessary to specify values for three parameters.

1. The elasticity of expected rate of return on capital in industry j with respect to an increase in planned capital stock in that industry (BETA_R$_j$).
2. The ratio of industry j's gross investment to future capital stock (INV_ELAST$_j$).
3. The ratio of the gross to the net rate of return (QCOEF$_j$).

In a standard short-run closure, the model redistributes exogenously given aggregate investment across industries (see section 4.28 in Chapter 4 for elaboration of this mechanism).

In the short-run simulations performed in this study, it is assumed that investment in each industry is given exogenously, and the capital stock in each industry is fixed. Hence, BETA_R$_j$ and INV_ELAST$_j$ have no role to play in these simulations. The parameter QCOEF$_j$ is still required to determine rates of return in industries. To implement the model, we assumed a uniform value of 2.0 for QCOEF$_j$. The assumed value has no effects on the results except for the rates of returns ($r0_j$).

5.4.6 Elasticities of substitution between different types of labour

No estimates were available for the elasticity of substitution between skilled and unskilled labour for Pakistan. Ahmed (1981)[5] estimated a production function and input elasticities for the construction of low-cost housing in six cities in developing countries. In the study, elasticities of substitution between capital and labour and between skilled and unskilled labour are estimated by CES production functions. The study concludes that, in general, both the elasticities are quite low. In Ahmed's study, the estimated substitution elasticity between skilled and unskilled labour is 0.66. To implement our model we chose a value of 0.5 for the substitution elasticity between skilled and unskilled labour; for both urban and rural regions.

5.4.7 All other parameters of the model

In this section, we discuss all the parameters of the model for which no reference values were available from other studies, and we used 'best guess' values for these parameters.

We assumed a low value (0.2) for substitution between less and more-flexible electricity industry groups (σIELE), and assumed a higher value of substitution (0.5) for electricity supply from industries within less-flexible and more-flexible electricity industry groups (σIELEL and σIELEM).

Elasticity of household migration (σREG_p) was another parameter set for which no estimated values were available. We assumed a value of 0.5 for migration of both skilled and unskilled groups of households.

In our data base, only the refinery industry has multiple outputs. Hence, the output transformation elasticity, σOUT, is relevant only for transformation possibilities for petroleum products. It was found appropriate to assume a low value (0.2) for σOUT in the refinery industry for the short-run simulations.

5.4.8 A complete list of parameters of the model

For a ready reference we have listed values of all the model's parameters except expenditure elasticities in table 5.9. The parameters appear in alphabetical order. To complete the list, we report the values for BETA_R_j and INV_ELAST$_j$ parameters which are generally used in the shot-run applications of ORANI.

Table 5.9
Parameters of the model

Parameter	Value	Description
σIELEL	0.30	Elasticity of substitution between two types of less-flexible electricity (steam and combined cycle electricity)·
σIIND1	0.20	Elasticity of substitution between fuels in the manufacturing, mining and construction industries.
σIIND2	0.20	Elasticity of substitution between composite fuels and electricity in the manufacturing, mining and construction industries.
BETA_R_j	5.0	Elasticity of expected rate of return on capital in industry j with respect to an increase in planned stock of capital in that industry.
EXP_ELAST$_i$	-20.0	Export demand elasticities.
INV_ELAST$_j$	0.50	The ratio of industry j's gross investment to its future capital stock.
QCOEF$_j$	2.0	Ratio of gross to net rate of return.
σAGR1	0.20	Elasticity of substitution between fertiliser and land in the agricultural industries.
σAGR2	0.50	Elasticity of substitution between capital and high speed diesel in the agricultural industries.
σAGR3	0.50	Elasticity of substitution between energy-capital composite, land, and labour in the agricultural industries.

.....*continued*

Table 5.9 (*continued*)

Parameter	Value	Description
σAGR4	0.20	Elasticity of substitution between light diesel oil and electricity in the agricultural industries.
σCOM1 to σCOM3 and σCOM5	0.50	Elasticity of substitution between domestic and imported goods for 4 consumer groups.
σFAC	0.50	Elasticity of substitution between primary factors.
σICCY	0.50	Elasticity of substitution between natural gas and furnace oil in combined cycle industry.
σIELE	0.50	Elasticity of substitution between less-flexible and more-flexible electricity.
σIELEM	0.70	Elasticity of substitution between two types of more-flexible electricity (hydro and gas turbine electricity)·
σIIND3	0.20	Elasticity of substitution between composite energy and capital in the manufacturing, mining and construction industries.
σIRDT1	0.20	Elasticity of substitution between gasoline and high speed diesel in the road transport industry.
σIRDT2	0.20	Elasticity of substitution between fuel-composite and capital in the road transport industry.
σIRDT3	0.50	Elasticity of substitution between fuel-capital composite , labour and land in the road transport industry.
σISTM	0.50	Elasticity of substitution between natural gas and furnace oil in steam electricity industry.
σOUT$_j$	0.20	Elasticity of transformation in industry j ∈ NONIELE.
σOUT$_j$	0.0	Elasticity of transformation in industry j ∈ IELE.
σPRF$_{rj}$	0.5	Elasticity of substitution between skilled and unskilled labour by region and industry.
σREG$_p$	0.50	Elasticity of migration for profession p.

Notes

[1] These FORTRAN programmes are available from Dr. Mark Horridge, Monash Univ., who prepared these programs.

[2] Kazi, Khan and Khan (1976), Kazmi (1981), Kemal (1981), Battes and Malik (1987), Khan(1989) and Mahmood (1990).

[3] Siddiqui (1982), Ali (1981, 1985), Burney and Akhtar (1990).

[4] For example Dervis, de Melo and Robinson (1982) and Vincent (1986).

[5] Ahmed (1981) made a survey of the low-cost housing industries in Rawalpindi (Pakistan), Colombo (Sri Lanka), Tunis (Tunisia), Nairobi (Kenya), Lusaka (Zambia), and Medllin (Colombia). In addition to other problems, the sample size of the survey is very small (35 observations).

6 A case study of energy tax reforms for Pakistan

6.1 Introduction

Pakistan like many developing countries relies heavily on indirect taxes to generate public funds and to change income distribution. This leads to selectivity in tax structure rather than uniformity which is economically more efficient. Our review of the prices of major energy products in Pakistan suggests that there are three types of major distortions in these prices.

1. There is a source-discrimination in taxes on petroleum products in the form of import taxes and subsidies (*i.e.* imported and domestic varieties of the same product are taxed differently).
2. There is a product-discrimination in taxes on petroleum products. Sales tax rates on different products are not uniform: for example the tax on HSD is different from that on FO.
3. There is user-discrimination in taxes on electricity and natural gas. The implicit tax rates on these products are not uniform for major consumer categories.

There are many ways to set up experiments to find out the effects of removing various distortions in energy taxes. Here, we make five experiments to simulate elimination of these three types of discriminations in taxes on energy products. Table 6.1 lists these five experiments and names of simulations, and briefly describes these simulations. Our analysis of these results focuses on the social equity effects of removing these distortions, along with the macro and micro economic effects of the reforms. Conversely the results show how far the discriminating taxes meet the announced objectives of energy pricing policy in Pakistan.

Table 6.1
List of simulations

Experiment No.	Simulation name	Description	Revenue neutral	Section/ subsection No.
1	SIM1a	Elimination of source-discriminating tax (import tax) on HSD.	No	6.3.1
1	SIM1b	Elimination of source-discriminating tax (import tax) on Gasoline.	No	6.3.2
1	SIM1c	Elimination of source-discriminating tax (import subsidy) on Kerosene.	No	6.3.3
1	SIM1d	Elimination of source-discriminating tax (import subsidy) on FO.	No	6.3.4
1	SIM1	Elimination of all source-discriminating taxes on petroleum products (SIM1a + SIM1b +SIM1c + SIM1d).	No	6.4
2	SIM2	Elimination of all product-discriminating sales taxes on petroleum products.	No	6.5
3	SIM3	Elimination of all source- and product-discriminating sales taxes on petroleum products (SIM1 + SIM2).	No	6.6
3	SIM3N	Elimination of all source- and product-discriminating sales taxes on petroleum products in revenue neutral environment (SIM3 + Revenue- neutralising taxes).	Yes	6.7.1
4	SIM4a	Elimination of user-discriminating tax (subsidy) on electricity sales to agricultural industries.	No	6.7.1
4	SIM4b	Elimination of user-discriminating tax (subsidy) on electricity sales to household sector.	No	6.7.2
4	SIM4c	Elimination of user-discriminating tax on electricity sales to large-scale manufacturing industries.	No	6.7.3
4	SIM4d	Elimination of user-discriminating tax on electricity sales to small-scale manufacturing industries.	No	6.7.4
4	SIM4e	Elimination of user-discriminating tax on electricity sales to services industries.	No	6.7.5

.... *continued*

Table 6.1 (*continued*)

Experi- ment No.	Simulation name	Description	Revenue neutral	Section/ subsecti on no.
4	SIM4	Elimination of all user-discriminating taxes on electricity in a revenue neutral environment (SIM4a + ...+SIM4e).	No	6.7.6
4	SIM4N	Elimination of all user-discriminating taxes on electricity (SIM4 + Revenue-neutralising taxes).	Yes	6.8
5	SIM5a	Elimination of user-discriminating tax on natural gas sales to households.	No	6.9.1
5	SIM5b	Elimination of user-discriminating tax on natural gas sales to all manufacturing industries.	No	6.9.2
5	SIM5c	Elimination of user-discriminating tax on natural gas sales to services industries.	No	6.9.3
5	SIM5d	Elimination of user-discriminating tax (subsidy) on natural gas sales to electricity industries.	No	6.9.4
5	SIM5	Elimination of all user-discriminating taxes on natural gas (SIM5a + ...SIM5d).	No	6.9.5
5	SIM5N	Elimination of all user-discriminating taxes on natural gas in a revenue neutral environment (SIM5 + Revenue-neutralising taxes).	Yes	6.10
6	SIM6a to SIM6h	One per cent increase in the indirect tax revenues through increase in the power of tax on an energy product.	No	6.11

In the sixth experiment, we increase the powers of taxes on all energy products to compute the social welfare cost of revenue generation from indirect taxes on these products. We take into account equity concern by computing these costs for two forms of the welfare function: (i) utilitarian, and (ii) mean of order (-1), and rank the energy products according to their social welfare costs. Our analysis of the results focuses on two aspects:

1. Which energy products have higher social welfare cost of generating tax revenue?
2. How much does the ranking of energy products alters with the change in equity concern?

169

As discussed in Chapters 2 and 4, the prices of major commercial energy products are regulated by the government. In all 21 simulations we assume that all prices are determined by market forces to capture the full impact of these reforms.

The simulation results of GE-PAK contain detailed information on the effects of an exogenous shock. This includes all endogenously determined macro variables and commodity-, industry-, and household-level micro variables. These results help us to understand how an exogenous shock affects the economy. However, it is not possible to report all these endogenously-determined variables. To evaluate the effects of the reforms in energy prices, we, main focus on the followings:

1. Equity or distributional effects.
2. The balance of trade.
3. Indirect tax revenues.
4. Economic growth in total, and by sector.

Thus, for each simulation, we are mainly interested in real GDP, the balance of trade, total real consumption, real consumption of households by income group and region, and sectoral output. Total real consumption is a simple weighted-average over all types of households. In the model there are 128 industries producing 131 commodities. To report the effects of the energy price reforms on output of industries, we group 128 industries into 10 sectors:

1. Agriculture.
2. Oil and gas.
3. Large-scale manufacturing, including coal and Other minerals industries and excluding energy producing and energy intensive industries.
4. Small-scale manufacturing.
5. Services.
6. Fertiliser.
7. Refinery.
8. Cement.
9. Natural gas.
10. Electricity.

In Appendix C, table C1 lists the names of industries in each sector.

Interactions of various factors determine the effects of a policy shock. In presenting our results, we reveal each part of the mechanism as we proceed.

As shown in table 6.1, all shocks to the tax rates are first given without a revenue-neutrality condition. Thus, any change in a tax rate reallocates income from the public budget to private consumption or vice versa. Hence, results in these simulations are the combined effects of changes in the tax on an energy product and in private consumption. We disaggregate the two effects and discuss them at length for SIM1a results (see section 6.3.1). For the remaining simulations, we discuss only the aggregate effects.

170

Similarly, the effects on real per capita consumption for 14 types of household are determined through changes in their nominal income, CPI, and the number of households in a household group. We discuss this mechanism in detail for SIM1 (see section 6.3.4), and only report changes in real per capita consumption for all other simulations.

An important part of our analysis is discussion of the distributional effects of a policy shock. We analyse these effects by comparing changes in real *per capita* consumption of 14 types of household. The households are grouped by region, employment category and income group (see fig. 4.2 in Chapter 4). There are several ways to make the comparisons across regions, income groups and employment categories. For example, we can compare effects on rural households and urban households in the low income group, or can compare the effects on the three income groups in the urban region. It is not possible for us to make all these comparisons. Therefore, we focus on the differences which stand out in a simulation result, and explain these differences. Thus, in some simulations we discuss in more detail inter-regional differences, while in others we compare effects on income groups within a region.

6.2   Macroeconomic environment: A short-term closure

The choice of exogenous variables, together with the values prescribed for them, and the values of user-specified parameters, determine the economic environment assumed for the experiment. We are interested in the effects of the tax reforms in the short term, as the adjustment cost of such reforms is generally perceived to be high. In line with the assumption of the short-term simulation period, the important assumptions made about the macroeconomic environment are as follows:

1. Industry-specific capital stocks are fixed implying that we are looking at the effects of changes in energy prices after a period which is sufficiently short for us to ignore induced changes (from the levels they otherwise would have reached) in industry's capital stocks available for use in production.
2. Real government spending and real investments by industries are fixed for two reasons. First, Pakistan's government makes investment plans at the outset of its five-year economic plan. Along with the investment projects in the public sector, the government sets some expected targets for private investment in major sectors of the economy. Second, the credit policy is also made by the government and is also set in line with the allocation of expected private investment among major sectors. Our assumption is that, in the short term, the credit policy and investment plan are not affected by the changes in energy prices.
3. Supplies of labour from households by profession and income groups are fixed, implying that the choice between leisure and work remains unchanged.

4. The average propensity to consume for each of the 14 types of households is fixed implying that choice between consumption and saving remains unaffected.
5. The nominal exchange rate is fixed and acts as the numeraire.
6. All the regulated prices are also determined endogenously.

Export quantities are held fixed at the base-year level for all but 13 commodities. We judge that, for each of these commodities, exports were a sufficiently important component of total sales to require that their domestic prices and export quantities be modelled as responding to changes in the domestic currency values of world prices. For these 13 commodities, more than 25 per cent of their total sales in the base year are exported. We assume that the export demand curves for these commodities are downward sloping and their export quantities are determined endogenously, while the export taxes on these commodities are exogenously given.

Table 6.2
Major exports of Pakistan and their shares in their base-year sales

Commodity Names	(1) Sectors	(2) Share exported[a]
Carpets and rugs	Large-scale manufacturing	0.81
Cotton fabrics	"	0.65
Wearing apparels	"	0.64
Fish and fish products	"	0.46
Sports goods	"	0.45
Rice (husked)	Small-scale manufacturing	0.41
Rice (milled)	Large-scale manufacturing	0.39
Leather and leather products	"	0.36
Silk and synthetics	"	0.33
Other textiles	"	0.32
Surgical instruments	"	0.31
Air transportation	Services	0.26
Thread balls	Large-scale manufacturing	0.25

a Basic values of exports as a proportion of the basic value of total output

Table 6.2 lists names of these commodities and the export shares in their base-year sales. These commodities form 60 per cent of total exports in the base year. For the remaining commodities, export quantities are given exogenously and export taxes are determined endogenously.

Consistent with the short-term focus, technological parameters, household preferences, industry-specific land stocks, direct tax rates, the number of households by profession, and the number of persons per household in each household type are assumed to be unaffected by the changes in energy prices. The rates of various types of indirect taxes are exogenous with zero change except for energy products. The taxes on energy products are exogenous and are given policy shocks which are discussed for each simulation before presenting the simulation results. In all simulations, we assume that prices of all commodities, including commodities with regulated prices (such as electricity and natural gas), are determined endogenously. The list of all exogenous variables is given in table 4.5.

6.3 The effects of removing source-discriminating taxes on petroleum products-Experiment 1

In this section we present the results of removing the import taxes (subsidies) on the four petroleum products. Table 6.3 shows the powers of import taxes on petroleum products in the base year and the corresponding shocks which set their import tax rates to zero level. The GE-PAK database has been framed so that import tax rates show the difference in the rate of indirect taxation between domestic and imported variants of each product. In these shocks, we remove only the difference in the import and sales tax rates. For example, there is no sales tax on Kerosene but there is a subsidy on its import. The power of the import tax on Kerosene was 0.83. We increase it by 20 per cent to remove the subsidy on Kerosene ($1.2 \times 0.83 = 1$).

Table 6.3
Values for the exogenous powers of import taxes on petroleum products

Petroleum products	(1) Power of import tax[a] in the base year	(2) Percentage change in power of import tax[b]	(3) Simulation
High speed diesel	1.06	-6.0	SIM1a
Gasoline	1.56	-36.0	SIM1b
Kerosene	0.83	20.0	SIM1c
Furnace oil	0.46	85.0	SIM1d

a The power of a tax is one plus the *ad valorem* tax rate
b All the four shocks are given in SIM1, SIM3 and SIM3N

Subsections 6.3.1 and 6.3.2 discuss the effects of eliminating import taxes on HSD (SIM1a) and Gasoline (SIM1b), respectively. Subsection 6.3.3 covers the effects of eliminating import subsidies from Kerosene (SIM1c) and FO (SIM1d), while subsection 6.3.4 presents the cumulative impact of all the shocks (SIM1).

In our short-term closure, we assume that the average propensity to consume in the 14 types of households is given exogenously and is held fixed in all simulations. Since all other tax rates (direct or indirect) are exogenously held fixed, the changes in the import taxes on petroleum products reallocate income from the public budget to private consumption or *vice versa*. Hence, our results are the combined effects of changes in the taxes on petroleum products and the effects of the change in private consumption. For SIM1a, we analyse these two effects separately to understand their combined net effects. To disaggregate the two effects, we repeat the SIM1a shock but assume that real consumption for each household group is fixed (we refer to this as Case 1 of SIM1a). These results are reported in column 1 of table 6.4. Results of Case 1 show decline in average propensities to consume for 14 types of households. The model defines a consumption function for each household group. With fixed real consumption, any increase in real income is offset by the decline in the average propensity to consume. In Case 2 of SIM1a, we increase real consumption for households to the same extent but without removing the tax on HSD. These results are reported in column 2 of table 6.4. In the next few paragraphs, we analyse the results of Case 1 and Case 2 before discussing the cumulative results (SIM1a).

Effects of removing import tax on HSD with fixed real consumption The purchaser's price of HSD falls by 3.2 per cent when the import tax on it is eliminated. A large share of HSD (about 80 per cent) is used as an intermediate input to two margin goods industries: Road transport and Rail transport. The shares of HSD in the total production costs of these industries are 22 per cent and 16 per cent, respectively. The fall in the purchaser's price of HSD reduces the production cost of these margin goods and, as a result, reduces the purchaser's prices of all commodities. This leads to reduction in domestic costs of production. Exports expand because, with their selling prices determined in the world markets, exporters enjoy a cost-price improvement. Import-competing industries also become more competitive and expand. Some of the non-traded goods industries which supply intermediate inputs to these traded-goods industries (such as some agricultural and electricity industries) also expand. The balance of trade improves, and so does the real GDP because the domestic absorption is fixed. An expansion in labour demand from the traded goods industries increases real wages for all four types of labour.

Our industry-level results show that increases in the output of the traded-goods industries from the large-scale manufacturing sector are smaller than those from industries in other sectors. This is caused by the difference in the energy consumption patterns of the industries. The industries in the small-scale manufacturing sector are all non-traded (except for the Rice-husking industry, which exports a large share of its output). This industry has higher electricity intensity than do other export industries in the large-scale manufacturing sector which have higher FO intensity. Our detailed results on energy prices show that there is a smaller increase in the price of electricity relative to that in the price of

174

FO. The production structure of the manufacturing industries allows substitution between FO and electricity. Owing to the higher share of electricity in their energy demand, there is a bigger substitution of electricity with FO in the Rice-husking industry than that in other export industries in the large-scale manufacturing sector. Thus, the export industry in the small-scale manufacturing sector enjoys a bigger decline in production costs. The increase in output of the Rice-husking industry outweighs the decline in the output of other non-traded goods in the sector and, consequently the sectoral output rises.

Wages, deflated by the CPI, increase for all four types of labour. However, the increase in real wages for unskilled labour is bigger than those for skilled labour. This is explained by the employment pattern in the industries. In the base year, the unskilled labour has a big share in the labour demand for traded goods industries, while most of the non-traded goods industries employ a balanced mix of the four types of labour. Expansion in the traded- and some of non-traded goods industries increases the demand for unskilled labour. The nominal and real wages for unskilled labour rise. But contractions in most of the non-traded goods industries reduce the demand for skilled labour, and their nominal wages decline. Nevertheless, there is a small increase in their real wages, owing to the bigger decline in the CPI relative to that in their nominal wages.

Effects of increase in real consumption   The results of Case 1 show that the average propensity to consume for 14 types of household declines between 0.02 and 0.15 per cent when we remove the import tax on HSD with fixed real consumption. It shows that this tax reform increases real income of the households between 0.02 and 0.15 per cent. We use these values to shock real consumption for 14 types of household in Case 2 of SIM1a to compute the effects generated by the increase in real consumption in SIM1a. In the short term, this expansion in domestic absorption has the following effects (see column 2 in table 6.4).

1.   Overall consumer prices and nominal wages increase. However, the increase in nominal wages is higher than the increase in consumer prices, as the latter are a weighted average of prices of domestic and imported goods. The result is an increase in real wages for four types of labour.
2.   Production in most of the non-traded goods industries increases; especially in industries with large sales to private consumption.
3.   The expansion in domestic production increases the basic prices of domestically produced goods. This reduces exports and increases imports as import-competing and export industries become less competitive. The trade balance declines by Rs. 0.37 billion.
4.   The structure of labour demands changes because of expansion in non-traded goods industries and the contraction of the traded-goods industries. The demand for skilled labour increases more than the demand for unskilled labour. As a result, the increase in the real wage for skilled labour is bigger than that for unskilled labour.

5. The contractions of the traded goods industries are shown by the decline in output of the large-scale manufacturing sector. The small-scale manufacturing and services sectors expand as the expansion of the non-traded goods industries in these sectors outweighs the decline in output of the traded goods industries.

Table 6.4
Disaggregation of effects of removing import tax on HSD in SIM1a
(percentage changes)

	(1) Removal of the import tax with fixed real consumption Case 1	(2) Exogenous change in real consumption Case 2	(3) = (1) + (2) Total effects SIM1a
Real GDP	0.01	0.01	0.02
Real private consumption	0.00	0.13	0.13
Trade balance[a]	0.03	-0.37	-0.34
Indirect tax revenue	-0.79	0.10	-0.69
CPI	-0.10	0.39	0.29
GDP deflator	-0.09	0.42	0.33
Real Wages			
Rural-skilled	0.05	0.18	0.23
Urban-skilled	0.02	0.21	0.23
Rural-unskilled	0.17	0.03	0.20
Urban-unskilled	0.11	0.03	0.14
Sectoral Output			
Agriculture	0.03	-0.01	0.02
Oil and gas	0.00	-0.01	-0.01
Large-scale manufacturing	0.02	-0.06	-0.04
Small-scale manufacturing	0.03	0.03	0.06
Services	0.03	0.02	0.05
Fertiliser	0.09	-0.05	0.04
Refinery	-0.15	-0.01	-0.16
Cement	-0.00	0.00	0.00
Natural gas	0.02	-0.01	0.01
Electricity	0.04	-0.06	-0.02

a   Rs Billion

176

Total effects of eliminating import tax on HSD-SIM1a Column 3 in table 6.4 shows the net effect of the two phenomena:

1. The reduction in the import tax on diesel that changes relative prices of commodities (case 1).
2. The increase in real private consumption as tax burden is reduced (case 2).

The increase in real consumption in Case 2 reverses some of the Case 1 effects, such as an improvement in the trade balance and a decline in domestic prices. The increase in real private consumption, however, outweighs the decline in the balance of trade. The net effect is 0.02 per cent increase in real GDP. The real wages for all four types of labour increase in both the cases but to a different extent. The total effect is a bigger increase in the real wage for skilled labour than that for unskilled labour, in both urban and rural regions. This is explained by the difference in the sectoral composition of GDP in the two cases (see Columns 1 and 2 in table 6.4). The sectoral output results show that most of the non-traded goods industries expand in both the cases, while export and import-competing industries expand only in Case 1. The net effects are an increase in output of the non-traded goods industries, and a decline in output of the traded-goods industries. This causes a bigger increase in the demand for skilled labour than that for unskilled labour.

The difference in real wages of unskilled labour in the two regions is due to their employment patterns. In the base-year, the traded goods industries of the large-scale manufacturing sector mainly employ urban-unskilled labour. The demand for this labour group increases due to expansion in the non-trading goods industries, but there is also a reduction in their demand from the traded goods industries. The rural-unskilled labourers are mainly employed in the agriculture sector, which supplies inputs to the non-traded and traded goods industries. The rural unskilled labourers enjoy an increase in the demand from those agricultural industries which, instead of supplying inputs to the export industries, now produce raw-materials for the non-traded goods industries.

Though total labour supply is fixed by profession, the labour supply function in a region is upward sloping for each profession. A change in the relative real wages for a profession between two regions induces migration of labour to the region with the higher real wage. Our labour migration results show that there is no inter-region migration of skilled labour. For unskilled labour, we observe an increase of 0.01 per cent in rural employment and a decline of 0.01 in urban employment. Owing to changes in sectoral composition of GDP, the increase in the demand for rural-unskilled labour is bigger than that for urban-unskilled labour. A relatively lower increase in the demand for urban-unskilled labour creates a difference between real wages of unskilled labour from the two regions. As a result, unskilled labour migrates from urban to rural region. An upward shift in the supply of unskilled labourers increases their wages, and there is a small decline in the employment of urban skilled labour. On the other hand, this migration improves the supply of unskilled labour in rural region, reducing upward pressure on their wages and increasing the employment of unskilled labour in the region.

With real government expenditure fixed, reduction of tax revenue by one base-period rupee increases the government deficit, as well as household incomes, by one rupee. With fixed propensities to save, household savings increase by less than one rupee. Since real investment is fixed, the gap between domestic savings and investments increases. This gap is filled by the deterioration of Rs 0.34 billion in the trade balance.

Table 6.5
Projected effects on household real *per capita* consumption of removing import taxes (subsidies) on petroleum products
(percentage change)

Power of tariff	(1) (SIM1a) HSD	(2) (SIM1b) Gasoline	(3) (SIM1c) Kerosene	(4) (SIM1d) FO	(5) (SIM1) Total effect of all shocks
	-6.0	-36.0	20.0	85.0	
Self-employed					
Rural-L[a]-income	0.15	0.11	-0.15	-0.01	0.10
Urban-L[a]-income	0.06	0.06	-0.14	-0.01	-0.03
Rural-M[a]-income	0.10	0.07	-0.06	-0.01	0.10
Urban-M[a]-income	0.10	0.10	-0.09	-0.01	0.10
Rural-H[a]-income	0.04	0.06	0.02	-0.01	0.11
Urban-H[a]-income	0.16	0.15	0.01	-0.02	0.28
Employed					
Rural-L[a]-income	0.15	0.11	-0.15	-0.01	0.10
Urban-L[a]-income	0.06	0.06	-0.14	-0.01	-0.03
Rural-M[a]-income	0.17	0.17	-0.12	-0.02	0.20
Urban-M[a]-income	0.19	0.25	-0.17	-0.03	0.24
Rural-H[a]-income	0.03	0.04	0.01	-0.01	0.07
Urban-H[a]-income	0.17	0.17	-0.01	-0.02	0.31
Others					
Rural	0.10	0.09	-0.06	-0.01	0.12
Urban	0.14	0.13	-0.05	-0.02	0.20

a   Low, Middle and High

The small increase in real GDP is explained by changes in its industry composition, since the supply of primary factors and technology is held fixed. The detailed results show that industry composition of GDP changes in favour of the high-tax commodities. Thus, resources initially used in production of the low-tax commodities now produce commodities which have higher worth in the market.

Distributional effects in SIM1a All the household groups enjoy an increase in real *per capita* consumption when we remove import tax on HSD (column 1 of table 6.5). The two urban low-income groups and the two rural high-income groups experience the smallest increase in consumption in their respective regions. These variations are caused by the differences between households in respect of the consumption pattern and sources of income. In both regions, the highest increase in real *per capita* consumption is enjoyed by the middle-income group in the employed category. Owing to a bigger increase in real wages of skilled labour in these groups, their income increases relatively more than their consumer price indices.

6.3.2 The effects of removing import tax on Gasoline-SIM1b

The economic effects of eliminating import tax on Gasoline are very similar to the effects observed for the elimination of import tax on HSD (see columns 1 and 2 in table 6.6). However, the mechanism through which the reduction in the import tax on Gasoline affects the economy is different from that for HSD. Gasoline is used mainly by the households for private transport. The elimination of the import tax on Gasoline reduces its purchasers' price by 15 per cent. Table 6.7 shows that households spend between 9 and 21 per cent of their total expenditure on non-durable transport; this is composed of expenditure on public transport and petroleum products (mainly Gasoline). The reduction in Gasoline price increases the real income and real consumption of households. This leads to the effects similar to those discussed for the reduction in the tax on HSD.

Our results show that the elimination of import tax on Gasoline, with fixed real household expenditure, causes a decline between 0.13 and 0.23 per cent in the nominal expenditure of the various types of household. This reduction is required to maintain real consumption at the base-year level. Conversely, we can say that 15 per cent decline in the price of Gasoline causes about 0.13 to 0.23 per cent increase in the income of various household groups. When we allow these changes in household income to affect their consumption, there is an expansion in private consumption. This leads to a small increase in the CPI. The increase in real private consumption increases the demand for both domestic and imported goods. The basic cost of production increases as the industries expand their production by substituting fixed capital stock with labour which is mobile across industries and regions. The demand for labour by these industries increases, leading to an increase in wages. The rise in domestic prices reduces demand for exports and increases imports. The demand for labour by these traded-goods industries declines. There is a reallocation of labour, between industries as well as between regions.

The results reported in columns 1 and 2 of table 6.6 show that the removal the import tax on HSD and Gasoline has a positive effect on real private consumption but also causes a deterioration in the indirect tax revenue and the balance of trade. The indirect-tax revenue is a major source of government income. With fixed real consumption of government and real investment (private + public), the reduction in

179

indirect tax revenue results in a public sector deficit and a deterioration in the trade balance.

As shown in table 6.3, there are import subsidies on two petroleum products. In the following sections, we first discuss the effects of removing the import subsidies on Kerosene and FO separately, then proceed to a discussion of the cumulative effects of removing all the import taxes and subsidies on petroleum products.

Table 6.6

Projected effects of removing import taxes on petroleum products (percentage changes)

Power of tariff	(1) (SIM1a) HSD	(2) (SIM1b) Gasoline	(3) (SIM1c) Kerosene	(4) (SIM1d) FO	(5) (SIM1) Total effect of all shocks
	-6.0	-36.0	20.0	85.0	
Real GDP	0.02	0.02	-0.00	0.00	0.04
Real private consumption	0.13	0.11	-0.10	-0.01	0.13
Trade balance[a]	-0.34	-0.30	0.25	0.05	-0.34
Indirect tax revenue	-0.69	-0.58	0.48	0.19	-0.61
CPI	0.29	0.19	-0.13	-0.02	0.34
GDP deflator	0.33	0.23	-0.15	-0.02	0.39
Real Wages					
Rural-skilled	0.23	0.30	-0.17	-0.03	0.33
Urban-skilled	0.23	0.30	-0.15	-0.04	0.34
Rural-unskilled	0.20	0.15	-0.12	-0.01	0.23
Urban-unskilled	0.14	0.13	-0.08	-0.02	0.18
Sectoral Output					
Agriculture	0.02	-0.00	-0.00	-0.00	0.02
Oil and gas	-0.01	-0.02	0.01	0.00	-0.01
Large-scale manufacturing	-0.04	-0.05	0.03	-0.00	-0.06
Small-scale manufacturing	0.06	0.02	-0.02	-0.01	0.04
Services	0.05	0.03	-0.01	-0.01	0.06
Fertiliser	0.04	-0.03	0.02	0.01	0.02
Refinery	-0.16	-0.28	0.20	0.03	-0.21
Cement	0.00	0.00	-0.00	0.00	0.00
Natural gas	0.01	-0.00	0.00	0.01	0.01
Electricity	-0.02	-0.06	0.04	0.01	-0.03

a Rs Billion

180

The reduction in the import subsidy on Kerosene decreases real private consumption by 0.10 per cent. The negative effect on real GDP is nearly zero. There is an improvement in the trade balance, of about Rs 250 million, and an increase in the government indirect tax revenue of about 0.5 per cent. The mechanism through which the reduction in Kerosene subsidy produces these results is the converse of the process discussed for Gasoline. Removal of the import subsidy decreases the real income of households, with a resulting contraction in private consumption.

The effects of removing the import subsidy on FO are very small compared to the effects of changes in the import taxes on HSD, Gasoline and Kerosene. FO is an intermediate input used in the manufacturing industries. It has a significant share (between 8 and 27 per cent) in the production costs of five small-scale manufacturing industries. Significant shares of the total supply of FO (24 and 15 per cent) are also consumed by the rail transport and steam electricity industries. The increase in the price of FO increases the basic price of the steam electricity industry's output. However, the purchasers' price of electricity does not increase significantly, for three reasons. First, in GE-PAK, four industries generate electricity, with the steam electricity industry generating only 30 per cent of the total supply. Second, there is a substitution possibility between steam-generated electricity and that generated by the combined cycle industry. Third, there is a substitution of FO by natural gas in the steam electricity industry. Among the transport industries, rail transport has only a small share in total transport margins, which are supplied mainly by road transport. Therefore, the increase in the price of FO increases the output prices of only five small-scale manufacturing industries.

These industries produce three investment goods and two consumer goods which are non-traded. Since investments in industries are given exogenously, the demand for investment goods is unaffected by the changes in their prices. Hence, the increases in the basic prices of investment goods produced by the FO intensive industries are passed on to the capital-goods-formation sector. The nominal investment expenditure increases. The increases in the basic prices of the two consumer goods produced by FO intensive industries generate the same qualitative effects as the change in the price of Kerosene.

6.3.4   The cumulative effects of removing import taxes (subsidies) on all petroleum products (SIM1)

In subsections 6.3.1 to 6.3.3, we discussed how shocks to each import tax/subsidy on petroleum products affect the economy. In this section we discuss the net effects of removing all these taxes and subsidies. The salient features of the simulation results are as follows:

1.   Removing import taxes and subsidies on petroleum products increases real GDP by 0.04 per cent and real private consumption by 0.13 per cent.

2. In the base year, the revenues generated by the import tax on two of the petroleum products are about the same as the subsidies on the other two. However, our results show that removal of taxes and subsidies on petroleum products gives a net loss of 0.34 per cent in indirect tax revenues. The resulting public sector deficit is accommodated by a deterioration in the trade balance amounting to Rs 340 million.

3. Fig. 6.1 shows the cumulative effects of these reforms on households. (a) In the self-employed category, these reforms have positive effects on all such households (except urban-low income for which there is a decline of 0.03 per cent in real *per capita* consumption). The largest gain is for the urban-high income group (0.31). As shown in table 6.5, the removal of the subsidy on Kerosene has a bigger negative effect on the low-income groups than on the high income groups. Since the urban-low income group enjoys only a small gain from the other two reforms they become net losers. (b) The pattern of changes in real *per capita* consumption of seven types of household in the employed category is similar to that in the self-employed category, except for three groups. First, the middle-income group in the employed category enjoys a bigger increase in the consumption than its counterparts in the self-employed category, in both urban and rural regions. This is caused mainly by a large increase in real wages of the skilled labour in both region's middle-income groups. Second, there is a smaller increase in real *per capita* consumption of the rural high-income group than that of this group in the self-employed category. (c) There are positive effects on real *per capita* consumption of households in the other category (for both regions); urban households have a relatively bigger increase in their consumption.

4. Among the 14 types of household, we observe that the urban high-income group has the biggest increase in real *per capita* consumption, in both the employment categories.

These non-uniform changes in real *per capita* consumption for 14 types of household are explained by differences in their income and consumption patterns. In table 6.7, columns 1 to 3 show changes in nominal *per capita* income, the CPI, and real *per capita* consumption by household type.

The import tax reforms increase nominal income for all 14 types of household, though to a different extent as the returns to primary factors rise. There is a bigger increase in the nominal income of urban households than that of rural households — with the exception of the low income groups. Relatively the bigger rises in rural-unskilled wages and a bigger share of wage-earning in their total income cause a big increase in the nominal income of the rural low-income groups. In the middle- and high-income groups, the shares of wage-earnings are smaller in the income of rural households than that for in urban households; therefore these households experience a smaller increase in their income despite a bigger increase in the wage rate for them. The nominal *per capita* income (column 1) is the nominal income of a household group net of changes to the number of households in that group.

In most of the groups, households migrate from the urban to the rural region. This is explained by the bigger increase in rural wages and a smaller increase in the consumer price indices for rural households.

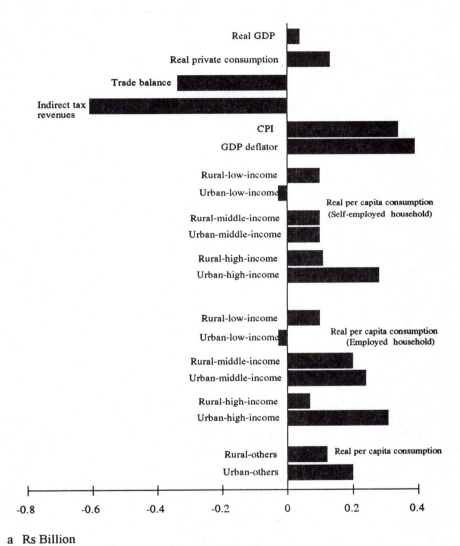

a   Rs Billion

Figure 6.1   Cumulative effects of removing import taxes (subsidies) on petroleum products (percentage change)

183

Table 6.7
Disaggregation of effects on real *per capita* consumption in SIM1

Household type	(1) Nominal *per capita* income	(2) CPI	(3) Real *per capita* consumption	(4) Number of households	(5) Share of skilled wages in total wages
Self-employed					
Rural-low-income	0.54	0.44	0.10	0.03	0.0
Urban-low-income	0.46	0.49	-0.03	-0.03	0.0
Rural-middle-income	0.45	0.35	0.10	0.02	0.0
Urban-middle-income	0.48	0.38	0.10	-0.02	0.0
Rural-high-income	0.33	0.21	0.11	0.00	0.0
Urban-high-income	0.45	0.17	0.28	0.00	
Employed					
Rural-low-income	0.54	0.44	0.10	0.03	0.0
Urban-low-income	0.47	0.50	-0.03	-0.03	0.0
Rural-middle-income	0.55	0.35	0.20	0.02	0.47
Urban-middle-income	0.63	0.38	0.24	-0.02	0.84
Rural-high-income	0.34	0.27	0.07	-0.01	0.0
Urban-high-income	0.49	0.18	0.31	0.01	0.0
Others					
Rural	0.44	0.32	0.12	0.00	0.0
Urban	0.47	0.27	0.20	0.00	0.0

The differences between household groups in real consumption become wide owing to the differences in their consumption patterns. The consumer price indices for all household groups rise the increase in the CPI is bigger for urban households in most of the income groups, with the biggest increase for the urban low-income groups (see column 2). The net effect is an increase in the real per capita consumption of all groups except the urban low-income groups.

Column 2 in table 6.7 shows that there is a non-uniform increase in the CPI across the income groups when the prices of consumer items are weighted by expenditure shares for each group. The biggest increase in the CPI is for the urban-low-income groups. This increase in the CPI outweighs the increase in the nominal *per capita* income of the urban-low-income groups, and there is a decline in their real consumption. Table 6.7 shows that the two rural-high income groups experience a bigger increase in nominal *per capita* income than do the two urban low-income groups. Further, these rural groups also enjoy a smaller increase in the CPI. Consequently, these groups enjoy an increase in real *per capita* consumption.

Of the 53 consumer items, table 6.8 shows the shares of kerosene, non-durable transport, wheat, and rice in the expenditure of all 14 types of household in the base year. These items are more affected by the import tax reforms than the other items. Table 6.8 shows the variation in the consumption pattern of households across income groups and across regions. The share of expenditure on kerosene is biggest for the two urban-low-income groups (in all 14 types of household). Contrary to this, the share of expenditure on non-durable transport is lower than that for most of the other groups.

Table 6.8
Shares of Kerosene and some other items in household expenditure

	Share in Household Expenditure			
	(1)	(2)	(3)	(4)
Household type	Kerosene	Non-durable transport	Wheat	Rice
Self-employed				
Rural-low-income	0.011	0.095	0.132	0.040
Urban-low-income	0.015	0.099	0.085	0.027
Rural-middle-income	0.007	0.126	0.098	0.037
Urban-middle-income	0.010	0.138	0.057	0.030
Rural-high-income	0.004	0.178	0.049	0.021
Urban-high-income	0.003	0.207	0.022	0.018
Employed				
Rural-low-income	0.011	0.094	0.134	0.040
Urban-low-income	0.015	0.099	0.085	0.027
Rural-middle-income	0.008	0.127	0.10	0.037
Urban-middle-income	0.011	0.136	0.58	0.030
Rural-high-income	0.004	0.148	0.57	0.023
Urban-high-income	0.003	0.203	0.23	0.018
Others				
Rural	0.007	0.136	0.088	0.032
Urban	0.007	0.173	0.040	0.023

Our results on the prices of consumer items show that biggest increase is in the price of kerosene and the biggest decline is in the price of non-durable transport, owing to the reduction in import tax on gasoline and HSD. The net effect is that the CPI increases more rapidly for the urban-low-income groups than for other household types. The CPI for the rural-low-income groups has a smaller increase than that for the urban-low-income groups. The rural low-income groups not only

185

spend less on kerosene but also more on wheat and rice. There are smaller increases in the prices of the latter two items than that for other items. The consumer price indices show the net effects on CPI for each household group.

Our results indicate that the removal of import taxes and subsidies from petroleum products has a negative impact on real *per capita* consumption for households in the urban-low-income group, owing to (i) the small increase in their income, and (ii) the big increase in prices of goods which have the bigger shares in their consumption baskets.

6.4   The effects of making sales tax rates on petroleum products uniform -SIM2

Our analysis of tax rates in the base year shows that there are high taxes on HSD and Gasoline, while there are subsidies on Kerosene, LDO and FO (see table 6.9). Sales tax rates on petroleum products vary between -3 and 23 per cent. The weighted-average of tax rates on all the petroleum products is about 13 per cent.

In SIM2, we shock the powers of taxes on all petroleum products to make the tax rates uniform at 13 per cent. Column 2 in table 6.9 reports these shock values.

Table 6.9
Values for powers of sales taxes on petroleum products in SIM2

Petroleum products	(1) Base year value	(2) Percentage change
Kerosene	0.99	14.0
High speed diesel	1.19	-5.0
Light Diesel Oil	0.99	14.0
Gasoline	1.23	-8.0
Furnace oil	0.97	16.0

a To make all tax rates equal to the weighted average -tax rate on petroleum products

Comparing the effects of reforms in import taxes and sales taxes on petroleum products gives the following insights (see table 6.10).

1. In the two simulations, the net effects of the tax reforms for petroleum products are qualitatively similar, but the impact of the sales-tax reforms is smaller than the effects of the import-tax reforms. This is explained by the smaller decline in the overall tax rates in SIM2, which results in a smaller increase in domestic absorption. The changes in the sales taxes differ from the changes in import taxes in two respects. First, there is an increase in sales tax on LDO in SIM2, while there is no change in its import tax in SIM1. Second, the increase in sales

186

tax on a commodity raises the tax on its domestic production and imports uniformly, while the import tax increases only the cost of its import. Therefore, the terms of trade effects are smaller in SIM2 than in SIM1

2. In line with the smaller increase in the domestic absorption, there are smaller increase in real wages of all four types of labour in SIM2. The rise in real wages for rural-unskilled labour is smaller than that for urban unskilled labour. This difference is mainly caused by the increase in the price of LDO in SIM2, and a smaller increase in the output from the agriculture sector. This sector is the main user of LDO and has a high intensity of rural-unskilled labour. A bigger rise in the price of LDO in SIM2 puts up the cost of production in this sector despite the substitution of LDO with electricity resulting in a smaller increase in its output in SIM2 than that in SIM1.

3. Most of the industries in the agriculture sector face no direct import-competition, but the rice and cotton industries (the latter in the large-scale manufacturing sector) supply raw material to the major export industries. The imports of cotton yarns become cheaper in SIM2 when there is an increase in the production costs of cotton due to the increase in the price of LDO Imports of cotton yarns rise and the domestic production of cotton and cotton yarn declines.

4. In the large-scale manufacturing sector, the smaller reduction in the output of major export industries is balanced by the decline in the output of the cotton yarn industry in SIM2. Therefore, the large-scale manufacturing sector contracts to the same extent in the two simulations.

5. The small-scale rice processing industry is one of the major export industries in the small-scale manufacturing sector. This industry has a higher electricity intensity than that of other export industries, but it also has a higher intensity of unskilled labour (both rural and urban). Thus, a smaller increase in labour wages in SIM2 than that in SIM1 outweighs the increase in electricity cost for this industry. The net effect is a much smaller decline in the industry's output, which leads to the expansion of the small-scale manufacturing sector in SIM2 to the same extent as in SIM1.

6. The demand for electricity increases as a result of its substitution for LDO in the agriculture sector and a smaller decline in the output of electricity-intensive industries than that in other sectors. Therefore, there is an increase in the output of electricity sector in SIM2, compared to the decline in SIM1. Consequently, the output of natural gas also increases, which is one of the major fuels in electricity production. The output of the natural gas industry in SIM2 shows a bigger increase than that in SIM1. In both simulations, there is a substitution of domestically produced fertiliser with imported fertiliser. Natural gas is used as a raw material in the fertiliser industry and comprises a big component of the production costs. There is a bigger increase in the price of fertiliser in SIM2 (relative to SIM1) when the price of natural gas rises. Therefore, there is a reduction in the domestic production and consumption of fertiliser in SIM2.

7. In SIM1, imports of HSD and Gasoline rise because of the reduction in import tax on these products. Consequently, the refinery industry contracts as these products constitute a big proportion of the industry's output Conversely in SIM2, the reduction in sales tax on these products increases production of these commodities and the refinery industry expands. We observe a lesser increase in imports of High speed diesel, and Gasoline and a smaller decline in imports of Kerosene and FO.

The above comparison reveals that the major difference between the two simulations is in their effect on energy-producing and energy-intensive industries. In SIM1, the output of the refinery and electricity industries declines and the output of the fertiliser industry increases. Conversely, in SIM2, the output of the refinery and electricity industries increases and the output of the fertiliser industry declines. In both simulations (but to a larger extent in SIM2) the output of the oil and gas industry declines, and the output of natural gas increases.

The comparison of the macro-economic effects in the two simulations shows that the positive effects of the reform in import taxes (SIM1) are bigger than that. Conversely, we can say that the source-discriminating taxes on petroleum products distort the economy more than the product-discriminating taxes do. In the next few paragraphs, we discuss the difference in the distributional impacts in the two simulations.

Comparison of the income distributional effects in the two simulations shows the following (see table 6.11).

1. The pattern of changes in the real *per capita* consumption is very similar in the two simulations. For example, in both simulations, all the household groups except the two urban low-income groups enjoy increase in real *per capita* consumption; the urban high-income groups enjoy the biggest increase. In both simulations, the effects for rural households are more uniform across the income groups in the self-employed category. Conversely, there are wide differences in the effects on the employed groups in both regions.

2. In SIM2, compared to SIM1, there is a smaller increase in real *per capita* consumption for the 12 types of household and a bigger declines for the urban-low income groups. This is mainly explained by the smaller increase in real wages for urban unskilled labour. There are smaller increases in the CPI and nominal income for most of the groups in SIM2; increases in income of the urban low-income groups are, however, much smaller than that in their CPIs.

Table 6.10
Projected economic effects of tax reforms in SIM1 and SIM2

Cumulative effects of:	(1) Removing import taxes	(2) Making sales tax rates uniform	(3)[b] = (1) + (2)
Real GDP	0.04	0.02	0.06
Real private consumption	0.13	0.11	0.24
Trade balance[a]	-0.34	-0.29	-0.63
Indirect tax revenue	-0.61	-0.54	-1.15
CPI	0.34	0.32	0.66
GDP deflator	0.39	0.36	0.75
Real Wages			
Rural-skilled	0.33	0.21	0.54
Urban-skilled	0.34	0.23	0.57
Rural-unskilled	0.23	0.17	0.39
Urban-unskilled	0.18	0.14	0.32
Sectoral Output			
Agriculture	0.02	0.01	0.03
Oil and gas	-0.01	-0.03	-0.04
Large-scale manufacturing	-0.06	-0.06	-0.12
Small-scale manufacturing	0.04	0.04	0.09
Services	0.06	0.05	0.11
Fertiliser	0.02	-0.04	-0.02
Refinery	-0.21	0.08	-0.12
Cement	0.00	0.00	0.00
Natural gas	0.01	0.02	0.03
Electricity	-0.03	0.01	-0.02
Energy prices			
Kerosene	12.00	10.73	22.74
High speed diesel	-3.00	-3.47	-6.44
Light diesel oil	0.89	4.63	5.52
Gasoline	-14.95	-5.31	-20.27
Furnace oil	6.61	5.98	12.60
Electricity	0.49	0.70	1.19
Natural gas	0.51	0.93	1.44

a Rs Billion
b Columns 1 and 2 might not add up to column 3 due to rounding off

Table 6.11

Projected changes in real *per capita* consumption in SIM1 and SIM2

Household Type	SIM1			SIM2		
	Nominal income	CPI	Real con-sumption.	Nominal income	CPI	Real con-sumption
Self-employed						
Rural-low-income	0.54	0.44	0.10	0.47	0.40	0.07
Urban-low-income	0.46	0.49	-0.03	0.41	0.45	-0.04
Rural-middle-income	0.45	0.35	0.10	0.42	0.33	0.09
Urban-middle-income	0.48	0.38	0.10	0.43	0.36	0.07
Rural-high-income	0.33	0.21	0.12	0.30	0.21	0.09
Urban-high-income	0.45	0.17	0.28	0.42	0.18	0.24
Employed						
Rural-low-income	0.54	0.44	0.10	0.46	0.40	0.06
Urban-low-income	0.47	0.50	-0.03	0.41	0.45	-0.04
Rural-middle-income	0.55	0.35	0.20	0.46	0.33	0.13
Urban-middle-income	0.63	0.38	0.25	0.51	0.36	0.15
Rural-high-income	0.34	0.27	0.07	0.30	0.26	0.04
Urban-high-income	0.49	0.18	0.31	0.42	0.19	0.23
Others						
Rural	0.44	0.32	0.12	0.39	0.30	0.09
Urban	0.47	0.27	0.20	0.43	0.27	0.16

3. Among the 14 types of household, only the urban high-income groups experience a bigger increase in their CPIs in SIM2. The consumption patterns of the households show that the two urban high-income groups spend a bigger share of their budget on non-durable transport, electricity and natural gas relative to the other groups. In SIM2, there are smaller increases in the prices of most of the consumer items except electricity and natural gas. Further, the price of non-durable transport declines in both simulations but this decline is smaller than that in SIM1.

4. Conversely, the relatively smaller increases in the prices of Kerosene and some food items in SIM2 benefit the low-income groups, as they consume these items the most. These low-income groups experience a smaller increase in consumer price indices in SIM2 than in SIM1. Within the low income groups, the increase in the CPI is of the same magnitude in the two regions. Expenditure patterns for these groups show that the rural households spend less on Kerosene and more on food than do the urban households. The smaller increases in the prices of these agriculture-based items benefit rural households more than their urban counterpart, which are benefited from the smaller increase in the price of Kerosene.

6.5   Cumulative effects of removing source- and product-discriminating tax rates on petroleum products-SIM3

As shown in fig. 6.2, there is an increase of 0.06 per cent in real GDP, and of 0.24 per cent rise in real private consumption, when all distortions in import and sales taxes on petroleum products are removed. However, there is a loss of Rs 630 million in the balance of trade and a decline of 1.15 per cent in total indirect tax revenues. Real *per capita* consumption rises for all 14 types of household except the urban low-income groups, which experience a decline of 0.07 per cent. The high-income group enjoys the biggest increase in real *per capita* consumption: 0.52 per cent. A similar pattern of changes in real *per capita* consumption emerges for the urban-employed category.

A different pattern of changes emerges for rural households. All seven types enjoy an increase in consumption. In the rural-self-employed category, real consumption increases to about the same extent for all the income groups. The middle-income group enjoys the biggest increase in the employed category.

Variations in real *per capita* consumption across income groups in a region are mainly explained by the differences in the wages of skilled and unskilled labour, the shares of skilled and unskilled labour in the income of households; and differences in the consumption pattern of households across income groups. The inter-regional differences in *per capita* consumption for households are mainly explained by the difference in the wages and household consumption pattern in the two regions. We have discussed these differences in the previous sections. In this section we point out only the major cause.

The major changes caused by removal of source- and product-discriminating taxes on petroleum products are an increase of 23 per cent in the price of Kerosene and a decline of 20 per cent in the price of Gasoline. The benefit generated by the reform in Gasoline price and the positive income effects of the reform in Kerosene price do not compensate the two urban-low income groups for the increase in their consumer prices.

The change in the price of HSD generates the least distributional effects, but the decline in its price of HSD is smaller than the changes in Kerosene and Gasoline prices. Another big increase is in the price of FO. but its effects are very small in every respect.

6.6   Effects of revenue-neutral reforms for source- and product-discriminating taxes on petroleum products-SIM3N

The results of SIM3 show a big negative effect on total indirect tax revenues when we abolish import taxes and subsidies (which are source-discriminating) and product-discriminating taxes on petroleum products. In SIM3N, the model computes a uniform change in the existing powers of taxes on all commodities to make up the loss in total indirect tax revenues which result from the reforms in the taxes on petroleum products.

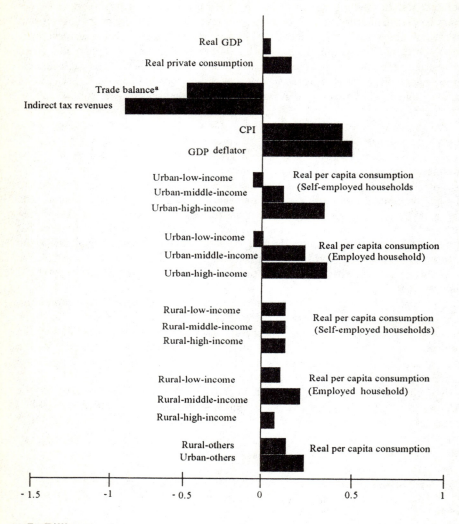

a Rs Billion

Figure 6.2   Cumulative effects of removing source- and product-discriminating taxes on petroleum products (SIM3)

192

Columns 1 and 2 in table 6.12 compares the cumulative effects of the reforms in petroleum product taxes (SIM3) with their effects when combined with a uniform tax on all commodities (SIM3N). The results of SIM3N show that an increase of 0.09 per cent is required in the power of indirect tax on all commodities to compensate for the loss in total indirect tax revenues. This additional tax does not completely wipe out the benefits of the reforms in the taxes on petroleum products. Real GDP and real private consumption rise by 0.04 per cent; without incurring any loss in total indirect-tax revenues.

Table 6.12
Effects of reforms in taxes on petroleum products

	(1) SIM3	(2) SIM3N	(3) = (2) - (1)
Real GDP	0.06	0.05	-0.01
Real private consumption	0.24	0.12	-0.12
Trade balance[a]	-0.63	-0.17	0.46
Indirect tax revenue	-1.15	0.00	1.15
Uniform tax rate	-	0.09	0.09
CPI	0.66	0.24	-0.42
GDP deflator	0.75	0.31	-0.44
Real Wages			
Rural-skilled	0.54	0.17	-0.37
Urban-skilled	0.57	0.15	-0.42
Rural-unskilled	0.39	0.21	-0.18
Urban-unskilled	0.32	0.11	-0.21
Sectoral Output			
Agriculture	0.03	0.04	0.01
Oil and gas	-0.04	-0.03	0.01
Large-scale manufacturing	-0.12	-0.05	0.07
Small-scale manufacturing	0.09	0.05	-0.04
Services	0.11	0.08	-0.03
Fertiliser	-0.02	0.00	0.02
Refinery	-0.12	-0.13	-0.01
Cement	0.00	-0.00	0.00
Natural gas	0.03	0.04	0.01
Electricity	-0.02	0.05	0.07

a Rs Billion

The additional tax in SIM3N maintains total indirect tax revenue at the base year level; as a result it off-sets the decline in the trade balance by Rs 460 million. However, there still remains a gap between savings and nominal expenditure on investment; the latter increases as a result of increases in the prices of investment goods while real investment is fixed. This causes a deterioration of Rs 170 million in the trade balance in SIM3N.

Since the model is linear, we can separate the effects of an additional uniform tax on all commodities by subtracting the result of SIM3 from SIM3N. Column 3 in table 6.12 shows these results. The additional tax reduces the increases in real wages of labour in the two regions. This reduction is bigger for the skilled labour compared to that for unskilled labour. The decline in domestic absorption, and the resulting decline in real wages, helps in expansion of exports and import-competing industries. We observe a significant increase in the output of the large-scale manufacturing industries and a decline in the non-traded good sectors such as small-scale manufacturing and services sectors when an additional tax is levied (see column 3 in table 6.12). The net effect of all the tax reforms (SIM3N) is a smaller decrease in the output of the large-scale manufacturing industries and a smaller expansion in the services and small-scale manufacturing industries.

Table 6.13
Projected changes in real *per capita* consumption by household type in SIM3 and SIM3N

Household Type	(1) SIM3	(2) SIM3N	(3) = (2) - (1)
Self-employed			
Rural-low-income	0.17	-0.01	-0.18
Urban-low-income	-0.07	-0.20	-0.13
Rural-middle-income	0.19	0.08	-0.11
Urban-middle-income	0.17	0.01	-0.16
Rural-high-income	0.21	0.21	0.00
Urban-high-income	0.52	0.38	-0.14
Employed			
Rural-low-income	0.16	-0.01	-0.17
Urban-low-income	-0.07	-0.20	-0.13
Rural-middle-income	0.33	0.12	-0.21
Urban-middle-income	0.40	0.04	-0.36
Rural-high-income	0.11	0.15	0.04
Urban-high-income	0.54	0.35	-0.19
Others			
Rural	0.21	0.11	-0.10
Urban	0.36	0.20	-0.16

Comparing the effect on real *per capita* consumption by household types in SIM3 and SIM3N (see table 6.13), we note the following.

194

1. There is a bigger negative impact (-0.20) on real *per capita* income of the low-income groups in the urban region in SIM3N. The positive effects for the rural-low-income groups are wiped out by the additional tax. The groups now experience a decline of -0.01 per cent in real *per capita* consumption.
2. The additional tax reduces the positive effects on real per capita consumption of households in most of the middle- and high-income groups but these households still enjoy a net gain in real *per capita* consumption between 0.04 and 0.38 per cent (see column 2).
3. The two urban high-income groups remain the biggest winners in SIM3N.
4. Only the rural high-income (employed) group experiences an increase in its real consumption in SIM3N, caused mainly by the smaller increase in its CPI .

6.7   Effects of removing user-discriminating taxes on electricity sales

Table 6.14 shows the powers of user-discriminating taxes on electricity sales to five consumer categories and the hypothetical percentage changes in them. Since there is a 3 per cent tax on electricity sales on the aggregate, the required changes are computed assuming that every consumer category pays a 3 per cent tax rate. We simulate the effects of these hypothetical changes in SIM4a to SIM4e. Table 6.15 reports these simulation results. In the following subsections, we discuss the effects of removing the tax (subsidy) on electricity sales to each consumer category, and then go on to a discussion on the cumulative effects of these tax reforms.

Table 6.14
Values for exogenous powers of user-discriminating taxes on electricity sales

User category	Power of tax in the base year	Percentage change in the power of tax[a]
Agriculture sector	0.76	36.0
Households	0.56	83.0
Large-scale manufacturing sector	1.61	-36.0
Small-scale manufacturing sector	1.38	-25.0
Services sector	1.46	-29.0

a   These shocks are given in SIM4a- SIM4e, SIM4 and SIM4N

6.7.1 Effects of removing subsidy on electricity sales to the agriculture sector
     -SIM4a

The power of the tax on electricity sales to the agriculture sector is increased by 36 percent to remove the implicit subsidy on electricity sales to this sector. The price of

195

electricity rises by 35 per cent for the agriculture sector and declines by 1 per cent for all other consumer categories. Real private consumption declines by 0.08 per cent and the trade balance improves by Rs 240 million. The reduction in domestic absorption due to increase in the tax rate on electricity sales reduces the CPI and the GDP deflator by 0.31 and 0.35 per cent, respectively. On the income side of GDP, total indirect tax revenue increases by 0.05 per cent while the returns to labour and land declining by 0.46 per cent, and the return to capital declining by 0.44 per cent.

The reduction in domestic prices improves competitiveness of the export industries and the import-competing industries. As a result, on the sectoral basis, we observe that there is an increase of 0.08 per cent in the output of the large-scale manufacturing industries, while there is a decline in the output of the non-traded goods industries. Apart from the electricity sector, the major decline occurs in the output of the small-scale manufacturing industries (-0.04), since most of these industries produce non-traded goods and final private consumption has the biggest shares in their sales. The agricultural industries provide inputs to both the large-scale and small-scale manufacturing industries. The demand for the agricultural inputs increases from the large-scale industries and declines from the small-scale manufacturing industries. The net effect is a decline in output of the agricultural industries. There is a substitution of electricity for LDO in the agricultural industries and a rise in the demand for it from the large-scale manufacturing industries. We observe that the refinery industry experiences the biggest increase in output. Conversely, the natural gas industry experiences a decline in its output because of the lower demand for natural gas by the electricity industries. Electricity production declines by 0.12 per cent as a result of removing the subsidy from its sales to the agricultural industries.

The changes in the pattern of demand and production of commodities affect the real wages of four types of labour. As shown in table 6.15, there are three noticeable changes in the real wages.

1. Real wages for urban-unskilled labour rise, mainly as a result of the expansion in the large-scale manufacturing industries. Urban-unskilled labour has 88 per cent share in total demand for labour in these industries.
2. Real wages for skilled labour decline in rural and urban regions. The contraction in the electricity and natural gas industries causes a reduction in overall demand for skilled labour as these industries are major employers of such labour. In particular, the steam-electricity industry is highly labour intensive; labour accounts for 48 per cent of total costs of which 26 per cent is paid to skilled labour.
3. There is a smaller decline (-0.15) in real wages of rural-unskilled labour than in those of skilled labour. This is caused by a smaller decline in the output of the agricultural industries than in the output of the electricity and services industries.

196

Table 6.15
Effects of removing user-discriminating taxes on electricity
(percentage changes)

Change in the power of implicit tax on	(1) SIM4a Agriculture	(2) SIM4b Households	(3) SIM4c Large-scale manufacturing	(4) SIM4d Small-scale manufacturing	(5) SIM4e Services
	36.0	83.0	-36.0	-25.0	-29.0
Real GDP	-0.00	0.06	0.06	0.02	0.01
Real private consumption	-0.08	-0.43	0.18	0.15	0.13
Trade balance[a]	0.24	1.61	-0.38	-0.44	-0.40
Indirect taxes	0.05	4.46	-2.41	-0.94	-1.06
CPI	-0.31	-0.86	0.90	0.86	0.36
GDP deflator	-0.35	-1.09	0.91	0.95	0.39
Real wages					
Rural-skilled	-0.24	-2.24	1.25	0.65	0.38
Urban-skilled	-0.23	-1.39	1.26	0.60	0.46
Rural-unskilled	-0.15	-0.71	0.30	0.38	0.14
Urban-unskilled	0.11	-0.20	0.40	0.24	0.20
Sectoral output					
Agriculture	-0.01	0.20	-0.06	0.07	-0.02
Oil and gas	-0.01	-0.08	-0.08	0.01	-0.01
Large-scale manufacturing	0.08	0.43	0.50	-0.29	-0.06
Small-scale manufacturing	-0.04	0.11	-0.13	0.24	0.04
Services	-0.00	0.03	-0.05	0.03	0.03
Fertiliser	-0.01	0.90	0.61	0.16	-0.06
Refinery	0.10	-0.06	0.03	-0.03	-0.02
Cement	0.00	0.00	0.00	0.00	0.00
Natural gas	-0.02	-0.29	-0.17	0.07	-0.02
Electricity	-0.12	-2.21	1.60	0.54	-0.05

In table 6.16, column 1 reports the effects on real *per capita* consumption by household type when we remove the subsidy on electricity sales to the agriculture sector. These effects are summarised below.

1. The urban middle-income group, in the employed category, experiences the biggest decline (-0.17) in real *per capita* consumption among 14 types of household. These households enjoy a bigger decline in their consumer prices

197

than do the other groups, owing to the decline in the price of electricity for households; but they also suffer a relatively bigger loss of income when wages of skilled and unskilled labour decline.

2. The two rural low-income groups also experience a big decline in real *per capita* consumption. These households experience a smaller decline in their nominal incomes, as there is a smaller decline in rural unskilled wages, but the decline in their consumer price indices are also smallest. Among all the commodities, the biggest decline is in the price of electricity (-0.87), and the rural low-income groups spend proportionally less on electricity than do any other groups.

3. Only the two rural high-income groups enjoy an increase in real *per capita* consumption, as their income is not affected by the declining wages, but they enjoy a decline in the CPI.

6.7.2 *Effects of removing subsidy on electricity sales to households - SIM4b*

The removal of subsidy on sales of electricity to households increases its price for them by 75 per cent, and decreases the price for all other user groups by 8 per cent. Consequently, the demand for electricity, on the aggregate, declines by 2.2 per cent.

The changes in electricity prices increase total indirect tax revenues by 4.5 per cent and real private consumption reduces by 0.43 per cent. This contraction in the domestic absorption leads to 0.86 per cent and 1.1 per cent reduction in the CPI and the GDP deflator, respectively. The trade balance improves by Rs 160 million. Real GDP rises by 0.06 per cent. The effects on sectoral output are similar to that of removing the subsidy from electricity sales to the agriculture sector, except that:

1. There is a decline in the output of the refinery industry.
2. There is an increase in the output of the agricultural, small-scale manufacturing and service sectors.

These differences are mainly due to the difference in the prices of electricity for the agriculture sector in the two simulations and its effects on the traded-goods industries. In SIM4b, the price of electricity declines for the agricultural industries as well as for other industries. Most of the export and import-competing industries buy intermediate inputs from the agricultural industries. The decline in electricity price greatly reduces the production costs of exports, and the demand for them grows. Further, the decrease in the price of electricity for the agriculture sector induces the substitution of electricity by LDO. The decline in the output of the refinery industry is mainly caused by the big reduction in the demand for LDO and FO. As shown in table 6.15, the reduction in electricity production causes a decline in the output of the natural gas and oil and gas industries. The industry-level results show a decline in the output of most of the non-traded goods industries in the small-scale and services sectors. However, this decline is outweighed by the increase in output from two export industries in these sectors.

Table 6.16
Projected effects on real *per capita* consumption of removing user-discriminating taxes on electricity (percentage change)

Change in power of implicit tax on:	(1) Agriculture	(2) House holds	(3) Large-scale manufac turing	(4) Small-scale manufac turing	(5) Services
	36.0	83.0	-36.0	-25.0	-29.0
Self-employed					
Rural-low-income	-0.14	-0.34	0.30	0.36	0.12
Urban-low-income	-0.05	-0.63	0.18	0.08	0.11
Rural-middle-income	-0.05	-0.03	0.00	0.07	0.10
Urban-middle-income	-0.06	-0.85	0.10	0.06	0.13
Rural-high-income	0.06	0.04	-0.15	-0.19	0.01
Urban-high-income	-0.05	-0.67	0.11	-0.05	0.14
Employed					
Rural-low-income	-0.14	-0.32	0.29	0.36	0.12
Urban-low-income	-0.05	-0.64	0.19	0.08	0.11
Rural-middle-income	-0.15	-0.99	0.62	0.39	0.20
Urban-middle-income	-0.17	-1.67	0.89	0.42	0.36
Rural-high-income	0.03	-0.04	-0.11	-0.12	-0.01
Urban-high-income	-0.05	-0.65	0.25	0.10	0.16
Others					
Rural	-0.04	-0.16	0.07	0.08	0.07
Urban	-0.06	-0.75	0.14	0.07	0.14

The industry-level results show a decline in output of all industries except export industries and their major intermediate inputs industries. Demand for, and the real wages of, all four types of labour decline, since most of the export industries are not labour intensive. Further, the biggest decline is in the output of the electricity sector, which is highly labour intensive. It employs, in particular, more rural skilled labour than urban skilled labour. Therefore, we observe the biggest decline in real wages of rural-skilled labour. On the other hand, most of the export industries demand urban unskilled labour and, therefore, the decline in real wage for this category is smallest.

The effects on real *per capita* consumption for the 14 types of household in SIM4b (column 2 in table 6.16) are discussed below:

1. Real *per capita* consumption declines for all 14 types of household except for one rural high-income group.
2. Most of the rural household groups experiences relatively a smaller decline in real *per capita* consumption compared to their counterparts in urban region.

Real wages for rural labour decline more than that for the urban labour in each category (see table 6.16) but, owing to their smaller expenditure on electricity, the CPIs for these groups decline more than those for the urban household groups.

3.   The urban-middle income group in the employed category experiences the biggest decline in real *per capita* consumption, because of the sharper decline in real wages for skilled labour and the bigger increase in their CPIs. This group derives income from both skilled and unskilled labour and spends on electricity more than other groups. For the same reasons, the rural middle-income group, in the employed category, experiences a relatively bigger decline (of 0.99 per cent) in real *per capita* consumption. This decline in consumption, however, is smaller than that of their counter parts, on account of their relatively smaller shares of electricity in their expenditure.

6.7.3   *Effects of removing the tax on electricity sales to the large-scale manufacturing sector-SIM4c*

A 36 per cent decrease in the power of the tax on electricity sales to the manufacturing industries lowers electricity price for them by 29 per cent, and increases this price for all other user groups by 6.7 per cent. On the demand side, the net effect is increase of 1.7 per cent in electricity consumption.

The reduction in the tax on electricity sales causes a decline of 2.4 per cent in indirect tax revenues, and an increase of 0.18 per cent in real private consumption. The rise in the domestic absorption increases the CPI and GDP deflator by 0.9 per cent, and it deteriorates the balance of trade by Rs. 0.4 billion.

The industry-level results show increases in the production of most of the industries, including some of the export industries. In this short-run closure, there are 13 industries for which exports are determined endogenously. For seven of the thirteen industries, the increase in the production costs is curtailed by the decline in the price of electricity for the large-scale manufacturing industries. As a result, the export component in their sales does not decline. The output of the remaining six export industries falls. Four industries experience an increase in their production costs, despite the reduction in the price of electricity, as expenditure on electricity is a small part of their production costs. The other two export industries (with endogenously determined exports) face higher electricity prices (as they are in the small-scale manufacturing and service sectors). This increase, coupled with the increase in other production costs, results in a decline in output.

The contraction in the rice industry causes a decline in agriculture sector output. The increase in the demand from the large-scale rice husking industry is outweighed by the decline in the demand from the corresponding small-scale industry. Owing to the increase in domestic absorption and expansion in some export industries, the output of the large-scale manufacturing sector increases. Apart from the two export industries in the small-scale manufacturing and service sectors, output of all industries increases in these sectors. The reduction in output from the two export industries causes a decline in the aggregate output of these sectors.

Table 6.15 shows that the real wages for all four types of labour increase as the output of most of the traded and non-traded goods industries increases. Since most of the service industries have a high intensity of skilled labour, increases in real wage for them are bigger than those for unskilled labour in the two regions.

The effects on real *per capita* consumption are summarised below.

1. Among the 14 types of household, only the two rural high-income groups experience a decline in real consumption (see column 3 in table 6.16). These groups do not enjoy an increase in income, owing to the small proportion of wages in their income, but they experience rise in CPI because of the big share of electricity in their expenditures compared to other groups.

2. The middle-income employed group, in urban region, enjoys the biggest increase in real *per capita* consumption (0.89 per cent), owing to the biggest increase in the real wages for skilled labour. The rural counterpart of this group enjoys the second biggest increase in real per capita consumption. The difference in the benefits across the two regions is explained by the relatively smaller increase in the real wages of rural-unskilled labour.

3. The rural low-income groups in the two employment categories experience a bigger increase in real *per capita* consumption than do their urban counterparts, despite smaller increases in wages for rural-unskilled labour. This difference is mainly due to the lower share of electricity in the rural household budget, and the resulting smaller increase in their consumer price indices.

6.7.4 *Effects of removing the tax on electricity sales to the small-scale manufacturing sector-SIM4d*

A 25 per cent reduction in the power of the tax on electricity sales to the small-scale manufacturing industries reduces electricity price for them by 21.9 per cent, and increases it by 3.1 per cent for all other users. Real private consumption increases by 0.15 per cent and there is a very small increase in real GDP as the production pattern of industries changes (see column 4 in table 6.15).

A comparison of SIM4c and SIM4d shows that the deterioration in the balance of trade is bigger the small-scale in electricity price. This is explained mainly by the difference in the effect of the tax reforms on exports industries.

As discussed in subsection 6.7.3, seven export industries enjoy expansions with the reduction of the tax on electricity sales to the large-scale industries. On the other hand, only one of the export industry enjoys reduced production costs when the tax on electricity sales to the small-scale manufacturing industries declines. Further, the increase in the price of electricity for other users (including the large-scale manufacturing sector) causes contractions in many exports industries.

The declines in exports and increases in imports are apparent from sectoral out put consumption shown in column 4. With the exception of the large-scale manufacturing sector and the refinery industry, the outputs of all sectors increase. The former sector comprises the major export and import-competing industries. In the refinery industry, the decline in output is caused mainly by the reduction in the demand for FO and other petroleum products. The major users of FO are electricity industries and some small-scale manufacturing industries. As electricity becomes cheaper for the latter, they substitute it for FO. Thus, this decline in the demand for FO outweighs the increase in its demand from electricity industries. The reduction in the demand for other petroleum products is due to the contraction in the air-transport industry; another export industry with endogenously determined exports. The competitiveness of this industry declines on account of the rise in domestic prices and labour wages.

A summary of the effects on real *per capita* consumption (column 4 of table 6.16) is given below.

1. Real per capita consumption increases for all except the two rural high-income and one urban high-income groups. In most cases, the increases are bigger for rural household that that for urban households.
2. The urban middle-income group, in the employed category, enjoys the biggest increase in real per capita consumption: 0.42 per cent. Its rural counterpart enjoys the second-biggest increase (0.39 per cent).
3. The two rural low-income groups also enjoy a 0.36 per cent increase in real per capita consumption.

As discussed in the previous sections, these differences in the effects on real *per capita* consumption are caused mainly by the differences in households incomes, the expenditure shares of electricity for them, and changes in the number of households in each group. As shown in column 4 of table 6.15, real wages of all four types of labour increase in SIM4d. Increases in the wages are bigger for rural labour than that for urban labour. This difference is bigger in the case of unskilled labour. All these differences are explained mainly by the employment pattern of the four labour categories in industries and the changes in the output of these industries.

Our detailed results show that there is a smaller increase in the CPIs for most of the rural household groups, owing to the smaller shares of electricity in their expenditures; they enjoy bigger increases in real income, and thus in real consumption. The bigger real wages in rural areas induce migration of households to the region. Thus, the benefit of bigger increase in real consumption of the rural groups is reduced on *per capita* basis as the number of households in rural region increases. Real *per capita* consumption for the two rural-high-income declines for two reasons. First, electricity shares in their budgets are bigger than that for other rural groups. these households spend more on electricity compared to the other rural groups. Second, these households are not benefited by the increase in the wages, as labour wages are but a small component of their income.

202

A 29 per cent decline in the power of the tax on electricity sales to the service industries reduces electricity price for these industries by 28.6 per cent, and increases it by 0.40 per cent for all other users.

Because of the smaller share of the service industries in total electricity consumption, the effects of reducing electricity price to these industries are smaller than the effects of reducing the tax on electricity sales to the manufacturing industries. A reduction in the price of electricity for this sector affects the non-traded goods industries, and only on traded good industry is benefited. All the other traded goods industries lose their competitiveness, owing to the increase in the production costs. As sectoral-output results show, there is a decline in the production of all except the small-scale manufacturing and service sectors which produce non-traded goods.

Most of the non-traded goods industries have a much bigger labour intensity than do the manufacturing industries. In the service industries, labour intensity of skilled-labour is relatively higher than that of unskilled labour. Consequently, expansion in the services industries increases wage for skilled labour more than those for unskilled labour.

In SIM4e the removal of the tax on electricity sales reduces the aggregate demand for electricity; unlike SIM4c and SIM4d, in which the aggregate electricity demand increases when we remove taxes on electricity sales to the two manufacturing sectors. We notice that, in SIM4e, the output of only the small-scale and services sectors increases. The demand for electricity from the small-scale manufacturing industries falls, despite the expansion in their output, owing to the changeover to other fuels as electricity price rises. Therefore, there is an increase in electricity demand from only the services industries, and this is outweighed by the decline in its demand from all other users.

The last column in table 6.16 shows the effect on real *per capita* consumption in SIM4e. There is an increase in the consumption for all groups, with the exception of one rural high-income group. There are two noticeable features of these results. First, the increase in real *per capita* consumption for the two middle-income employed groups (rural and urban) is much bigger than that for the other 11 groups. This is caused by the bigger increase in real wages of skilled labour, which belongs to this group only. All the other household groups own only unskilled labour. Second, there are not big differences between the regions in the increases in real consumption of the low-income groups. This is explained by the small difference in real wages for unskilled labour in the two regions.

*6.7.6 Cumulative effects of removing user-discriminating taxes on electricity sales
- SIM4*

The cumulative effects of removing all the user-discriminating taxes on electricity sales is a 0.55 per cent increase in total indirect tax revenues (fig. 6.3). The loss in indirect tax revenues through the removal of taxes on electricity sales to the manufacturing and services industries is less than the revenues generated by removing the subsidies on electricity sales to households and the agriculture sector (see table 6.15).

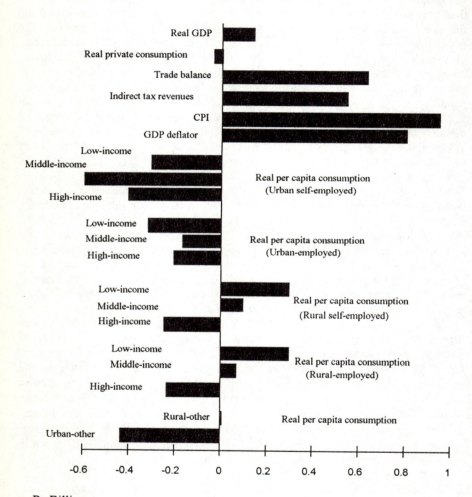

a   Rs Billion

Figure 6.3   Cumulative effects of tax reforms in electricity prices (SIM4)

Removal of the discrimination in taxes against the manufacturing sectors improves the competitiveness of seven of the major export industries, which are relatively more electricity intensive, and all import-competing industries. On the other hand, removal of subsidies on electricity sales to households reduces their real consumption and contracts the non-traded goods industries which are highly labour intensive. The re-allocation in electricity consumption across sectors relocates labour from the non-trade goods industries to the traded goods industries with a small increase in real wages since the latter type of industries is not labour-intensive. Because the tax rates on the traded goods are higher than those on non-traded goods, real GDP increases and the balance of trade improves by Rs 0.64 billion.

Real GDP from the expenditure side is the weighted average of final consumption and the balance of trade deflated by the GDP deflator. The latter is the weighted average of price indices for final consumers, exporters and importers. In this simulation the CPI for final consumption increases but the export price index declines owing to the reduction in electricity prices for the traded good industries. As a result, there is a smaller increase in the GDP deflator relative to CPI for final consumers. The net effect is an increase in real GDP.

We deflate the nominal wages by the overall CPI to derive real wages for producers. The increase in real wage of urban-skilled labour is bigger than that for rural skilled wages, owing to the fact that the output of large-scale manufacturing industries expands more than that of the agriculture sector. The former industries employ only urban labour, and 88 per cent of these labours are unskilled. On the other hand, the agriculture sector employs mainly rural labour, about 95 per cent of which is unskilled. The rural-skilled labour is employed mainly in the services and energy sectors. Their share in the electricity sector's employment is double of the share of urban-skilled labour. Contraction in the electricity sector caused a decline in real wage of rural skilled labour. The contraction reduces the demand for urban-skilled labour as well, but this is compensated for by the increase in the demand from the large-scale manufacturing sector.

Aggregate household real private consumption declines by 0.04 per cent as all seven urban income groups experience a decline in real *per capita* consumption. The biggest decline (0.60 per cent) is for the urban middle-income group in the self-employed category. The two urban low-income groups experience a relatively smaller decline (0.30 per cent) in real *per capita* consumption while their rural counterparts enjoy the biggest increase (about 0.30 per cent). All the rural groups enjoy an increase in real per capita consumption, with the exception of the high-income group. Conversely, these results show that the distortions in electricity prices favour all the urban groups at the expense of the low- and middle-income groups of the rural region.

The differences in real *per capita* consumption for households by income and region are caused mainly by the differences in the consumption patterns of these households. The share of electricity in the total expenditure for the urban households is bigger than that of rural households, in all categories. For example, electricity accounts for 1.5 per cent of the expenditure of the urban low-income group, compared to 0.2 per cent for the rural low-income group. In the rural region, the share of electricity increases with income and the highest income group got the biggest electricity share in its expenditure. Thus, increases in the consumer price indices for most of the rural groups are much smaller than those for the urban groups when the price of electricity rises. In urban households, on the other hand, the middle-income group has the biggest share of electricity in its expenditure (1.6 per cent) and the highest income group has the smallest (1.3 per cent).

The biggest decline is in the consumption by the urban middle-income group in the self-employed category, owing to nominal wages of urban-unskilled labour and the big share of electricity in their consumption.

6.8   Effects of revenue-neutral reforms on user-discriminating taxes on electricity-SIM4N

Column 1 in table 6.17 shows that total indirect tax revenue increases by 0.55 per cent when user-discriminating taxes on electricity are abolished. A decrease of 0.05 per cent in the powers of indirect taxes on all commodities balances out this surplus. The cumulative effect of these taxes is an increase of 0.02 per cent in real private consumption. As a result, improvement in the balance of trade comes down to Rs 0.42 billion from Rs 0.64 billions in SIM4. Similarly, there is a bigger increase in the CPI (1.14 per cent) and the GDP deflator relative to those in SIM4.

Column 2 in table 6.17 shows that, outputs of all non-energy sectors rise, while that of the energy sectors (electricity, natural gas, and oil and gas industries) decline. The industry-level results show that most of the export industries in the large-scale manufacturing sector experience a bigger increase in their outputs than do all other industries. The price of electricity for the large-scale manufacturing industries declines by 36 per cent as the net effect of all the tax reforms. These industries, such as the cotton-fabrics industry, are relatively more electricity intensive. Similarly, some of the electricity intensive import-competing industries (such as the other chemical and fertiliser industries) also enjoy a reduction in their production costs.

There is an increase in the output of the non-traded goods industries, mainly due to the increase in real private consumption. In the agriculture sector, most industries experience increase in the demand for their products from the domestic and export markets. However, some of the import-competing industries in this sector (such as oil seed and pulses industries) become less competitive and reduce their output as electricity price for the agriculture sector increases along with an increase in labour wages. The demands for electricity by the manufacturing and service industries increase, but are out-balanced by the reduction in the demand from households. The electricity sector has the biggest share (18 per cent) in the total demand for natural gas. The decline in electricity production reduces the demand for natural gas. As a

206

result, we observe a decline in the output from the natural gas and oil and gas industries.

The patterns of changes in real wages for all labour categories are similar in SIM4 and SIM4N. The expansion in domestic absorption increases the real wages, for all four types of labour, in SIM4N more than that in SIM4. As a result, there is a smaller decline in the real wages of rural skilled labour and an increase in real wages for rural unskilled labour.

Table 6.17
Cumulative effects of revenue-neutral reforms in user-discriminating taxes on electricity (percentage change)

Cumulative effects in:	(1) SIM4	(2) SIM4N	(3) = (2) - (1)
Real GDP	0.14	0.15	0.01
Real private consumption	0.04	0.12	0.06
Trade balance[a]	0.64	0.42	-0.22
Indirect tax revenue	0.55	0.00	-0.55
Uniform tax rate	0.00	-0.05	-0.05
CPI	0.95	1.14	0.19
GDP deflator	0.81	1.02	0.30
Real Wages			
Rural-skilled	-0.19	-0.14	0.05
Urban-skilled	0.70	0.90	0.20
Rural-unskilled	-0.04	0.04	0.08
Urban-unskilled	0.53	0.63	0.10
Sectoral Output			
Agriculture	0.17	0.17	0.00
Oil and gas	-0.17	-0.17	0.00
Large-scale manufacturing	0.66	0.63	-0.03
Small-scale manufacturing	0.21	0.23	0.02
Services	0.14	0.15	0.01
Fertiliser	1.60	1.59	-0.01
Refinery	0.02	0.02	0.00
Cement	0.00	0.00	0.00
Natural gas	-0.43	-0.43	0.00
Electricity	-0.24	-0.27	0.03

a Rs Billion

Table 6.18
Cumulative effects on real *per capita* consumption in SIM4 and SIM4N
(percentage change)

Household type	(1) SIM4	(2) SIM4N	(3) = (2) - (1)
Self-employed			
Rural-low-income	0.30	0.38	0.08
Urban-low-income	-0.31	-0.26	0.05
Rural-middle-income	0.10	0.15	0.05
Urban-middle-income	-0.60	-0.53	0.07
Rural-high-income	-0.25	-0.25	0.00
Urban-high-income	-0.41	-0.34	0.07
Employed			
Rural-low-income	0.30	0.38	0.08
Urban-low-income	-0.32	-0.26	0.06
Rural-middle-income	0.07	0.17	0.10
Urban-middle-income	-0.17	-0.01	0.16
Rural-high-income	-0.24	-0.25	-0.02
Urban-high-income	-0.21	-0.12	0.09
Others			
Rural	0.01	0.05	0.04
Urban	-0.44	-0.37	0.07

Column 3 in table 6.17 shows the effect of a 0.05 per cent uniform reduction in the power of tax on all commodities. This tax reduction increases real private consumption by 0.06 per cent. A negligible increase in real GDP is caused by reallocation of resources from the low tax rate industries to the high tax rate industries as the consumption pattern changes. Removal of the user-discriminating taxes on electricity improves the balance of trade. The additional uniform reduction in the powers of taxes on all commodities reduces this gain by 0.22 percentage point but does not wipe it out completely.

Table 6.18 shows that the pattern of changes in real *per capita* consumption for 14 types of household are similar in SIM4 and SIM4N. The reduction in taxes increases real *per capita* consumption for all groups except the rural high-income group (see column 3). The income groups that experience a decline in real *per capita* consumption in SIM4 now experience a lower decline in SIM4N, and the rest of the groups enjoy, a bigger increase in consumption. The major income sources of the rural high-income groups are wages of unskilled labour and remittances from abroad. The groups experience a smaller increase in income, on account of a smaller rise in rural unskilled wages, but face a bigger increase in CPIs resulting from the expansion in domestic absorption.

6.9 Effects of removing user-discriminating taxes on natural gas sales

Table 6.19 shows the powers of taxes on natural gas for four consumer categories and the hypothetical percentage changes in them. Because on the average, there is no tax on natural gas, the hypothetical changes in the powers of taxes are calculated to abolish the taxes or subsidies on natural gas for all consumer categories. According to table 6.19, the powers of the taxes on natural gas sales should be decreased for three consumer groups and increased for one group. We simulate the effects of these hypothetical changes in SIM5a to SIM5d.

Table 6.19
Values for exogenous powers of user-discriminating taxes on natural gas sales

User category	*Ad valorem* power of tax in the base year	Percentage change in power of tax[a]
Manufacturing	1.12	-11.0
Services	1.62	-38.0
Electricity industries	0.77	29.0
Households	1.09	-8.0

a These shocks are given in SIM5a to SIM5d, SIM5 and SIM5N to the user-discriminating tax variables for natural gas

In the following sub-sections, we discuss separately the effects of removing tax (subsidy) to each consumer category and then go on to a discussion on the cumulative effect of these tax reforms.

6.9.1 Effects of removing user-discriminating tax on natural gas sales to the manufacturing industries-SIM5a

An 11 per cent reduction in the power of the tax on natural gas sales to the manufacturing industries, both small- and large-scale, has no significant effect on real GDP. However, real private consumption increases by 0.02 per cent. There is a negative effect on the balance of trade which declines by Rs 70 million. Similarly, total indirect tax revenue declines by 0.55 per cent (see column 1 of table 6.20).

Among the manufacturing industries, there are three export industries in which natural gas has one to two per cent shares in the total costs. The industry-level results show that the rise in domestic prices causes a decline in the demand for all major export industries except these three. Total exports decline resulting in the trade deficit. Expansion in these three industries increases the output of the large-scale manufacturing sector. The small increase in private consumption increases the output of only the service sector as the competing effects of domestic and foreign demands are cancelled out by the agriculture and small-scale manufacturing sectors.

Table 6.20
Effects of reforms in user-discriminating taxes on natural gas

Power of implicit tax on:	(1) SIM5a Manufacturing industries -11.0	(2) SIM5b Services industries -38.0	(3) SIM5c Electricity industries 30.0	(4) SIM5d Households -8.0
Real GDP	0.00	0.01	-0.00	0.00
Real private consumption	0.03	0.09	-0.07	0.01
Trade balance[a]	-0.07	-0.28	0.18	-0.03
Indirect taxes	-0.55	-0.71	0.39	-0.06
CPI	0.10	0.25	-0.25	0.02
GDP deflator	0.09	0.28	-0.29	0.02
Real Wages				
Rural-skilled	0.11	0.26	-0.33	0.03
Urban-skilled	0.13	0.33	-0.28	0.01
Rural-unskilled	-0.01	0.09	-0.11	0.02
Urban-unskilled	0.03	0.14	-0.05	-0.00
Sectoral Output				
Agriculture	0.00	-0.02	0.01	-0.00
Oil and gas	0.24	-0.01	-0.16	0.01
Large-scale manufacturing	0.02	-0.04	0.04	-0.01
Small-scale manufacturing	0.00	0.03	-0.02	0.00
Services	0.01	0.02	0.00	0.00
Fertiliser	0.39	-0.04	0.24	-0.03
Refinery	0.00	-0.02	0.15	0.00
Cement	0.00	0.00	-0.00	0.00
Natural gas	0.66	-0.01	-0.44	0.03
Electricity	-0.11	-0.04	-0.27	-0.00

a   Rs Billion

An 11 per cent reduction in the power of the tax on natural gas sales to the manufacturing industries reduces its price to them by 5.16 per cent, while the price for all other users increases by 5.84 per cent. In GE-PAK, the production structures of the manufacturing industries allow substitution between natural gas and electricity. The decline in the price of natural gas for the manufacturing industries, along with the increase in the price of electricity due to the higher natural gas price, induces substitution of electricity by natural gas. Hence, at sectoral level, we notice a fall in the output of the electricity industries.

The fertiliser industry, which faces import competition, enjoys the reduction in price of natural gas which has a high share in its total production costs.

6.9.2 Effects of removing user-discriminating tax on natural gas sales to the service industries-SIM5b

Column 2 in table 6.20 reports the results of SIM5b and shows that the sectoral effects are different from those observed in SIM5a. The bigger rise in real private consumption in SIM5b increases the output of the small-scale manufacturing sector. The traded goods industries now face high production costs, due to the increase in the price of their natural gas supplies. As a result, the large-scale manufacturing sector and the fertiliser industry contract in SIM5b.

Unlike SIM5a, there is a small reduction in the output of the natural gas industry, caused by the contraction in the demands from the major consumers such as the large-scale manufacturing industries (-0.05 per cent) and the fertiliser industry (-0.06 per cent).

All labour categories enjoy a bigger increase in real wages compared to SIM5a, due to a bigger increase in private consumption. The wages for rural unskilled labour also increase, as there is a smaller contraction in the electricity industries.

6.9.3 Effects of removing user-discriminating subsidy on natural gas sales to the electricity industries-SIM5c

The removal of the user-discriminating subsidy on natural gas sales to the electricity industries reduces real private consumption by 0.06 per cent. This improves the balance of trade by Rs 180 million, and increases total indirect tax revenues by 0.39 per cent. The CPI goes down by 0.25 per cent and the GDP deflator declines by 0.29 per cent.

The reduction in domestic absorption lowers domestic prices, while there is an expansion in the output of the export and import-competing industries. Among the energy industries, only the refinery industry shows an expansion in its output. The electricity industries experience a 0.27 per decline and the biggest reduction is in the output of the natural gas industry (-0.44). The fertiliser industry enjoys the reduction in the price of natural gas for users other than the electricity sector, and this also benefits the agriculture sector.

6.9.4 Effects of removing user-discriminating tax on natural gas sales to households-SIM5d

The last column in table 6.20 shows that removal of user-discriminating tax on natural gas sales to households has very small effects on the economy. The small increase in the price of natural gas for all production sectors and the small increase in real private consumption do not change the production structure much. There is also a small increase in energy consumption as outputs from the natural gas and oil and gas industries rise. Relative to all other effects, there is a bigger decline in the indirect tax revenues.

211

6.9.5 Cumulative effect of removing user-discriminating taxes on natural gas sales -SIM5

Fig. 6.4 shows the cumulative effects of removing all user-discriminating taxes on natural gas sales. Real GDP increases by 0.01 per cent, and real private consumption rises by 0.06 per cent. A loss of 0.94 per cent in total indirect tax revenue, and of Rs 190 million in the balance of trade, occurs as a result of removing all user-discriminating taxes and the subsidies on natural gas sales. There are increases in domestic prices; CPI increases by 0.12 per cent, and the GDP deflator rises by 0.10 per cent. Except the rural high-income group, all income groups in the employed category enjoy a rise in *per capita* consumption.

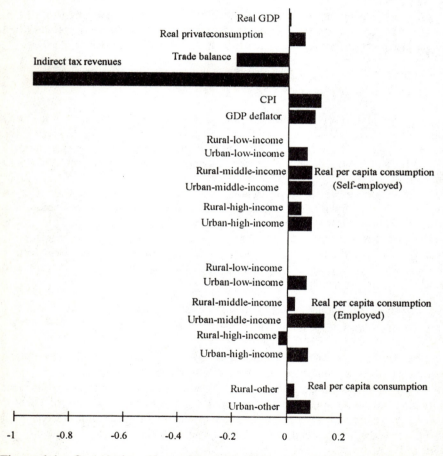

Figure 6.4   **Cumulative effects of tax reforms in natural gas prices (SIM5)**

There are three noticeable changes in the real *per capita* consumption of 14 types of household:

1. In most of the household groups, the urban groups enjoy a bigger increase in real *per capita* consumption than do their counterparts in the rural region.
2. Among the seven types of urban households, the middle-income groups from the two employment categories enjoy the highest increase in real *per capita* consumption, compared to all other groups.
3. A different pattern of changes in real *per capita* emerges for rural households. The consumption for the two low-income groups remains unchanged, while the two rural middle-income groups enjoy an increase in real *per capita* consumption. Only one high-income group enjoys an increase in real *per capita* consumption while the other group experiences a decline.

These results show that the removal of user-discriminating taxes on natural gas benefits urban households more than the rural households, and benefits households in the middle-income group more than those in the other two income groups, in both the regions. Of the 14 household groups, the three rural groups are net losers.

6.10 Cumulative effects of revenue-neutral reforms in user- discriminating taxes on natural gas -SIM5N

In SIM5N, we repeat all SIM5 simulations in a revenue-neutral environment. Table 6.21 reports the results of SIM5 and SIM5N. The following paragraphs discuss the results of SIM5N.

A uniform 0.08 per cent increase in the power of indirect tax rate on all commodities makes up the loss incurred in total indirect tax revenues caused by the reforms in taxes on natural gas. The net effect of all the tax reforms is a negligible increase in real GDP, and a decline of -0.07 percent in real private consumption. There is a positive effect on the trade balance; it improves by Rs 180 million.

The reduction in real private consumption reduces domestic prices; the CPI declines by 0.22 per cent and the GDP deflator goes down by 0.25 per cent. The pattern of sectoral production also changes. There is an increase in the output of all sectors except the small-scale manufacturing sector (-0.01) and the electricity sector (-0.39). The output of the energy industries, other than electricity, rises. The output of the natural gas industry increases by 0.25 per cent. The changes in production and consumption patterns affect the real wages of all four labour categories. Real wages of all four types of labour decline. The decline in the real wage of urban unskilled labour is smaller (-0.05) than the decline in the real wages of the other three categories (between 0.15 and 0.23 per cent). This difference is caused mainly by a big increase in the demand for urban unskilled labour from the large-scale manufacturing industries. (mainly refinery and fertiliser). These industries have a high proportion of urban-unskilled labour in their total labour demand.

Table 6.21
Cumulative effects of revenue-neutral reforms in user-discriminating taxes on natural gas

	(1) SIM5	(2) SIM5N	(3) = (2) - (1)
Real GDP	0.01	0.00	-0.01
Real private consumption	0.06	-0.07	-0.13
Trade balance[a]	-0.19	0.18	0.37
Indirect taxes	-0.94	0.0	
Uniform indirect tax rate	-	0.08	
CPI	0.12	-0.22	-0.34
GDP deflator	0.10	-0.25	-0.35
Real Wages			
Rural-skilled	0.07	-0.23	-0.30
Urban-skilled	0.19	-0.15	-0.34
Rural-unskilled	-0.01	-0.16	-0.15
Urban-unskilled	0.12	-0.05	-0.17
Sectoral Output			
Agriculture	-0.01	-0.00	0.01
Oil and gas	0.08	0.09	0.01
Large-scale manufacturing	0.01	0.07	0.06
Small-scale manufacturing	0.02	-0.01	-0.03
Services	0.03	0.01	-0.02
Fertiliser	0.56	0.58	0.02
Refinery	0.15	0.14	-0.01
Cement	0.00	0.00	0.0
Natural gas	0.24	0.25	0.01
Electricity	-0.43	-0.39	0.04

a   Rs Billion

Table 6.22 shows the effects on household real *per capita* consumption by income, region and employment categories in SIM5 and SIM5N. The results of SIM5N are summarised below:

1.   Contrary to SIM5, real *per capita* consumption for all 14 types of household decline, except for one rural high income group. The biggest decline is in the consumption for the rural middle-income group, in the employed category. Real consumption of this group declines by 0.15 per cent.

214

2. The two rural low-income groups experience the second biggest decline in real *per capita* consumption, *i.e* -0.14 per cent. This decline is much higher than the decline in real consumption for the two urban low-income groups (0.03 per cent).
3. In the rural self-employed category, the high-income group enjoys a 0.05 per cent increase in real *per capita* consumption.

Table 6.22

Cumulative effects on household real *per capita* consumption in SIM5 and SIM5N (percentage change)

Household Type	(1) SIM5	(2) SIM5N	(3) = (2) - (1)
Self-employed			
Rural-low-income	-0.00	-0.14	-0.12
Urban-low-income	0.07	-0.03	-0.12
Rural-middle-income	0.09	-0.01	-0.09
Urban-middle-income	0.09	-0.03	-0.15
Rural-high-income	0.05	0.05	0.02
Urban-high-income	0.09	-0.03	-0.14
Employed			
Rural-low-income	-0.00	-0.14	-0.12
Urban-low-income	0.07	-0.03	-0.12
Rural-middle-income	0.03	-0.15	-0.16
Urban-middle-income	0.14	-0.09	-0.25
Rural-high-income	-0.03	-0.01	0.04
Urban-high-income	0.08	-0.06	-0.16
Others			
Rural	0.03	-0.04	-0.05
Urban	0.09	-0.04	-0.15

In brief, the removal of user-discriminating taxes on sales of natural gas inflicts big adverse effects on most of the rural low income groups. As shown in table 6.22, the negative effects of removing these taxes on rural households vary between -0.15 and -0.01 per cent. These variations in negative impacts on household consumption show two things. First, the user-discriminating taxes favour rural households over the urban households. Second, these tax discriminations have income distributional effects only among rural households, as they favour the low-income groups. Contrary to this, among urban household groups, these taxes favour the middle- and

215

high-income groups more than the low-income groups in the employed category, while they favour all the income groups in the self-employed category.

6.11   Elasticity of social welfare cost with respect to indirect tax revenues -SIM6

In most developing countries, the governments rely on indirect taxes to raise public funds. In the sixth experiment, we compute the social cost of raising public fund by increasing the tax rates on energy products. For the computation of welfare cost, we simulate a 1 per cent increase in the indirect tax revenues through an increase in the powers of taxes on eight petroleum products in SIM6a to SIM6h. We form two scenarios of equity concern. In scenario 1 (referred to as Case A), we use a utilitarian welfare function and, the Atkinson welfare function of Mean of order 1 is used in scenario 2 (referred to as Case B). The two social welfare functions differ in their degrees of inequality aversion. Hence, the purpose of analysing these two scenarios is to show that the social welfare effects of imposing a tax on a commodity without (case A) and with due consideration of the income distributional impacts (case B) will be different. Subsection 6.11.1 describes the elasticity of social welfare with respect to indirect tax revenues and the social welfare function used to compute these elasticities. The results of cases A and B are discussed in subsections 6.11.2 and 6.11.3, respectively.

Before proceeding to our results, it is worthwhile to summarise the environment in which the welfare cost elasticities are computed.

1.   In our model government income is composed of indirect tax revenues, direct tax revenues and returns to capital and land owned by the government. There is a change in the government income from all sources when the tax rate on a commodity is increased. However, we only consider indirect tax revenue because it has the biggest share in the government income.

2.   The government expenditure includes purchase of commodities and some transfers to households. We assume that the government expenditure on commodities is fixed in real terms. However, its transfer to households changes with changes in its total income, but these payments are not made to compensate the loss in income of households due to the increase in indirect taxes.

3.   The changes in government income or private savings do not effect the investment expenditure which is assumed to be constant in real terms.

Thus, in this experiment we increase distorted indirect tax on each commodity to reduce the existing trade deficit.

216

6.11.1. Computation of social welfare elasticities and alternative social welfare functions

We define the elasticity of social welfare with respect to the real value of public funds as:

$$SWE = - \frac{\%\text{change in social welfare}}{\%\text{change in real indirect tax revenue}}.$$

Social welfare is measured by the function proposed by Atkinson (1970) which is defined as:

$$W\,(PERCONR_1, \ldots\ldots\ldots, PERCONR_{POP}) = (\frac{1}{POP_i}\sum_{=1}^{POP} PERCONR_i^{\tau})^{\frac{1}{\tau}},$$

$$\tau \le 1 \text{ and } \tau \ne 0, \qquad\qquad (6.11.1.1)$$

where $PERCONR_i$ is real consumption of individual i, POP is total population, and τ is the 'inequality aversion' parameter. Table 6.23 reports various types of welfare functions which can be defined using eq. (6.11.2.1).

Table 6.23
Welfare functions

Atkinson inequality parameter (t)	Welfare function type	Implication
1	Utilitarian	A dollar increase in real consumption has equal weight for all persons.
$\rightarrow 0$	Relativist	1 % increase in real consumption for a rich person is equal to 1 % increase for a poor person.
-1	Mean of order 1	A one per cent increase in real consumption for a low-income person has a higher weight than a one per cent increase in consumption for a high-income person.
$\rightarrow (-\infty)$	Rawlsian	When changes in real consumption of only the low-income group is counted.

In these various functional forms as τ decreases and becomes negative, more importance is given to the welfare of the poor and less to the welfare of the rich. When τ tends towards minus infinity, the function tends toward the Rawlsian welfare function (Rawls, 1971), which takes into account welfare of the low income groups only. When $\tau = -1$, the value of the weight given to a household group depends on the income disparities in the base year. The bigger is the real *per capita* consumption of a household group relative to that of the low-income group, the smaller is the weight given to the effects on its welfare when computing the welfare of the society. The value of the 'inequality aversion' parameter depends either on judgement or can be inferred from government policies such as the personal income tax structure [1].

We illustrate the implication of computing social welfare using the alternative functional forms through an example. Table 6.24 shows two states of income distribution in a society comprising of two persons. D1 refers to an initial state, while D2 refers to the state after a redistribution of the total income.

Table 6.24
A hypothetical income distribution

	Expenditure in Rs. in state	
Person	D1	D2
I	10	11
II	20	19

In the initial state, person I is half of the expenditure of person II. In the state D2, a rupee is taken from the rich person and is given to the poor. First row in table 6.25 shows that welfare index of the society does not change in the state D2 when we assume a utilitarian function. However if the society is assumed to be sensitive to the distribution of income, and we assume a welfare function of 'Mean of order -1', then the welfare index increases with the redistribution of income (see eq. 6.11.2.1 for computation of the index).

Table 6.25
Welfare measures according to two welfare functions

	Welfare index in state	
Welfare functions	D1	· D2
Utilitarian	15.0	15.0
Mean of order -1	13.3	14.3

In our model there are 14 types of household which are categorised by region and income group. Thus, the welfare function corresponding to equation (6.11.1.1) becomes:

$$W^\tau = \sum_{r \in REGn} \sum_{\in INC} \frac{POP_{rn}}{POP} PERCONR_{rn}^\tau \qquad \text{if } \tau \leq 1 \text{ and } \tau \neq 0, \quad (6.11.1.2)$$

where $PERCONR_{rn}$ is real *per capita* consumption in group n in the region r. POP_{rn} is the population of that group, and POP is total population. The two sets REG and INC contain number of regions and income groups, respectively (see Appendix F for deriving W in the percentage change form).

As mentioned all variables in GE-PAK are in percentage changes. We can compute the elasticity of social welfare cost with respect to indirect tax revenue by defining:

$$SWE_{i\tau} = \frac{w}{torev - xigdp}, \qquad (6.11.1.3)$$

where w is percentage change in social welfare and in the denominator is percentage change in real indirect tax revenues; torev and xigdp are the percentage changes in nominal indirect tax revenue and the GDP deflator, respectively.

6.11.2 Ranking of energy products according to their social welfare cost elasticities (SWC) -Case A

Case A assumes that there is no inequality aversion, *i.e.*, a dollar decrease in real *per capita* consumption, at the margin, has equal weight for all persons irrespective of their consumption level in the base year. Column 2, in table 6.26, reports the SWE values in Case A with respect to one per cent increase in real indirect tax revenues by increasing the tax rates on eight energy products. The ranking of energy products according to the SWE value is given in column 3. Among the eight energy products, the product with the biggest SWE value is given the rank of 8. The energy product with the lowest SWE value is ranked 1. The higher is the rank of a product, the biggest is the welfare cost to the society of increasing tax rate on that product. In our analysis in this section, we focus on two aspects:

1.   What energy products have low elasticities of welfare with respect to public funds?
2.   What are the mechanisms that produce these results?

In table 6.26, the positive value of SWE for kerosene shows gain to the society, on aggregate, for increasing the revenue by increasing the tax on kerosene. Among the remaining seven products, increasing the tax on natural gas has the lowest social welfare cost, while this cost is relatively bigger for electricity and gasoline.

In these simulations, the increase in the tax on a commodity changes the structure of domestic production and imports. The tax rates on commodities in the base year are not uniform. Real GDP can rise, despite of fixed factor supplies, if a tax-shock changes the production/import structure towards the high-tax commodities at the expense of reductions in the supplies of the low-tax commodities. For example, if a unit of imports in the domestic market costs Rs.10, including Rs.2 for the tariff, then it costs the society Rs.8 worth of resources. For an additional unit of imports, the society has to produce additional exports worth of Rs. 8. The society can reallocate resources to exports industries from some other activity, where they were initially producing output worth of Rs. 8. This will leave an extra Rs.2 worth of absorption with no deterioration in the balance of trade[2].

Contrary to this, if the commodity supply structure changes away from the high-tax commodities towards the low-tax commodities, real GDP will decline. In Pakistan, the major sources of indirect tax revenues are crude oil, petroleum products and refined/natural gas. There are high sales taxes and tariff on these commodities except for some of the petroleum products which enjoy subsidies. There are wide differences in the tax rates on these commodities. For example, the tax rate on LDO is 16 percent compared to 35 percent on HSD. Thus in our simulations, the effect on real GDP of an increase in the tax rate on an energy product depends on the changes in the pattern of commodity supplies in general and of energy products in particular. GE-PAK allows substitution among different energy products used as intermediate inputs to production. Therefore, substitution possibilities also affect the production and import pattern of energy products.

Table 6.26
Ranking of energy products according to social welfare
elasticities (SWE)-Case A

Increase in the power of tax on	(1) Percentage change in Real GDP	(2) SWE	(3) Rank
Light speed diesel	-0.00918	-0.010549	8
High speed diesel	-0.00892	-0.009521	7
Gasoline	-0.00643	-0.007362	6
Electricity	-0.00130	-0.002046	5
Other petroleum products	-0.00204	-0.001712	4
Furnace oil	-0.00163	-0.001473	3
Natural gas	-0.00022	-0.000274	2
Kerosene	0.00477	0.006296	1

220

In SIM6a, we increase real indirect tax revenues by increasing the sales tax on kerosene. Kerosene is mainly used by the households, and a big share of its supply is imported. Our results show that the kerosene-tax shock contracts the refinery industry's activity level. The refinery industry is a multiple output industry, with constant elasticities of transformation between its six products. It is an import-competing industry as significant shares of all petroleum product supplies, except LDO, are imported. Since we have assigned small values to the elasticities of transformation, an increase in the tax on one product of the industry decreases its activity level. In SIM6a, domestic production of all petroleum products decline with a relatively bigger decline in kerosene production. On the import side, there are two effects: (i) imports of all petroleum products increase while import of kerosene declines, (ii) the contraction of the refinery industry reduces import as well as domestic production of crude oil. The oil and gas industry is also a multiple-output industry with the low transformation elasticities between crude oil and natural gas. Because the demand for crude oil declines, the industry increases production of natural gas. In the base year, the tax rate on kerosene is much smaller than that on other petroleum products, and there is an import subsidy on it compared to the high tariff rates on other imported petroleum products such as gasoline and HSD. In SIM6a, the real GDP increases due to (i) a decline in the production of and import of kerosene (ii) an increase in the import of gasoline which has a relatively higher tariff rate compared to the sales tax, and (iii) an increase in the natural gas production which has a relatively higher tax compared to crude oil. The detailed results show that production of some of the high-tax consumption goods such as beverages and cigarettes also increases which shows the second round effects of the increase in real GDP and the consequent effects on real private consumption.

In this short-term closure, the average propensity to consume increases to absorb the increase in real GDP because the balance of trade, real investment and government consumption are fixed. Column 1 in table 6.26 reports real GDP elasticities with respect to real indirect tax revenues for the eight simulations. Real private consumption constitutes 83 per cent of real GDP. Therefore, an increase in real GDP is translated into a bigger increase in real private consumption.

For the kerosene-tax shock, real GDP increases by 0.00477 per cent, therefore we expect real private consumption to increase by 0.00575 per cent. However, we observe an increase of 0.00630 in real private consumption (see in column 2). The additional increase is caused by an improvement in the terms of trade. The export demand curves for 13 major export commodities are assumed downwardly sloping. Since the nominal exchange rate is fixed, domestic and foreign prices of export commodities move together. A decline in the export of a commodity implies an increase in its foreign price and vice versa. In all simulations the foreign prices of all imports are assumed fixed. The increase in real GDP and private consumption drives up the domestic prices. This makes the traded goods industries less competitive leading to an increase in imports. But, the increase in imports of other commodities is outweighed by the decline in the imports of crude oil and kerosene. The total import bill declines. To keep the balance of trade fixed, the export bill also declines causing a decline in export quantities. Resources from these export industries are reallocated to other industries to supply goods for private consumption.

Table 6.26 shows that for the rest of the seven energy products (SIM6b to SIM6H), the increase in the tax rates reduces real GDP. The mechanism discussed above is reversed in these simulations. Most of these products, except gasoline, are used as intermediate inputs. Variations in the effects on real GDP can be explained by the compositional effects on commodity supplies which are related to each energy product's consumption and substitution pattern. For example, LDO is mainly used by the agriculture sector and is not imported. However, it can be substituted with electricity. The increase in the tax on LDO (i) reduces domestic production of all petroleum products except FO, (ii) increases imports of all petroleum products with a relatively bigger increase in furnace oil imports, and (iii) decreases domestic crude oil production while natural gas production rises. In the model, there are four electricity industries. The input 'Fuel' in the steam electricity and combined cycle industries is a CES composite of FO and natural gas. Substitution of LDO with electricity increases the demand for FO, which not only has a smaller tax rate relative to LDO but also enjoys an import subsidy. Further, contrary to the kerosene-tax shock, imports of kerosene also increase in this simulation. Thus indirectly the LDO-tax shock increases the consumption of energy products that have lower taxes and import subsidies. The net effect is a decline in real GDP and real private consumption.

One might expect that the increase in the taxes on gasoline and HSD would cause a bigger decline in real GDP since these products have the high tax rates. In the following paragraphs we discuss the differences in the effects generated by the tax shocks to HSD and gasoline compared to the LDO-tax shock.

The major user of HSD is the road transport industry, a significant share of it is used in the agriculture sector and the combined cycle electricity industry. Only in the Road transport industry, HSD is substitutable; gasoline is a substitute for motor fuel. For electricity generation, HSD is used in the Combined cycle electricity industry with a fixed input coefficient. In the agriculture sector, HSD is substitutable by capital which is assumed to be fixed. An increase in the tax rate on HSD induces consumption of gasoline which is a high-tax commodity. Thus, the production and import patterns in the HSD-tax simulation show an increase in domestic production and the import of gasoline. Contrary to the LDO-tax shock, the production and import of FO declines when the tax on HSD is increased.

Gasoline is mainly used for private transportation and a significant share of its supply is used in public transportation. Increase in gasoline prices induces substitution towards HSD, resulting in an increase in domestic production and the import of HSD. Unlike the LDO-tax shock, the increase in gasoline price falls mainly on the household sector and increases domestic prices. This makes import-competing industries less competitive and induces an expansion in imports; most of which have high tariff rates. Thus the decline in real GDP due to lower production and import of gasoline is cushioned by the increase in the imports of HSD and other commodities that have high import taxes. Therefore, we observe a smaller decline in real GDP for the gasoline-tax shock as compared to that for the LDO-tax shock.

Among all the energy products, the gas-tax shock generates the smallest decline in real GDP and private consumption. Natural gas is mainly used by the manufacturing and electricity sectors. In the manufacturing sector, it is substitutable with FO and electricity. An increase in gas price induces substitution towards FO directly and indirectly through electricity usage. Consequently, the refinery industry expands. There is an increase in the production of crude oil and a decline in natural gas production. Like the LDO-tax shock, increase in the price of raw natural gas increases production and the imports of FO. However, unlike the LDO-tax shock, production of the other five petroleum products also increases and their imports decline which is enough to compensate for the loss in real GDP due to the increase in FO production. The small loss in real GDP reported in our result is due to the decline in the imports of some high-import-tax commodities such as oil seed and other crops. Natural gas has a significant share in the cost of some of the import-competing industries such as edible oil, confectionery, rubber footwear, other rubber products. Increase in refined gas price falls on these import-competing industries and their domestic production declines.

6.11.3 Social welfare elasticities incorporating distributional effects - Case B

In case B, we repeat SIM6a to SIM6h, but take a welfare function of mean of order-1instead of the utilitarian. Hence in SWE calculation, a lower weight is given to the effects on consumption of the high- and middle income groups. Our analysis in this subsection focuses on two issues:

1.   Does the ranking of the products, according to SWE, change when distributional effects of taxes are taken into account?
2.   What are the differences in the income and consumption patterns of household groups which generate these results?

In table 6.27, columns 3 and 4 report the SWE values and their ranks in Case B while column 5 gives the change in the rank of a commodity relative to Case A. In case B, the rank a decline in the rank of a commodity shows that it has become a better candidate to increase public funds if social equity is a concern in social welfare effects.

Column 5, in table 6.27, shows that the ranks of all energy products change in Case B, indicating that the effects of a tax-shock are not uniform for all income groups. The biggest increase is in the rank of kerosene which becomes the most undesirable commodity to tax in case B. Contrary to this, the biggest decline in the rank of gasoline shows that it is a better candidate to increase tax revenues. The detailed results of the kerosene-tax shock show that real *per capita* consumption declines for all the four low-income groups, while it increases for all other household groups. Hence, the decline in social welfare in Case B shows worsening of the income inequality.

Table 6.27
Ranking of energy products according to elasticities of social welfare in Case A and Case B

Case A: $\tau = 1$			Case B: $\tau = -1$			
	(1)	(2)		(3)	(4)	(5) = (4) - (2)
Increase in the tax on	SWE	Rank	Increase in the tax on	SWE	Rank	Change in the rank
LDO	-0.01055	8	Kerosene	-0.03050	8	+7
HSD	-0.00952	7	LDO	-0.02410	7	-1
Gasoline	-0.00736	6	Electricity	-0.00083	6	+1
Electricity	-0.00205	5	HSD	-0.00076	5	-2
Other s	-0.00171	4	FO	0.00668	4	+1
FO	-0.00147	3	Gasoline	0.01092	3	-3
Nat. gas	-0.00027	2	Others	0.01646	2	-2
Kerosene	0.00630	1	Nat. gas	0.01671	1	-1

These effects on real *per capita* consumption can be disaggregated into effects on nominal income, nominal consumption, and CPI. Table 6.28 shows these effects for 6 groups of households as a sample. Columns 1 to 3 show that nominal income and the CPI increase for all the groups in SIM6a. In this short-term closure, we assume that the average propensity to consume changes uniformly for all groups to keep the balance of trade fixed. There is an increase of 0.152 per cent in the economy-wide average propensity to consume. Thus, the tax-shock gives in an increase in consumer prices for all groups. However, the increase in consumer prices is bigger for the low-income groups relative to the other groups as kerosene has a bigger share (0.011 and 0.015) in their consumption relative to that for other income groups (.0003 to 0007). Among the middle- and high-income groups, the urban middle-income group also experiences a decline in its real consumption. The share of kerosene in the urban group's consumption is also high (0.010). Thus, the increases in nominal income of the low-income groups and the urban middle-income group are not enough to compensate for the rise in their cost of living.

Table 6.28
Effects on real consumption of households for the
kerosene-tax shock SIM6a

Household type (Self-employed)	(1) Household disposable income	(2) Nominal consumption	(3) CPI	(4) Real consumption
Low Income				
Rural	0.025	0.177	0.224	-0.046
Urban	0.028	0.180	0.304	-0.124
Middle Income				
Rural	0.024	0.176	0.168	0.008
Urban	0.030	0.182	0.225	-0.043
High Income				
Rural	0.008	0.160	0.108	0.052
Urban	0.043	0.196	0.099	0.097

As shown in table 6.27, natural gas becomes the best candidate to raise public fund in Case B. The increase in the tax on natural gas helps to improve the social equity. The detailed results show that the real burden of imposing a tax on natural gas falls on the middle- and high-income groups, and there is a redistribution of income in favour of the low-income groups. As illustrated in the example in section 6.11.1, this redistribution improves the welfare of the society. In the next few paragraphs, we discuss how an increase in the tax on natural gas causes this redistribution.

In table 6.29, columns 1, 2 and 3 report disposable income, nominal consumption and consumer prices for the 6 household groups. Since the model incorporates a regional migration function, the number of households in the regions changes with the changes in the relative wages in the two regions. Column 4 in table 6.29 reports *per capita* consumption for these income groups taking into account the number of households in each group.

Table 6.29 shows that the increase in the tax on natural gas has a negative effect on the nominal income of all the income groups. However, there is a relatively bigger decline in the income of the middle- and high-income groups in the two regions. In particular, the rural middle-income group experiences the biggest decline in its income. The detailed results show that the rental to capital and land

225

decline by 0.147 and 0.436 per cent, respectively, compared to 0.10 per cent decline in labour wages. This causes a bigger decline in the disposable income of the middle- and high-income groups as rentals to capital and land constitute about 37 to 68 percent of the income of groups. Contrary to this, these factors have zero shares in the income of the low income groups, which mainly rely on labour wages.

Our industry level results show that most of the non-traded goods industries contract with the increase in the price of natural gas. The increase first falls on most of the traded goods industries which are gas-intensive and the households. Since the households are main users of the non-traded good industries, the decline in their expenditure reduces demands for the non-traded goods industries. The distribution of labour, land and capital across industries shows that their major shares are employed in the non-traded goods industries. This drives down the rental to all the three factors. These industries are labour intensive, therefore, contraction in their demand reduces labour wages. Since labour is mobile across industries, reduction in labour wages induces substitution towards it in the traded goods industries. There is an expansion in those export and import-competing industries which are less intensive in their use of natural gas and electricity. The price of electricity increases due to its intensive use of natural gas. Thus absorption of labour in the traded goods industries causes a lower decline in their wages.

Table 6.29
Effects on real consumption of households for the gas-tax shock-SIM6h (Case B)

Household Type (Self-employed)	(1) Household disposable income	(2) Nominal consumption	(3) CPI	(4) Real consumption
Low Income				
Rural	-0.072	0.001	-0.023	0.024
Urban	-0.067	0.006	-0.017	0.023
Middle Income				
Rural	-0.099	-0.026	-0.026	-0.001
Urban	-0.087	-0.014	-0.014	-0.0001
High Income				
Rural	-0.079	-0.006	-0.028	0.021
Urban	-0.085	-0.012	-0.017	0.005

According to the results, a 0.073 per cent increase in the average propensity to consume is required to keep the balance of trade fixed when real GDP declines. Table 6.29 shows that this increase in the average propensity to consume increases the nominal consumption for the low-income groups only. The nominal consumption of the middle- and high income groups declines as the decline in their nominal income is bigger than that for the low-income groups.

Column 3, in table 6.29 shows that the consumer price indices decline for all income groups. The small decline in the CPI for the low-income group makes them further better off. The decline in the CPI for the high-income group is big enough to compensate the loss in nominal income, and the real consumption of the two groups increase. The decline in the CPI helps the middle income groups in the two regions but the net effect is a small decline in their real consumption.

We have contained our discussion on the elasticities of social welfare cost of public funds to energy products. A similar analysis can be done for all other commodities. However, there is one limitation of this ranking procedure if investment goods are also included in the set of commodities. As discussed, real investments are fixed in the short-term closure, therefore, an increase in the tax on investment goods do not affect the demand for these commodities which results in a big increase in tax revenues. The real *per capita* consumption is not affected very much because it does not include future consumption. The elasticities of the social welfare cost of investment goods will be smallest in the ranking. There are many ways to solve this problem. For example, we can change the closure in the short-term to assume exogenously fixed balance of trade, or balance of payment, and endogenously determined real investment. However, these estimates can best be made in an inter-temporal model.

Notes

[1]   For example Piggott (1982) estimated the elasticity of the social marginal valuation of income to derive welfare weights for different individuals in different income groups for Australia.

[2]   See Dixon, Parmenter, Powell and Wilcoxen (1992) for further detail.

7   Conclusion

7.1   Introduction

The two objectives of this book were development of a computable general equilibrium model of energy, economy and equity interaction in Pakistan and application of the model to conduct a case study on energy pricing policy in the country. In the case study, we estimated distortions in energy prices and evaluated the effects of removing these distortions. In the analysis, the focus was on effectiveness of the pricing policy to achieve its announced objective of equity, besides the micro- and macro-economic effects caused by these distortions in energy prices. This application of GE-PAK shows how the model can be used to provide useful and detailed inputs for informed policy-making. In this sense, the relevance of this study is not confined to the energy sector or to Pakistan but has implications for many developing countries that face similar policy issues relating to other sectors. One can apply the model for an analysis of the pricing policy of other commodities as it contains detailed disaggregation of production activities, user groups and primary factors.

This final chapter briefly reviews the major findings of the simulation results (section 7.2), and describes the important strengths and weaknesses of the model (section 7.3). Furthermore, it also discusses some possible applications of the model to point out the directions for future research.

7.2 Major findings

Our review of the taxes on energy products showed that the household sector consistently receives a subsidy or pays the lowest tax rate on energy products as compared to other sectors. Since energy is considered a basic necessity, these discriminating taxes are intended to counterbalance the large imbalances in the income distribution. In our case study, we simulated the effects of removing three types of discriminations in the taxes on energy products to assess how far these discriminations meet the motive behind them. As detailed in Chapter 6, we simulated the effects of removing these discriminations in energy taxes with and without the revenue-neutrality condition. In the summary of the major findings given in table 7.1, we report the simulation results of the revenue-neutral reforms.

Table 7.1
Summary of results

| | Effects of revenue-neutral reforms in taxes on | | | | | |
	Petroleum products		Electricity		Natural gas	
Real GDP	+		+		+	
Trade balance	-		+		+	
Equity across Region and income[a]:	Rural	Urban	Rural	Urban	Rural	Urban
Low-income	-	-	+	-	-	-
Middle-income	+	+	+	-	-	-
High-income	+	+	-	-	-	-

a We report the results for the self-employed category since the pattern of changes for this category is qualitatively similar to that for the other categories

Table 7.1 shows that only the tax reforms for petroleum products have negative effects on real *per capita* consumption of the low-income groups, while there are positive effects on the middle and high-income groups. Conversely, it shows that the distortions in the taxes on petroleum products meet the social equity objective. As far as macro-economic effects are considered, positive effects on real GDP shows that these distortions generate efficiency losses but keep a check on the balance of trade.

Contrary to the petroleum products, the removal of the distortions in the taxes on electricity have positive effects on the low- and middle income groups of rural households, and have negative effects on real *per capita* consumption of all urban income groups. Conversely, the discriminations in the taxes on electricity are against the social equity objective for the rural region. Furthermore, this tax structure is against the equity across regions as they favour the urban households against most of the rural households. The positive effects on real GDP and the balance of trade show that the loss in economic efficiency and trade deficit are incurred due to the distortions in the taxes on electricity. The tax reforms for natural gas have negative impacts on real *per capita* consumption of all household groups. Conversely they favour all income groups. But the removal of these tax-distortions improves the balance of trade and increases real GDP.

Ranking of energy products Our simulation results show that the distributional effects of eliminating the discriminations in taxes on energy products vary across

230

these products. Like many other developing countries, Pakistan relies heavily on indirect taxes for generation of public funds and at the same time to foster the welfare of the low-income groups. In our study, we computed the social welfare cost of increasing indirect tax revenues through an increase in the tax rate on each energy product. Our results showed that kerosene is the best candidate to increase tax revenues when social equity is not considered, while the second best candidate is natural gas.

These results changed when we took into account the income distributional effects of these taxes. Increase in the tax on kerosene becomes least desirable as it changes the distribution of income against the low income groups, and thus causing the biggest social welfare cost. Natural gas becomes the best candidate to increase the tax revenues as it causes negative impacts on all income groups and the minimum welfare cost on the aggregate. In Pakistan, traditionally the taxes on HSD and gasoline are increased whenever there is a need for additional public funds. If income distributional effects are considered, gasoline is a good candidate to raise revenues, but HSD remains a bad candidate to raise indirect tax revenues as compared to natural gas and FO.

We acknowledge that there are certain limitations of this analysis, and these findings are subject to certain conditions. Nevertheless, this analysis serves our purpose of demonstrating how the GE-PAK can be applied to help in informed policy making.

7.3 Other possible applications of the model

In this book, we applied the model to analyse the effects of changes in domestic tax-mix and consumer subsidies on energy products. Similar exercises can be done for all other commodities. The model can be used to analyse the impact of a single exogenous shock or cumulative effects of more than one shock. For example, during the 1970s oil crisis, the jumps in world oil prices were accompanied by an increase in the demand for Pakistani workers in the oil exporting countries. Hence, there was a reduction in domestic labour supply and an increase in remittances along with a rise in the import price of oil. The model can be used to simulate the individual and cumulative effects of these shocks.

Like other developing countries, trade liberalisation and deregulation of the economy are on the agenda of economic planning in Pakistan. The macro and micro economic effects of these changes in economic policies can be evaluated by the model in detail. For example, the reductions in tariffs, the introduction of export subsidies or taxes can be simulated for a large set of commodities. Further, the disaggregation of households by region and income group helps in evaluating the short-run adjustment costs in terms of real household consumption along with the income-distributional effects.

These issues are important for Pakistan and many other developing countries that are under pressure from the international aid giving agencies to liberalise their economies. It is important to evaluate various economic and social-equity effects of these changes in economic policies in the short-term as the adjustment costs of these changes are typically thought to be high by the public, politicians and policy makers.

7.4 Limitations of the model

Various CGE models have been built and applied in developing countries to address a variety of issues[1]. However, each model has its own limitations. Here we outline some limitations of the theoretical structure of GE-PAK and its application in this book.

Limitation of the theory In GE-PAK, we are limited in the specification of labour supply function. We assume that the labour supply curve for each profession can be either horizontal or vertical. This limitation is primarily due to the lack of empirically estimated labour-supply functions for Pakistan. We tried to get around this problem by allowing inter-region household migration that makes the regional labour supply curves upward sloping. Nevertheless, these labour supply functions do not allow any change in the hours of labour supply from a household group in response to an increase in real wages.

In common with many other CGE models, money is absent from GE-PAK; the model is limited to the real side of the economy where decisions are based on relative prices. It is implicitly assumed that the government adjusts the money supply of the economy in a way consistent with the changes in the domestic price level emerging from the results of the policy simulations. The introduction of equations for the financial sector linking money supply, the domestic price level, GDP, the balance of trade, exchange rate and aggregated investment would be a major extension of the model.

At present the model is suitable only for a comparative-static analysis and is not capable of forecasting. In the static model the investment decisions do not change as the rate of return changes across industries in a policy simulation. Thus, the effects of reallocation of resources in capital formation for future production are not taken into account. The introduction of dynamics into the model would be an important improvement.

Although, non-commercial energy products meet a significant fraction of energy demand, mainly in the household sector, production and consumption pattern of these traditional fuels have not been model in GE-PAK for two reasons. First, a major portion of these traditional fuels are not purchased but rather collected by the family members especially children and women. In the short-term, any marginal change in the economy in terms of demand for and wages of labour will not substantially affect the opportunity cost of family hours used in supplying these fuels. Second, substitution of non-commercial fuels with commercial fuels is determined mainly by a household's access to the distribution system of natural gas and electricity and its income level to bear initial cost of getting connection and gadgets. Thus, changes in the government pricing policy and the resultant marginal effects on household income will not affect this substitution pattern. Hence, the government policies in the short-term will not neither effect the demand for and supply of these fuels. A small fraction of energy demand in Pakistan is also meet by coal which is mainly used in the brick industry. Substitution of coal with any other fuel is not possible in the existing production technology. Though, a separate coal industry has been defined in the model, consumption pattern of coal has not been modeled in detail. Incorporation of non-commercial fuels in the model will be required to analyse the long-term energy policies issues, particularly for energy demand projection.

Limitation of data The model is based on two sets of data; (i) a social accounting matrix that includes an Input-Output matrix and various income-expenditure matrices of major institutions of the economy, and (ii) a set of elasticity parameters. To prepare the PDB, we used the SAM of 1983-84 and modified it using various sources of data. However, some data values were based on 'best guess'. An example is the disaggregation of returns to fixed factors into land and capital in the agriculture, mining and hydro electricity industries.(see chapter 5 for details). Use of a recent SAM incorporating all such data will enable the researchers to get more reliable results from the model's application for policy formulation. Similarly, improved estimates of the values of the model's parameters would considerably enhance the usefulness of the model. Ideally, this would involve the estimation of the elasticity parameters econometrically. That would require more time and research resources than were available for this study. Nevertheless, these estimated values of parameter will only improve the precision and the reliability of the model's results.

Note

[1]   Bandara (1989) has made a comprehensive survey of CGE models applications for the developing countries. He has given a summary of major features of 61 such CGE models and major results of their studies.

Bibliography

Adelman, I. and S. Robinson (1978), *Income Distribution Policy in Developing Countries*, Oxford: Oxford University Press.

Ahmad, S.E. and N.H. Stern (1984), 'The Theory of Reform and Indian Indirect Taxes', *Journal of Public Economics*, Vol. 25, pp. 254-298.

_____ (1986), 'The Analysis of Tax Reform for Developing Countries: Lessons from Research on Pakistan and India', *DEP NO. 2*, London School of Economics and Political Science.

_____ (1990), 'Tax Reform and Shadow Prices for Pakistan', *Oxford Economic Papers*, Vol. 42, pp. 135-159.

Ahmad, S.E. and S. Ludlow (1988), 'On changes in Inequality In Pakistan: 1979-84', *DEP No. 13*, The Development Economic Research Program, London School of Economics.

Ahmed, E. (1981), 'Production Functions and Input Elasticities in the Construction of Low-Cost Housing: A Comparison of building Firms in Pakistan with Firms in Five other Countries', *The Pakistan Development Review*, Vol. xx, No. 4, winter, pp. 417-426.

Ahmed, E., et al. (1985), Input-output matrices for Pakistan 1980-81, Development Economic Research Centre, discussion paper 68, University of Warwick, UK.

Ali, M. S. (1981), 'Rural-urban Consumption Pattern in Pakistan', *The Pakistan Development Review*, Vol. 19, No. 2, pp. 85-94.

____ (1985), 'Household Consumption and Saving Behaviour in Pakistan: An Application of the Extended Linear Expenditure System', *The Pakistan Development Review*, Vol. XXIV, No. 1, Spring 1985, pp. 24-37.

Armington, P. S. (1969), 'The Geographic Pattern of Trade and the Effects of Price Changes', *IMF Staff Papers*, XVI, July, pp. 176-199.

____ (1970), 'Adjustments of Trade Balances: Some Experiments with a Model of Trade Among Many Countries', *IMF Staff Papers*, XVII, November, pp. 488-523.

Atkinson, A. B. (1970), 'On the Measurement of Inequality', *Journal of Economic Theory*, Vol. 2, pp. 244-263.

Bacharach, M. (1970), *Bi proportional Matrices and Input-output Change*, Cambridge University Press, UK.

Bahatia, R. (1984), 'Energy Pricing in Developing Countries: Role of Prices in Investment Allocation and Consumer Choices', in C.M. Sidayyo (ed.), *Criteria for Energy Pricing*, Graham & Trotman, Bangkok.

Ballard, C. L. and S.G. Medema (1993), 'The Marginal Efficiency Effects of Taxes and Subsidies in the Presence of Externalities: A Computational General Equilibrium Approach', *Journal of Public Economics*, Vol. 52, No. 2, pp. 199-216.

Ballard, C. L., J.B. Shoven, and J. Whalley (1985), 'General Equilibrium Computation of the Marginal Welfare Costs of Taxes in the United States', *The American Economic Review*, Vol. 75. No. 1, pp. 128-138.

Bandara, S. J. (1989), *A Multi sectoral General Equilibrium Model of the Sri Lankan Economy With Application to the Analysis of the Effects of External Shocks*, Ph.D. thesis, School of Economics, La Trobe University, Victoria, 3083, Australia.

Bardhan, P.K. (1984), *Land, Labour, and Rural Poverty: Essays in Development Economics*, New York: University of Colombia Press, USA.

Batra, R.N. and N. Naqvi (1987), 'Urban Employment and the Gains from Trade', *Economica*, Vol. 54, pp. 381-396.

Battese, G.E. and S.J. Malik (1987), 'Estimation of Elasticities of Substitution for CES Production Functions using Data on Selected Manufacturing Industries in Pakistan', *The Pakistan Development Review*, Vol. XXVI, No. 2, pp. 163-177.

Beladi, H. (1988), 'Variable Returns to Scale, Urban Unemployment and Welfare', *Southern Economic Journal*, Vol. 55, pp. 412-423.

Beladi, H. and N. Naqvi (1988), 'Urban Unemployment and Non-immiserizing Growth', *Journal of Development Economics*, Vol. 28, pp. 365-376.

Bell, C. (1991), 'Markets, Power and Productivity in Rural Asia: A review article', *Journal of Development Economics*, Vol. 36, pp. 373-393.

Benjamin, N.C., S. Devarajan, and R.J. Weiner (1989), 'The Dutch Disease in a Developing Country: Oil Revenues in Cameroon' *Journal of Development Economics*, Vol. 30, January, pp. 71-92.

Bergman, L. (1978), 'Energy Policy in a Small Open Economy: The Case of Sweden.' *Research Report*, No. 16, International Institute of Applied Systems Analysis, Laxenburg, Austria.

Bergman, L. (1986), 'ELIAS — A Model of Multi-sectoral Economic Growth', in B.C. Ysander (ed.), *Two Models of an Open Economy*, Stockholm, The Institute for Economic and Social Research, Sweden.

Bergman, L. (1988), 'Energy Policy Modelling: A Survey of General Equilibrium Approaches', *Journal of Policy Modelling*, Vol. 10, No. 3, pp. 377-399.

Bergman, L., D. Jorgenson, and E. zalai (eds.) (1990a), *General Equilibrium Modelling and Economic Policy Analysis*, Basil Blackwell Inc., Oxford, UK.

Bergman, L. and S. Lundgren (1990b), 'General Equilibrium Approaches to Energy Policy Analysis in Sweden', in L. Bergman, D. Jorgenson, and E. zalai (eds.), *General Equilibrium Modelling and Economic Policy Analysis*, Basil Blackwell Inc., Oxford, UK.

Bilquees, F. (1992), 'Trends in Intersectoral Wages in Pakistan', *The Pakistan Development Review*, Vol. 31, No. 4, Part II, Winter, pp. 1243-1253.

Binswanger H. and M. Rosenzweig (eds.) , (1984), *Contractual Arrangements, Employment and wages in Rural Labour Markets in Asia*, New Haven: Yale University Press, USA.

Blackorby, C. and D. Donaldson (1978), 'Measures of Relative Equality and their Meaning in terms of Social Welfare', *Journal of Economic Theory*, Vol. 18, pp. 59-80.

Blitzer, C. (1984), 'Energy Demand in Jordan: A Case study of Energy-Economy Linkages', *The Energy Journal*, Vol. 5, No. 4, pp. 1-19.

Blitzer, C. (1986), 'Energy-Economy Interactions in Developing Countries', *The Energy Journal*, Vol. 7, No. 1, pp. 35-50.

Blitzer, C. and R. Eckaus (1983a), 'Energy-Economy Interactions in Mexico: A Multiperiod General Equilibrium Model', *Working Paper* No. MIT-EL 8301WP, Cambridge, MA: Massachusetts Institute of Technology, USA.

Blitzer, C. and R. Eckaus (1983b), 'Modelling Short-Run Energy Policy in Mexico: A General Equilibrium Approach', *Working Paper*, No. 83-017, Energy Laboratory MIT, USA.

Blitzer, C. and R. Eckaus (1985), *Modelling Energy-Economy Interactions in Small Developing Countries: A Case Study of Sri Lanka*, June, Energy Laboratory, MIT, USA.

Bovenberg, L. (1978), 'Indirect Taxation in Developing Countries: An Applied General Equilibrium Approach', *Staff Papers*, International Monetary Fund, Washington, D.C., USA

Browing, E. K. (1976), 'The Marginal Cost of Public Funds', *Journal of Political Economy*, April, Vol. 84, pp. 283-98.

Burney, N. A. and A. H. Khan (1991), 'Household Consumption Pattern in Pakistan: An Urban-Rural Comparison Using Micro Data', *The Pakistan Development Review*, Vol. 30, No. 2, Summer, pp. 145-171.

Burney, N A. and N. Akhtar. (1990), 'Fuel demand Elasticities in Pakistan: An Analysis of Households' Expenditure Using Micro Data', *The Pakistan Development Review*, Vol. 29, No. 2, pp. 155-1741.

Chamber, M.M. (1985), 'An Energy Economy Model of Pakistan', in *Proceeding of the Seventh Annual North American meeting of the International Association of Energy Economists*, Philadelphia, Pennsylvania 10-13 December, 1985.

Chao, C. and E.S.H. Yu (1992), 'Capital Markets, Urban Unemployment and Land', *Journal of Development Economics*, Vol. 38, pp. 407-413.

Chaudhry, M.G. (1982), 'Green Revolution and Redistribution of Rural Income: Pakistan's Experience', *The Pakistan Development Review*, Vol. 21, No. 3.

Chaudhry, M.G. and G.M. Chaudhry (1992), 'Trend of Rural Employment and Wages in Pakistan', *The Pakistan Development Review*, Vol. 31, No. 4, Part II, Winter, pp. 803 - 815.

Chern, W.S. (1987), 'Macroeconomic Impacts of Oil Shocks in Pakistan', *Natural Resource Forum*, Vol. 11, No. 1, pp. 85-91.

Clarete, R. L. and P. G. Warr (1992), *The Theoretical Structure of the APEX Model of the Philippine Economy*. Unpublished Manuscript presented at the Workshop on the APEC Computable General Equilibrium Model of the Philippine Economy, Manila, Philippines.

Corden, W.M. and J.P. Neary (1982), 'Booming Sector and De-industrialisation in a Small Open Economies', *Economic Journal*, Vol. 92, pp. 825-848.

Dahl, H., S. Devarajan and S. van Wijnbergen (1986), 'Revenue-Neutral Tariff Reform: Theory and an Application to Cameroon', Country Policy Department *Discussion Paper* No. 25, World Bank, Washington, D.C. USA.

Dervis, K., J. de Melo and S. Robinson (1982), *General Equilibrium Models for Development Policy*, Cambridge: Cambridge University Press.

Devarajan, S. (1988), 'Natural Resources and Taxation in Computable General Equilibrium Models of Developing Countries', *Journal of Policy Modelling*, Vol. 10, No. 4, pp. 505-528.

Devarajan, S. and J. de Melo (1987), 'Adjustment with a Fixed Exchange Rate: Cameroon, Cote d'Ivorie and Senegal', *World Bank Economic Review* 1: pp. 447-488.

Dhanani, S. (1986a), 'An Updated Input-Output Table for Pakistan 1983-84', *Report No. 17*, Institute of Agricultural Economics, University of Oxford.

_____(1986b), 'Construction of A Disaggregated Pakistan SAM for 1983-84', *Report No. 18*, Institute of Agricultural Economics, University of Oxford.

_____(1989), 'A SAM-based General Equilibrium Model of the Pakistan Economy, 1983-84', *Fifth Meeting of Pakistan Society of Development Economists*, Pakistan Institute of Development Economics, Islamabad, Pakistan.

Diamond, P. and J. Mirrlees (1971), 'Optimal Taxation and Public Production', *American Economic Review*, Vol. 61, pp. 8-27.

Diewert, W. E. (1971), 'An Application of the Shephard Duality Theorem: A Generalised Leontief Production Structure', Vol. 79, pp. 481-507.

Diewert, W. E. (1985), 'Measurement of Waste and Welfare', in J. Piggott and J. Whalley (eds), *New Developments in Applied General Equilibrium Analysis*, Cambridge: Cambridge University Press, pp. 42-103.

Dixit, A. and D. Newbery (1984), 'Setting the Price of Oil in a Distorted Economy', *Economic Journal*, Vol. 95, pp. 71-92.

Dixon, P.B., B.R. Parmenter, J. Sutton and D.B. Vincent (1982), *ORANI: A Multisectoral Model of the Australian Economy*, Amsterdam: North-Holland.

Dreze, J.P. and A. Mukherjee (1989), 'Labour Contracts in Rural India: Theories and Evidence', in S. Chakravarty (ed.) *The Balance between Industry and Agriculture in Economic Development*, Vol 3, Manpower and Transfers I.E.A. and Macmillan, London.

Duff, I.S. (1977), MA 28 - *A Set of FORTRAN subroutines for Sparse Unsymmetric Systems of Linear Equations*, Report 8730, A.E.R.E., Harwell HMSO, London.

_____ (1981), ' A Sparse Future', in I.S. Duff (ed.) *Sparse Matrices and Their Uses*, London: Academic Press, pp. 1-30.

ENAR Petro Tech (1979), 'Energy Supply and Demand Analysis', A report prepared for the Ministry of Planning and Development Division, Islamabad, Pakistan.

ENERPLAN (1988), 'The Pricing Impacts of Changing Energy Prices in Pakistan', A *report of a project of* Ministry of Planning and Development Division, Islamabad, Pakistan.

Far Eastern Economic Review (1986), 'The Choice: a Meagre Wage or Unemployment', in Asian Unions, 3 April, pp-43-67.

Faulhaber, G. (1975), 'Cross Subsidisation: Pricing in Public Enterprise', *American Economic Review*, December, pp. 966-977.

Fishbone, L.G., G. Giesen, G. Goldstein, H.A. Hymmen, K.J. Stocks, H. Vos, D. Wilde, R. Zolcher, C. Balzer, and H. Abilock (1983), 'User's Guide for MARKAL (BNL/KFA Version 2.0)', BNL 51701, Brookhaven National Laboratory, Upton, N.Y. 11973 and Forschungsanlage KFA-Julich, D-5170 Julich.

Fortin, B., M. Truchon, and L. Beausejour (1993), 'On reforming the Welfare System: Workfare Meets the Negative Income tax', *Journal of Public Economics*, Vol. 51, pp. 119-151.

Ginsburgh, V.A. and J.L.Waelbroeck (1981), *Activity Analysis and General Equilibrium Modelling*, Amsterdam: North-Holland.

GOP (Government of Pakistan), (1979), *National Accounts of Pakistan*, Federal Bureau of Statistics, Islamabad, Pakistan.

_____(1983), *Household Income and Expenditure Survey 1979*, Federal Bureau of Statistics, Islamabad, Pakistan.

_____ (1985), *Energy Year Book 1984*, Directorate General of Energy Resources, Ministry of Petroleum and Natural Resources, Islamabad, Pakistan.

_____(1985a), *Government Sponsored Corporations 1983-84*, Ministry of Finance, Islamabad, Pakistan.

_____(1985b), *Pakistan Economic Survey 1984-85*, Ministry of Finance, Islamabad, Pakistan.

_____ (1985c), *National Accounts of Pakistan*, Federal Bureau of Statistics, Islamabad, Pakistan.

_____(1986), *Household Income and Expenditure Survey, 1984-85*, Federal Bureau of Statistics, Islamabad, Pakistan.

_____(1987), *Survey of Small and Household Manufacturing Industries 1983-84*, Vol. 1 and 2, Federal Bureau of Statistics, Islamabad, Pakistan.

_____ (1988a), *Census of Mining Industries 1984-85*, Federal Bureau of Statistics, Islamabad, Pakistan.

_____ (1989), *Energy Year Book 1988*, Directorate General of Energy Resources, Ministry of Petroleum and Natural Resources, Islamabad, Pakistan.

_____ (1990), *Economic Survey 1989-90*, Ministry of Finance, Islamabad, Pakistan.

_____ (1992a), *Energy Year Book 1991*, Hydrocarbon Development Institute of Pakistan, Ministry of Petroleum and Natural Resources, Islamabad.

_____ (1992b), *Pakistan Economic Survey 1991-92*, Ministry of Finance, Islamabad, Pakistan.

_____ (1994a), *Report of Prime Minister's Task Force on Energy*, Cabinet Secretariat, Islamabad.

_____ (1994b), *Eighth Five Year Plan (1993-98), and earlier issues*, Planning Commission, Islamabad, Pakistan.

_____ (1994c), Policy Framework and Package of Incentives for Private Sector Power Generaion Projects in Pakistan, Private Power and Infrastructure Board, Islamabad, Pakistan.

_____ (1995a), Policy Framework and Package of Incentives for Private Sector Transmission Line Projects in Pakistan, Private Power and Infrastructure Board, Islamabad, Pakistan.

_____ (1995b), Policy Framework and Package of Incentives for Private Sector Hydel Power Generation Projects in Pakistan, Private Power and Infrastructure Board, Islamabad, Pakistan.

_____ (1996a), *Energy Year Book 1995*, Hydrocarbon Development Institute of Pakistan, Ministry of Petroleum and Natural Resources, Islamabad, Pakistan.

_____ (1996b), *Economic Survey 1995-96*, Ministry of Finance, Islamabad, Pakistan.

Guisinger, S. (1978), 'Long Term Trends in Income Distribution in Pakistan', *World Development*, Vol. 6, pp. 1271-1280.

Hamilton, L. D., G.A. Goldstein, J. Lee, A. S. Manne, W. Marcuse, S.C. Morris, and Clas-Ott Wene (1992), 'MARKAL-MACRO: An Overview'. A project *Report* of U.S. Department of Energy under Contract No. DE-AC02-76CH00016, November, 12.

Hanson, I. and C. Stuart (1985), 'Tax Revenue and Marginal Cost of Public Funds in Sweden', *Journal of Public Economics*, Vol. 27, pp. 331-353.

Harris, J.R. and M. Todaro (1970), 'Migration, Unemployment and Development: A two sector analysis', *American Economic Review*, Vol. 60, pp. 126-142.

Hazari, B.R. and P.M. Sgro (1991), 'Urban-rural Structural Adjustment, Urban Unemployment with Traded and Non-traded Goods', *Journal of Development Economics*, Vol. 35, pp. 187-196.

Harberger, A.C. (1962), 'The Incidence of the Corporate Income Tax', *Journal of Political Economy*, Vol. 70, No. 3, pp. 215-40.

Horridge, M., B.P. Parmenter, and K.R. Pearson (1993), 'ORANI-F: A General Equilibrium Model of the Australian Economy', *Economic and Financial Computing*, Summer 1993.

Hudson E. A . and D.W. Jorgenson (1975), 'U.S. Energy Policy and Economic Growth', *Bell Journal of Economics and Management Science*, Vol. 5, No. 2: pp. 461-514.

Hughes, G. (1986a), 'The Impact of Fuel Taxes in Tunisia', *Mimeograph*, Department of Economics, University of Edinburgh, UK.

Hughes, G. (1986b), 'A New Method for Estimating the Effects of Fuel Taxes: An Application to Thailand', *World Bank Economic Review*, No. 1, pp. 665-701.

IAEA (International Atomic Energy Agency), (1984), *Expansion Planning for Electrical Generating Systems: A Guide Book*, Technical Report Series No. 241, Vienna, Austria.

IEDC (International Energy Development Corporation), (1983), 'A long Term Plan for Energy Sector', A *report* prepared for Planning and Development Division, Government of Pakistan, Islamabad, Pakistan.

Impact Project (1993), *GDP-1, Introduction to GEMPACK*, First edition, April, Monash University, Melbourne.

_____ (1993), *GDP-2, User's Guide to TABLO and TABLO generated Programs*, First edition, April, Monash University, Melbourne.

_____ (1993), *GDP-3, How to Create and Modify GEMPACK Header Array Files using the Program MODHAR*, Third edition, April, Monash University, Melbourne.

_____ (1993), *GDP-4, Implementing Levels Models Directly Using GEMPACK Programs*, First edition, April, Monash University, Melbourne.

Industry Commission, (1991), 'Costs and Benefits of Reducing Greenhouse Emissions', *Report No.* 15, a.g.p.s, Canberra, Australia.

Irfan, M. (1980), *Wage Structure in Pakistan*, unpublished Ph.D. thesis, Cornell University Ithaca, New York (USA).

Irfan, M. (1982), 'Wages, Employment and Trade Unions in Pakistan', *The Pakistan Development Review*, Vol. 21, No. 1.

Irfan, M. and M. Ahmed (1985), 'Real Wages in Pakistan: Structure and Trends, 1970-84', *The Pakistan Development Review*, Vol. 24, No. 3&4.

Jalal, A.I. (1988), *A Computable General Equilibrium Model for the Evaluation of Energy pricing Policies in Pakistan*, thesis for the Degree of Engineer, Stanford University, USA.

Jetha, N. S. Akhtar, and G. Rao (1984), 'Domestic Resource Mobilisation in Pakistan', *World Bank Staff Working Paper* 632, World Bank, Washington, D.C., USA.

Johansen, L. (1960), *A Multi-sectoral Study of Economic Growth*, Amsterdam: North-Holland Publishing Company.

Jorgenson, D. W. (1982), 'Econometric and Process Analysis Models for Energy Policy Assessments', in R. Amit and M. Avriel (eds.) , *Perspectives on Resource Policy Modelling: Energy and Minerals*, Cambridge, MA: Ballinger, pp. 9-62.

Jorgenson, D. W. and D. T. Slesnick (1984), 'Aggregate Consumer Behaviour and the Measurement of Inequality', *Review of Economic Studies*, Vol. 51, pp. 369-392.

Katz, J. (1969), *Production Functions, Foreign Investment and Growth*, Amsterdam: North Holland Publishing Company.

Kazi, S., Z.S. Khan and S.A. Khan (1976), 'Production Relationships in Pakistan's Manufacturing Industries', *The Pakistan Development Review*, Vol. xv, No. 41 pp. 406-423.

Kazmi, N. (1981), 'Substitution Elasticities in Small and Household Manufacturing Industries in Pakistan', *Research Report Series*, No. 109, Pakistan Institute of Development Economics.

Kemal, A.R. (1981), 'Substitution Elasticities in the Large-Scale Manufacturing Industries of Pakistan', *The Pakistan Development Review*, Vol. xx, No. 1 pp. 1-36.

Khan, A. H.(1989), 'The Two-level Production Function for the Manufacturing Sector of Pakistan', *The Pakistan Development Review*, Vol. 28, No. 1 pp. 1-12.

Khan, A.M., M. Jameel, F. Naqvi, and A. Mumtaz (1986), 'Projection of Energy Demand for the Long Term Plan 1984-85 to 2007-08', A *Report* prepared for the Planning and Development Division, Government of Pakistan, Islamabad, Pakistan.

Khan, A.R. and E. Lee, (1984), 'Introduction', in *Poverty in Rural Asia*, A.R. Khan and E. Lee (eds.), International Labour Organisation, Asian Employment Programme.

Khan, A. and S.N.H. Naqvi (1983), 'Capital Market and Urban unemployment and Specific Factors of Production', *Journal of International Economics*, Vol. 15, pp. 367-385.

Kim, S. (1984), 'Models of Energy-Economy Interactions for Developing Countries: A Survey', *Working Paper*, No. 84-007, August, Energy Laboratory, MIT, USA.

Kosmo, M. (1989), 'Commercial Energy Subsidies in Developing Countries: Opportunity for Reforms', *Energy Policy*, June, pp. 244-253.

Kuijper, M.A.M. (1982), 'The Pricing of Petroleum Products in Pakistan', *The Pakistan Development Review*, Vol. xxi, No. 3, pp. 231-244.

Lluch, C., A.A. Powell, and R.A. Williams (1977), *Patterns in Household Demand and Savings,* Oxford: Oxford University Press.

Longva, S., L. Lorentsen and O. Olsen (1985), 'The Multi-Sectoral Growth Model MSG-4, Formal Structure and Empirical Characteristics', in F. Forsund, *et al.*, (eds.), *Production, Multi-Sectoral Growth and Planning*, Amsterdam: North-Holland.

de Lucia, R.J. and M.C. Lesser (1985), 'Energy Pricing Policies in Developing Countries', *Energy Policy*, August, pp. 345-349.

de Lucia, R. and H. Jacoby (1982), *Energy Planning for Developing Countries: A study of Bangladesh*, Baltimore: Johns Hopkins University Press.

Lundgren, S. (1985), *Model Integration and the Economics of Nuclear Power*, Stockholm: Economic Research Institute, Stockholm School of Economics, Sweden.

Mahmood, Z. (1990), 'Derived Demand for Factors in the Large-Scale Manufacturing Sector of Pakistan', *Sixth Annual General Meeting, Pakistan Society of Development Economist*, Pakistan Institute of Development Economics, Islamabad, Pakistan.

242

Mahmood, Z. (1990), 'Derived Demand for Factors in the Large-Scale Manufacturing Sector of Pakistan', *Sixth Annual General Meeting, Pakistan Society of Development Economist*, Pakistan Institute of Development Economics, Islamabad, Pakistan.

Manne, A. (1977), 'ETA-Macro: A Model of Energy Economy Interactions', *EA-592 Research Report*, No. 1014, Palo Alto: Electric Power Research Institute, USA.

Marcuse, W. L. Bodin, E. Cherniavsky, and Y. Sanborn (1976), 'Dynamic Time dependent Model for the Analysis of Alternative Energy Policies', in K.B. Haley (ed.) , *Operational Research' 75*, Amsterdam: North Holland.

Marjit, S. (1991), 'Agro-based Industry and Rural-urban migration: A case for an urban employment subsidy', *Journal of Development Economics*, Vol. 5, pp. 393-398.

Martin, R. and S. van Winjbergen (1986), 'Shadow Prices and the Intertemporal Aspects of Remittances and Oil Revenues in Egypt', in J.P. Neary and S. van Wijnbergen (eds.) , *Natural Resources and the Macroeconomy*, Cambridge, MA: MIT Press.

Munasinghe, M. (1985), 'Supply and Demand Management', in R. Codon, H. Park and K. V. Ramani (eds.), *Integrated Energy Planning: A Manual*, Asian and Pacific Development Centre, Kualalumpur.

Nazli, E. and S. Lahiri (1990), 'Short-Run Energy-Economy Interactions in Egypt', in L. Taylor, *Socially Relevant Policy Analysis: Structuralist Computable General Equilibrium Model for the Developing World*, MIT Press, USA.

Newbry, D. M.G. and N. H. Stern (eds.) (1987), *The Theory of Taxation for Developing Countries*, Oxford University Press.

Nordhaus, W. D. (1974), 'The Allocation of Energy Resources', *Brookings Papers on Economic Activity*, 4: 529-577.

OCAC (Oil Company Advisory Committe), (1988), *Petroleum Products Statistics*, Ministry of Petroleum and Natural Resources, Islamabad, Pakistan.

Panda, M. and H. Sarkar (1990), 'Resource Mobilisation through Administered Prices in an Indian CGE', in Taylor L. (ed.), *Socially Relevant Policy Analysis: Structuralist Computable General Equilibrium Models for the Developing World*, Cambridge: The MIT Press, USA.

Pearson, K. R. and R. J. Rimmer (1983), 'Sparse Matrix Method for Computable General Equilibrium Models of the Johansen Class', *Impact Preliminary Working Paper*, OP-43, Impact Project, University of Melbourne.

_____ (1985), 'An Efficient Method for the Solution of Large Computable General Equilibrium Models', *Journal of International Association of Math. Comp. Sim.*, 27, 223-229.

Piggot, J. (1982), 'The Social marginal Valuation of Income: The Australian Estimates from Government Behaviour', *The Economic Record*, March, pp. 92-99.

Piggot, J. and J. Whalley (1977), 'General Equilibrium Investigation of UK. Tax-subsidy Policy: Progress Report', in M. J. Artis and A. R. Nobay (eds.) *Studies in Modern Economic Analysis*, Oxford: Blackwell, pp. 259-99.

243

Rawls J. (1971), *A Theory of Justice*, Cambridge Mass, Harvard University Press.

Riaz, T. (1984), *The Energy Sector: A Study in Sector Planning*, Ferozsons Ltd., Lahore, Pakistan.

Robert, K.W.S. (1980), 'Interpersonal Comparability and Social Choice Theory', *The Review of Economic Studies*, Vol. 47, pp. 421-439.

Sabih, F. (1986), *Welfare Implication of Electricity Pricing and Power Outages in Pakistan*, Ph.D. thesis, Boston University.

Saleem, M. (1983), Revised PIDE Input-Output Table of Pakistan's Economy *1975-76*, Pakistan Institute of Development Economics, Islamabad, Pakistan.

Salma, U. (1992), *Agricultural Price Policy in Bangladesh: General Equilibrium Effects on growth and income distribution*, unpublished Ph. D. thesis, Australian National University, Canberra, Australia.

Sarkar, H. and G.K. Kadekodi (1988), *Energy Pricing in India: Perspective,* Issues and Options, United Nation Development Programme and Economic and Social Commission for Asia and the Pacific, International Labour Organisation (Asian Employment Program), New Delhi, India.

Scarf, H.E. (1967), 'On the Computation of Equilibrium Prices', in W. J. Feliner (ed.), The Economic Studies in the Tradition of Irving Fisher, New York: Wiley.

Shoven, J. B. and J. Whalley (1972), 'A General Equilibrium Calculation of the Effects of Different Taxation of Income from Capital in the US', *Journal of Public Economics*, Vol. 9, pp. 281-321.

_____(1973), 'General Equilibrium with Taxes: A Computation Procedure and Existence Proof', *Review of Economic Studies*, Vol. 60, October, pp. 475-90.

_____ (1984), 'Applied General Equilibrium Models of Taxation and Trade: An Introduction and Survey', *Journal of Economic Literature*, Vol. 22, September, pp. 1007-51.

Sidayyo, C.M. (1983), 'Pricing Policy and Efficient Energy Use', *Energy*, Vol. 8, No. 1, pp. 45-68.

_____(1988), 'Energy Policy Issues in Developing Countries: lesson from ASEAN's Experience', *Energy Policy*, December 1988, pp. 608-620.

Siddiqui, R. (1982), 'An Analysis of consumption Pattern in Pakistan', *The Pakistan Development Review*, Vol. XXI, No. 4, pp 275-296.

Stern, N.H. (1990), 'Uniformity versus Selectivity in Tax Structure: Lesson from Theory and Policy', *Economics and Politics*, Vol. 2, No. 1, March 1990.

Stuart, C. E. (1984), 'Welfare Cost per Dollar of Additional Tax Revenues in the United States', *The American Economic Review*, Vol. 74, pp. 352-62.

UNDP/World Bank (1987), 'Power System Planning for Pakistan', a report prepared for WAPDA, Pakistan.

Vincent, D.P. (1986), 'Stabilisation and Adjustment in Commodity Dependent Developing Countries: Findings from a Collection of Studies Centered around Country-specific General Equilibrium Models', *Paper* presented to the University of Melbourne, Department of Economics, Impact Research Centre, IAESR Workshop in Computable General Equilibrium Modelling, June , 1986.

WAPDA (Water and Power Development Authority) (1986), 'Study for Restructuring of Tariff', *A Report prepared for the Government of Pakistan*, WAPDA, Lahore, Pakistan.

_____ (1996), *Power System Statistics Fourteenth Issue 1995 and earlier issues*, WAPDA, Lahore, Pakistan.

Webb, M.G (1978), 'Policy on Energy Pricing', *Energy Policy*, March, pp. 53-65.

Appendix A   Equations of GE-PAK

Block 1 Equations for region-profession specific labour demand

$$x1lab_{rpj} = x1lab\_rp_j + a1lab\_p_{rj} + a1lab_{rpj}$$

$$- \sigma PRF_{rj} [\{p1lab_{rpj} + a1lab_{rpj}\} - p1lab\_p_{rj}],$$

$$r \in REG, \ p \in PRF, \ j \in IND, \qquad (1.1)$$

$$p1lab\_p_{rj} = \frac{1}{V1LAB\_p_{rj}} \sum_{p \in PRF} \{V1LAB_{rpj} \times (p1lab_{rpj} + a1lab_{rpj})\},$$

$$r \in REG, \ j \in IND, \qquad (1.2)$$

$$p1lab\_rp_j = \frac{1}{V1LAB\_rp_j} \sum_{r \in REG} V1LAB\_p_{rj} \times \{p1lab\_p_{rj} + a1lab\_p_{rj}\},$$

$$j \in IND. \qquad (1.3)$$

Block 2 Demand equations for capital, land and composite labour

$$x1cap_j = x1prm_j + a1cap_j - \sigma FAC_j [\{p1cap_j + a1cap_j\} - p1prm_j],$$

$$j \in IND, \qquad (2.1)$$

$$x1lnd_j = x1prm_j + a1lnd_j - \sigma FAC_j [\{p1lnd_j + a1lnd_j\} - p1prm_j],$$

$$j \in IND, \qquad (2.2)$$

247

$$x1lab\_rp_j = x1prm_j + a1lab\_rp_j - \sigma FAC_j \left[\{plab\_rp_j + a1lab\_rp_j\} - p1prm_j\right],$$

$$j \in IND, \tag{2.3}$$

$$p1prm_j = \frac{1}{V1PRM_j} \left(V1CAP\_c_j \times \{p1cap_j + a1cap_j + a1prm_j\} \right.$$

$$+ V1LND\_d_j \times \{p1lnd_j + a1lnd_j + a1prm_j\}$$

$$\left. + V1LAB\_rp_j \times \{p1lab\_rp_j + a1lab\_rp_j + a1prm_j\} \right), \ j \in IND. \tag{2.4}$$

Block 3 Equations of intermediate demand by source

$$x1_{isj} = x1\_s_{ij} + a1_{isj} - \sigma SRC1_i \left[\{p1_{isj} + a1_{isj}\} - p1\_s_{ij}\right],$$

$$i \in COM, \ s \in SRC, \ j \in IND, \tag{3.1}$$

$$p1\_s_{ij} = \frac{1}{V1BAS\_s_{ij}} \sum_{s \in SRC} V1BAS_{isj} \, (p1_{isj} + a1_{isj}),$$

$$i \in COM, \ j \in IND. \tag{3.2}$$

Block 4 Composite-inputs demand equations

$$x1oct_j = atot_j + a1oct_j + z_j, \quad j \in IND, \tag{4.1}$$

$$x1prm_j = atot_j + a1prm_j + z_j, \quad j \in IND, \tag{4.2}$$

$$x1\_s_{ij} = atot_j + a1\_s_j + z_j, \qquad i \in COM, \ j \in IND, \tag{4.3}$$

$$p0ind_j - a_j = \frac{1}{COSTS_j} \left(\sum_{i \in COM} \sum_{s \in SRC} PUR1_{isj} \times p1_{isj} \right.$$

$$+ \sum_{r \in REG} \sum_{p \in PRF} V1LAB_{rpj} \times p1lab_{rpj}$$

$$+ V1CAP\_c_j \times p1cap_j$$

$$\left. + V1LND\_d_j \times p1lnd_j + V1OCT_j \times p1oct_j \right), \qquad j \in IND, \tag{4.4}$$

248

$$a_j - atot_j = \sum_{i \in COM} (PUR1\_s_j \times a1\_s_j + \sum_{s \in SRC} PUR1_{isj} \times a1_{isj})$$

$$+ V1PRM_j \times a1prm_j + \sum_{r \in REG} \sum_{p \in PRF} V1LAB_{rpj} \times a1lab_{rpj}$$

$$+ LAB\_rp_j \times a1lab\_rp_j + V1CAP\_c_j \times a1cap_j + V1LND\_d_j \times a1lnd_j$$

$$+ V1OCT_j \times a1oct_j, \quad j \in IND, \tag{4.5}$$

$$p1oct_j = xi3 + f1oct_j, \quad j \in IND. \tag{4.6}$$

Block 5 Equations for output-mix in multiple-output industries

$$x0_{ij} = z_j + \sigma OUT_j (p0dom_i - p0ind_j), \quad i \in NONCELE,$$
$$j \in NONIELE, \tag{5.1}$$

$$p0ind_j = \frac{1}{MAKE\_ij} \sum_{i \in COM} MAKE_{ij} \times p0dom_i,$$

$$j \in NONIELE, \tag{5.2}$$

$$x0dom_i = \frac{1}{MAKE\_ji} \sum_{j \in NONIELE} MAKE_{ij} \times x0_{ij},$$

$$i \in NONCELE. \tag{5.3}$$

Block 6 Equations of electricity supply structure

$$x0_{ij} = x0elec\_lflex - \sigma IELEL (p0ind_j - p0elec\_lflex),$$

$$i = electricity, j \in ILFLX, \tag{6.1}$$

$$p0elec\_lflex = \frac{1}{\sum\limits_{j \in ILFLX} MAKE_{ij}} \left(\sum\limits_{j \in ILFLX} MAKE_{ij} \times p0ind_j \right),$$

$$i = electricity, \qquad (6.2)$$

$$x0_{ij} = x0elec\_hflex - \sigma IELEM\ (p0ind_j - p0elec\_hflex),$$

$$i = electricity,\ j = IMFLX, \qquad (6.3)$$

$$p0elec\_hflex = \frac{1}{\sum\limits_{j \in IHFLX} MAKE_{ij}} \left(\sum\limits_{j \in IHFLX} MAKE_{ij} \times p0ind_j \right),$$

$$i = electricity, \qquad (6.4)$$

$$x0elec\_lfflex = x0dom_i - \sigma IELE\ (p0elec\_lflex - p0dom_i), \quad i = electricity, \quad (6.5)$$

$$x0elec\_hflex = x0dom_i - \sigma IELE\ (p0elec\_hflex - p0dom_i), \quad i = electricity\ , \quad (6.6)$$

$$podom_i = \frac{1}{\sum\limits_{j \in IELE} MAKE_{ij}} \left(\sum\limits_{j \in IELE} MAKE_{ij} \times p0ind_j \right), \quad i = electricity. \quad (6.7)$$

Block 7 Equations of demand for commodities for capital formation

$$x2_{isj} = x2\_s_{ij} + a2_{isj} - \sigma SRC2_i\ [\{p2_{isj} + a2_{isj}\} - p2\_s_{ij}],$$
$$i \in COM,\ s \in SRC,\ j \in IND, \qquad (7.1)$$

$$p2\_s_{ij} = \frac{1}{PUR2\_s_{ij}} \left(\sum\limits_{s \in SRC} PUR2_{isj}\ \{p2_{isj} + a2_{isj}\} \right),$$

$$i \in COM,\ j \in IND, \qquad (7.2)$$

250

$$x2\_s_{ij} = y_j + a2\_is_j + a2\_s_{ij}, \quad i \in COM, j \in IND, \tag{7.3}$$

$$p2\_is_j = a2\_is_j + \frac{1}{PUR2\_is_j} \left(\sum_{i \in COM} PUR2\_s_{ij} \{p2\_s_{ij} + a2\_s_{ij}\} \right),$$
$$j \in IND. \tag{7.4}$$

Block 8 Coefficients in household demand equations

$$ALPHA\_I_{krn} = ALPHA_{rn} \times EPS_{krn}, \quad k \in ITM, r \in REG, n \in INC, \tag{8.1}$$

$$ALPHA_{rn} = (-1/FRISCH_{rn}), \quad r \in REG, n \in INC, \tag{8.2}$$

$$DELTA_{krn} = EPS_{krn} \times \frac{VITEM_{krn}}{VITEM\_k_{rn}}, \quad k \in ITM, r \in REG, n \in INC. \tag{8.3}$$

Block 9 Equations for household demand

$$xitem_{krn} = [1 - ALPHA\_I_{krn}] [q\_p_{rn} + aitemsub_{krn}]$$
$$+ ALPHA\_I_{krn} \times [luxexp_{rn} + aitemlux_{krn} - pitem_k],$$
$$k \in ITM, r \in REG, n \in INC, \tag{9.1}$$

$$aitemlux_{krn} = aitemsub_{krn} - \sum_{l \in ITM} (DELTA_{lrn} \times aitemsub_{lrn}),$$
$$k \in ITM, r \in REG, n \in INC, \tag{9.2}$$

$$aitemsub_{krn} = aitem_{krn} - \sum_{l \in ITM} (VITEM_{lrn} \times aitem_{lrn}),$$
$$k \in ITM, r \in REG, n \in INC, \tag{9.3}$$

$$utility_{rn} = luxexp_{rn} - q\_p_{rn} - \sum_{k \in ITM} (DELTA_{krn} \times pitem_k),$$
$$r \in REG, n \in INC, \tag{9.4}$$

$$chou_{rn} = \frac{1}{VITEM\_k_{rn}} \sum_{k \in ITM} \left(VITEM_{krn} \times \{xitem_{krn} + pitem_k\} \right),$$
$$r \in REG, n \in INC. \tag{9.5}$$

Block 10 Demand equations for formation of items

$$xitem\_rn_k = \frac{1}{VITEM\_k_{rn}} \left(\sum_{r \in REG} \sum_{n \in INC} VITEM_{krn} \times xitem_{krn} \right),$$
$$k \in ITM, \qquad (10.1)$$

$$x3item\_s_{ki} = xitem\_rn_k, \quad k \in ITM, \ i \in COM, \qquad (10.2)$$

$$pitem_k = \frac{1}{COMITEM\_is_k} \left(\sum_{i \in COM} COMITEM\_s_{ki} \times p3item\_s_{ki} \right),$$
$$k \in ITM, \qquad (10.3)$$

$$x3item_{kis} = x3item\_s_{ki} - \sigma SRC3_i \ [p3_{is} - p3item\_s_{ki}],$$
$$k \in ITM, \ i \in COM, \ s \in SRC, \qquad (10.4)$$

$$p3item\_s_{ki} = \frac{1}{COMITEM\_s_{ki}} \left(\sum_{s \in SRC} COMITEM_{kis} \times p3_{is} \right),$$
$$k \in ITM, \ i \in COM, \qquad (10.5)$$

$$x3_{is} = \frac{1}{COMITEM\_k_{is}} \left(\sum_{k \in ITM} COMITEM_{kis} \times x3item_{kis} \right),$$
$$i \in COM, \ s \in SRC. \qquad (10.6)$$

Block 11 Equations for exports demand and government consumption

$$x4_i - feq_i = EXP\_ELAST_i \ [pe_i - fep_i], \quad i \in COM, \qquad (11.1)$$

$$pe_i + phi = \frac{1}{PUR4_i} \Big((V4BAS_i + V4TAX_i) \times (p0dom_i + t4_i)$$
$$+ \sum_{m \in MAR} V4MAR_{im}[p0dom_i + a4mar_{im}] \Big), \quad i \in COM, \qquad (11.2)$$

252

$$x5_{is} = \text{chour\_rn} + f5_{is} + f5\text{tot},$$

$$i \in \text{COM}, s \in \text{SRC}. \tag{11.3}$$

Block 12 Equations of demands for margin-goods

$$x1\text{mar}_{isjm} = x1_{isj} + a1\text{mar}_{isjm},$$

$$i \in \text{COM}, s \in \text{SRC}, j \in \text{IND}, m \in \text{MAR}, \tag{12.1}$$

$$x2\text{mar}_{isjm} = x2_{isj} + a2\text{mar}_{isjm},$$

$$i \in \text{COM}, s \in \text{SRC}, j \in \text{IND}, m \in \text{MAR}, \tag{12.2}$$

$$x3\text{mar}_{ism} = x3_{is} + a3\text{mar}_{ism},$$

$$i \in \text{COM}, s \in \text{SRC}, m \in \text{MAR}, \tag{12.3}$$

$$x4\text{mar}_{im} = x4_i + a4\text{mar}_{im},$$

$$i \in \text{COM}, m \in \text{MAR}, \tag{12.4}$$

$$x5\text{mar}_{ism} = x5_{is} + a5\text{mar}_{ism},$$

$$i \in \text{COM}, s \in \text{SRC}, m \in \text{MAR}. \tag{12.5}$$

Block 13 Equations for purchasers' prices

$$p0_{is} = p0\text{dom}_i, \quad s = \text{domestic}, \quad i \in \text{COM}, \tag{13.1}$$

$$p0_{is} = p0\text{imp}_i, \quad s = \text{imported}, \quad i \in \text{COM}, \tag{13.2}$$

$$p1_{isj} = \frac{1}{\text{PUR1}_{isj}} \Big([\text{V1BAS}_{isj} + \text{V1TAX}_{isj}] \times \{p0_{is} + t1_{isj}\}$$

$$+ \sum_{m \in \text{MAR}} (\text{V1MAR}_{isjm}\{p0\text{dom}_m + a1\text{mar}_{isjm}\}) \Big),$$

$$i \in \text{COM}, s \in \text{SRC}, j \in \text{IND}, \tag{13.3}$$

253

$$p2_{isj} = \frac{1}{PUR2_{isj}} \Big([\, V2BAS_{isj} + V2TAX_{isj}] \Big) \{ p0_{is} + t2_{isj} \}$$

$$+ \sum_{m \,\in\, MAR} (V2MAR_{isjm} \{ p0dom_m + a2mar_{isjm} \}) \Big)$$

$$i \in COM, s \in SRC, j \in IND, \tag{13.4}$$

$$p3_{is} = \frac{1}{PUR3_{is}} \Big([\, V3BAS_{is} + V3TAX_{is} \,] \times \{ p0_{is} + t3_{is} \}$$

$$+ \sum_{m \,\in\, MAR} V3MAR_{ism} \{ p0dom_m + a3mar_{ism} \} \Big),$$

$$i \in COM, s \in SRC, \tag{13.5}$$

$$p5_{is} = \frac{1}{PUR5_{is}} \Big([\, V5BAS_{is} + V5TAX_{is} \,] \times \{ p0_{is} + t5_{is} \}$$

$$+ \sum_{m \,\in\, MAR} V5MAR_{ism} \{ p0dom_m + a5mar_{ism} \} \Big),$$

$$i \in COM, s \in SRC, \tag{13.6}$$

$$p0imp_i = pm_i + phi + tm_i, \quad i \in COM. \tag{13.7}$$

Block 14 Equations for indirect taxes

$$t1_{isj} = t_{is} + t1\_isj + t0 + t1\_e_{ij},$$
$$i \in COM, s \in SRC, j \in IND, \tag{14.1}$$

$$t2_{isj} = t_{is} + t2\_isj + t0 + t2\_e_{ij}, \quad i \in COM, s \in SRC, j \in IND, \tag{14.2}$$

$$t3_{is} = t_{is} + t3\_is + t0 + t3\_e_i, \quad i \in COM, s \in SRC, \tag{14.3}$$

$$t5_{is} = t_{is} + t5\_is + t0, \quad i \in COM, s \in SRC. \tag{14.4}$$

254

Block 15 Tax rate equations for commodities with regulated prices

$$fp0pub_{as} = t_{as} + p0_{as}, \quad a \in ADM, \ s \in SRC, \qquad (15.1)$$

Block 16 Market clearing equations for commodities

$$x0dom_m = \frac{1}{SALES_j} \Big[\sum_{j \, \in \, IND} V1BAS_{mlj} \times x1_{mlj} + \sum_{j \, \in \, IND}$$

$$V2BAS_{mlj} \times x2_{mlj} \quad + V3BAS_{ml} \times x3_{ml} + V4BAS_m \times x4_m$$

$$+ \ V5BAS_{ml} \times x5_{ml} \quad + \sum_{i \, \in \, COM} \Big\{ V4MAR_{im} \times x4mar_{im}$$

$$+ \sum_{s \, \in SRC} V3MAR_{ism} \times x3mar_{ism} \ + \sum_{s \, \in SRC} V5MAR_{ism} \times x5mar_{ism}$$

$$+ \sum_{s \, \in SRC} \sum_{j \, \in IND} V1MAR_{ismj} \times x1mar_{ismj}$$

$$+ \sum_{s \, \in SRC} \sum_{j \, \in IND} V2MAR_{ismj} \times x2mar_{ismj} \Big\} \Big],$$

$$l=\text{domestic}, \ m \in MAR, \qquad (16.1)$$

$$x0dom_i = \frac{1}{SALES_j} \Big[\sum_{j \, \in IND} V1BAS_{ilj} \times x1_{ilj} + \sum_{j \, \in IND} V2BAS_{ilj} \times x2_{ilj}$$

$$+ \ V3BAS_{il} \times x3_{il} \quad + \ V4BAS_i \times x4_i + V5BAS_{il} \times x5_{il} \Big],$$

$$l=\text{domestic}, \ i \in NONMAR, \qquad (16.2)$$

$$x0imp_i = \frac{1}{V0IMP_j} \Big[\sum_{j \, \in IND} V1BAS_{ilj} \times x1_{ilj} + \sum_{j \, \in IND} V2BAS_{ilj} \times x2_{ilj}$$

$$+ \ V3BAS_{il} \times x3_{il} \quad + V5BAS_{il} \times x5_{il} \Big], \quad l=\text{imported}, \ i \in COM. \qquad (16.3)$$

Block 17 Demand equations for aggregate primary factors

$$\text{lambda}_{rp} = \frac{1}{\text{V1LAB\_j}_{rp}} \sum_{j \in \text{IND}} \text{V1LAB}_{rpj} \times \text{x1lab}_{rpj},$$

$$r \in \text{REG}, \ p \in \text{PRF}, \tag{17.1}$$

$$\text{x1cap\_j}_c = \frac{1}{\text{V1CAP\_j}_c} \sum_{j \in \text{IND}} \text{V1CAP}_{cj} \times \text{x1cap}_j, \quad c \in \text{CAP}, \tag{17.2}$$

$$\text{x1lnd\_j}_d = \frac{1}{\text{V1LND\_jd}} \sum_{j \in \text{IND}} \text{V1LND}_{dj} \times \text{x1lnd}_j, \quad d \in \text{LND}, \tag{17.3}$$

$$\text{lambda\_p}_r = \frac{1}{\text{V1LAB\_pjr}} \sum_{p \in \text{PRF}} \text{V1LAB\_rjp} \times \text{lambda}_{rp}, \quad r \in \text{REG}, \tag{17.4}$$

$$\text{lambda\_r}_p = \frac{1}{\text{V1LAB\_rjp}} \sum_{r \in \text{REG}} \text{V1LAB\_pjr} \times \text{lambda}_{rp}, \quad p \in \text{PRF}.$$

$$\tag{17.5}$$

Block 18 Equations of aggregate demand for final consumption, exports, imports and indirect-tax revenues

$$\text{exp} = \frac{1}{\text{PUR4\_i}} \sum_{i \in \text{COM}} \text{PUR4}_i \times [\text{pe}_i + \text{x4}_i], \tag{18.1}$$

$$\text{imp} = \frac{1}{\text{V0IMP\_i}} \sum_{i \in \text{COM}} \text{V0IMP}_i \times [\text{pm}_i + \text{x0imp}_i], \tag{18.2}$$

$$\text{expvol} = \text{exp} + \text{phi} - \text{xi4}, \tag{18.3}$$

$$\text{impvol} = \text{imp} + \text{phi} - \text{xim}, \tag{18.4}$$

$$\text{chour}_{rn} = \text{chou}_{rn} - \text{xiitem}_{rn}, \quad r \in \text{REG}, \ n \in \text{INC}, \tag{18.5}$$

$$\text{perconr}_{rn} = \text{chour}_{rn} - \text{q\_p}_{rn} - \text{hsize}_{rn}, \quad r \in \text{REG}, \ n \in \text{INC}, \tag{18.6}$$

$$\text{chour\_rn} = \frac{1}{\text{VITEM\_krn}} \sum_{r \in \text{REG}} \sum_{n \in \text{INC}} \text{VITEM\_k}_{rn} \times \text{chour}_{rn}, \quad (18.7)$$

$$\text{chou\_rn} = \frac{1}{\text{VITEM\_krn}} \sum_{r \in \text{REG}} \sum_{n \in \text{INC}} \text{VITEM\_k}_{rn} \times \text{chou}_{rn}, \quad (18.8)$$

$$\text{inv} = \text{invr} + \text{xi2}, \quad (18.9)$$

$$\text{invr} = \frac{1}{\text{PUR2\_isj}} \sum_{j \in \text{IND}} \text{PUR2\_is}_j \times y_j, \quad (18.10)$$

$$\text{oth} = \text{othr} + \text{xi5}, \quad (18.11)$$

$$\text{oth} = \frac{1}{\text{PUR5\_is}} \sum_{i \in \text{COM}} \sum_{s \in \text{SRC}} \text{PUR5}_{is} \times \text{x5}_{is}, \quad (18.12)$$

$$\text{labrev} = \frac{1}{\text{V1LAB\_rpj}} \sum_{j \in \text{IND}} \sum_{r \in \text{REG}} \sum_{p \in \text{PRF}} \text{V1LAB}_{rpj} \times (\text{p1lab}_{rpj}$$
$$+ \text{x1lab}_{rpj}), \quad (18.13)$$

$$\text{caprev} = \frac{1}{\text{V1CAP\_cj}} \sum_{j \in \text{IND}} \sum_{c \in \text{CAP}} \text{V1CAP}_{cj} \times (\text{p1cap}_j + \text{x1cap}_j),$$
$$(18.14)$$

$$\text{lndrev} = \frac{1}{\text{V1LND\_dj}} \sum_{j \in \text{IND}} \sum_{d \in \text{LND}} \text{V1LND}_{dj} \times (\text{p1lnd}_j + \text{x1lnd}_j),$$
$$(18.15)$$

$$\text{octrev} = \frac{1}{\text{V1OCT\_j}} \sum_{j \in \text{IND}} \text{V1OCT}_j \times (\text{p1loct}_j + \text{x1oct}_j), \quad (18.16)$$

$$t1rev\_isj = \frac{1}{V1TAX\_isj} \sum_{i \in COM} \sum_{s \in SRC} \sum_{j \in IND}$$

$$\left(V1TAX_{isj} \times \{ p0_{is} + x1_{isj} \} + [V1TAX_{isj} + V1BAS_{isj}] \times t1_{isj} \right), \quad (18.17)$$

$$t2rev\_isj = \frac{1}{V2TAX\_isj} \sum_{i \in COM} \sum_{s \in SRC} \sum_{j \in IND}$$

$$\left(V2TAX_{isj} \times \{ p0_{is} + x2_{isj} \} + [V2TAX_{isj} + V2BAS_{isj}] \times t2_{isj} \right), \quad (18.18)$$

$$t3rev\_is = \frac{1}{V3TAX\_is} \sum_{i \in COM} \sum_{s \in SRC} \left(V3TAX_{is} \times \{ p0_{is} + x3_{is} \} \right.$$

$$\left. + [V3TAX_{is} + V3BAS_{is}] \times t3_{is} \right), \quad (18.19)$$

$$t4rev\_i = \frac{1}{V4TAX\_i} \sum_{i \in COM} \left(V4TAX_i \times \{ p0dom_i + x4_i \} \right.$$

$$\left. + [V4TAX_i + V1BAS_i] \times t4_i \right), \quad (18.20)$$

$$t5rev\_is = \frac{1}{V5TAX\_is} \sum_{i \in COM} \sum_{s \in SRC} \left(V5TAX_{is} \times \{ p0_{is} + x5_{is} \} \right.$$

$$\left. + [V5TAX_{is} + V5BAS_{is}] \times t5_{is} \right), \quad (18.21)$$

$$tmrev\_i = \frac{1}{V0TAR\_i} \sum_{i \in COM} V0TAR_i \{ pm_i + phi + x0imp_i \}$$

$$+ \sum_{i \in COM} IMPORTS_i \times tm_i, \quad (18.22)$$

$$t0rev = \frac{1}{V0TAX} (V1TAX\_isj \times t1rev\_isj + V2TAX\_isj \times t2rev\_isj$$

$$+ V3TAX\_is \times t3rev\_is + V4TAX\_i \times t4rev\_i + V5TAX\text{-}i \times t5rev\_is$$

$$+ V0TAR \times tmrev\_i + V1OCT\_j \times octrev. \quad (18.23)$$

Block 19 Equations for GDP and the balance of trade

$$delB = (PUR4\_i \times exp - V0IMP\_i \times imp) \times 100.0 / 1000.0, \quad (19.1)$$

$$gdpexp = \frac{1}{GDPEXP} \Big(VITEM\_krn \times chou\_rn + PUR2\_isj \times inv + PUR5\_is \times oth$$

$$+ PUR4\_i \times (exp + phi) - V0IMP\_i \times (imp + phi) \Big), \quad (19.2)$$

$$gdpinc = \frac{1}{GDPINC} \Big(V1LND\_dj \times lndrev + V1CAP\_cj \times caprev$$

$$+ V1LAB\_rpj \times labrev + V0TAX \times t0rev \Big), \quad (19.3)$$

$$gdpreal = gdpexp - xigdp, \quad (19.4)$$

$$x1cap\_cj = \frac{1}{V1CAP\_cj} \sum_j V1CAP\_cj \times x1cap_j, \quad (19.5)$$

$$x1lab\_rpj = \frac{1}{V1LAB\_rpj} \sum_j V1LAB\_rpj \times x1lab\_rp_j, \quad (19.6)$$

$$x1lnd\_dj = \frac{1}{V1LND\_dj} \sum_j V1LND\_dj \times x1lnd_j. \quad (19.7)$$

Block 20 Equations for investment allocation

$$r0_j = QCOEF_j \times [p1cap_j - p2\_is_j], \quad j \in IND, \quad (20.1)$$

$$r0_j - rtot = BETA\_R_j \times [x1cap_j - x1cap\_cj] + fr0_j,$$
$$j \in IND, \quad (20.2)$$

$$x1cap_j = INV\_ELAST_j \times y_j + fx1cap_j, \quad j \in IND. \quad (20.3)$$

Block 21 Equations of price indices

$$xi2 = \frac{1}{PUR2\_isj} \sum_{i \in COM} \sum_{s \in SRC} \sum_{j \in IND} PUR2_{isj} \times p2_{isj}, \quad (21.1)$$

$$xi3 = \frac{1}{PUR3\_is} \sum_{i \in COM} \sum_{s \in SRC} PUR3_{is} \times p3_{is}, \qquad (21.2)$$

$$xiitem_{rn} = \frac{1}{VITEM\_k_{rn}} \sum_{k \in ITM} VITEM_{krn} \times pitem_k,$$
$$r \in REG, n \in INC, \qquad (21.3)$$

$$xi5 = \frac{1}{PUR5\_is} \sum_{i \in COM} \sum_{s \in SRC} PUR5_{is} \times p5cs_{is}, \qquad (21.4)$$

$$xi4 - phi = \frac{1}{PUR4\_i} \sum_{i \in COM} PUR4_i \times pe_i, \qquad (21.5)$$

$$xim - phi = \frac{1}{V0IMP\_i} \sum_{i \in COM} V0IMP_i \times pm_i, \qquad (21.6)$$

$$ximp0 = \frac{1}{IMPORTS\_i} \sum_{i \in COM} IMPORTS_i \times p0imp_i, \qquad (21.7)$$

$$xigdp = \frac{1}{GDPEXP} (PUR2\_isj \times xi2 + PUR3\_is \times xi3 + PUR4\_i \times xi4$$
$$+ PUR5\_is \times xi5 - V0IMP\_i \times xim), \qquad (21.8)$$

$$xifac = \frac{1}{V1PRM\_j} \sum_{j \in IND} V1PRM_j \times p1prm_j. \qquad (21.9)$$

Block 22 Equations for factor prices indices

$$p1lab\_j_{rp} = \frac{1}{V1LAB\_j} \sum_{j \in IND} V1LAB_{rpj} \times p1lab_{rpj},$$
$$r \in REG, p \in PRF, \qquad (22.1)$$

$$p1cap\_j_c = \frac{1}{V1CAP\_j_c} \sum_{j \in IND} V1CAP_{cj} \times p1cap_j, \qquad c \in CAP, \quad (22.2)$$

$$p1lnd\_j_d = \frac{1}{V1LND\_j_d} \sum_{j \in IND} V1LND_{dj} \times p1lnd_j, \qquad d \in LND. \quad (22.3)$$

Block 23 Rural-urban migration and real wages

$$q_{rnp} = q\_r_{np} + \sigma REG_p \, (p1labr\_j_{rnp} - p1labr\_rj_{np}),$$

$$r \in REG, n \in INC, p \in PRF, \tag{23.1}$$

$$p1labr\_rj_{np} = \frac{1}{VYHOULAB\_r_{np}} \sum_{r \in REG} VYHOULAB_{rnp} \times p1labr\_j_{rnp},$$

$$n \in INC, p \in PRF, \tag{23.2}$$

$$q\_P_{rn} = \frac{1}{VYHOULAB\_P_{rn}} \sum_{p \in PRF} (VYHOULAB_{rnp}) \times q_{rnp},$$

$$r \in REG, n \in INC, \tag{23.3}$$

$$p1labr\_j_{rnp} = p1lab\_j_{rp} + xiitem_{rn}, \quad r \in REG, n \in INC, p \in PRF, \tag{23.4}$$

$$p1lab_{rpj} = xi3 + f1wag\_j_{rp}, \quad r \in REG, p \in PRF, j \in IND. \tag{23.5}$$

Block 24 Equations determining factor supplies from institutions

$$ehoulab_{rnp} = ulab\_j_{rp} + q_{rnp}, \quad r \in REG, n \in INC, p \in PRF, \tag{24.1}$$

$$ehoucap_{rnc} = ucap\_j_c + q\_P_{rn}, \quad r \in REG, n \in INC, c \in CAP, \tag{24.2}$$

$$ehoulnd_{rnd} = ulnd\_j_d + q\_P_{rn}, \quad r \in REG, n \in INC, d \in LND, \tag{24.3}$$

$$ecorcap_{oc} = ucap\_j_c, \quad o \in COR, c \in CAP, \tag{24.4}$$

$$ecorlnd_{od} = ulnd\_j_d, \quad o \in COR, d \in LND, \tag{24.5}$$

$$egovcap_c = ucap\_j_c, \quad c \in CAP, \tag{24.6}$$

Block 25 Market clearing equations for primary factors

$$\text{lambda}_{rp} = \frac{1}{\text{VYHOULAB\_n}_{rp}} \sum_{n \in \text{INC}} \text{VYHOULAB}_{rnp} \times \text{ehoulab}_{rnp}$$

$$r \in \text{REG}, p \in \text{PRF}, \quad\quad\quad (25.1)$$

$$\text{x1cap\_j}_c = \frac{1}{\text{V1CAP\_j}_c} \Big(\sum_{r \in \text{REG}} \sum_{n \in \text{INC}} \text{VYHOUCAP}_{rnc} \times \text{ehoucap}_{rnc}$$

$$+ \sum_{o \in \text{COR}} \text{VYCORCAP}_{oc} \times \text{ecorcap}_{oc} + \text{YGOVCAP}_c \times \text{egovcap}_c$$

$$+ \text{VYROWCAP}_c \times \text{erowcap}_c \Big), \quad\quad c \in \text{CAP}, \quad (25.2)$$

$$\text{x1lnd\_j}_d = \frac{1}{\text{V1LND\_j}_d} \Big(\sum_{r \in \text{REG}} \sum_{n \in \text{INC}} \text{VYHOULND}_{rnd} \times \text{ehoulnd}_{rnd}$$

$$+ \sum_{o \in \text{COR}} \text{VYCORLND}_{od} \times \text{ecorlnd}_{od} + \text{VYGOVLND}_d \times \text{egovlnd}_d$$

$$+ \text{VYROWLND}_d \times \text{erowlnd}_d \Big), \quad d \in \text{LND}. \quad (25.3)$$

Block 26 Equations determining institutions' income by source

$$\text{yhoulab}_{rnp} = \text{ehoulab}_{rnp} + \text{p1lab\_j}_{rp}, \quad r \in \text{REG}, n \in \text{INC}, p \in \text{PRF},$$
$$(26.1)$$

$$\text{yhoucap}_{rnc} = \text{ehoucap}_{rnc} + \text{p1cap\_j}_c, \quad r \in \text{REG}, n \in \text{INC}, c \in \text{CAP}, \quad (26.2)$$

$$\text{yhoulnd}_{rnd} = \text{ehoulnd}_{rnd} + \text{p1lnd\_j}_d, \quad r \in \text{REG}, n \in \text{INC}, d \in \text{LND}, \quad (26.3)$$

$$\text{ycorcap}_{oc} = \text{ecorcap}_{oc} + \text{p1cap\_j}_c, \quad o \in \text{COR}, c \in \text{CAP}, \quad\quad (26.4)$$

$$\text{ycorlnd}_{od} = \text{ecorlnd}_{od} + \text{p1lnd\_j}_d, \quad o \in \text{COR}, d \in \text{LND}, \quad\quad (26.5)$$

$$\text{ygovcap}_c = \text{egovcap}_c + \text{p1cap\_j}_c, \quad c \in \text{CAP}, \quad\quad\quad (26.6)$$

$$\text{ygovlnd}_d = \text{egovlnd}_d + \text{p1lnd\_j}_d, \quad d \in \text{LND}, \quad\quad\quad (26.7)$$

$$yrowcap_c = erowcap_c + p1cap\_j_c, \quad c \in CAP, \tag{26.8}$$

$$yrowlnd_d = erowlnd_d + p1lnd\_j_d, \quad d \in LND, \tag{26.9}$$

$$yhouhou_{rnuv} = fyhouhou_{rnuv} + yh_h,$$
$$r \in REG, n \in INC, u \in REG, v \in INC, \tag{26.10}$$

$$yhoucor_{rno} = drate_o + ycor_o, \quad r \in REG, n \in INC, o \in COR, \tag{26.11}$$

$$yhougov_{rn} = fyhougov_{rn} + ygov, \quad r \in REG, n \in INC, \tag{26.12}$$

$$yhourow_{rn} = fyhourow_{rn} + phi, \quad r \in REG, n \in INC, \tag{26.13}$$

$$ygovhou_{rn} = tyhou_n + yhou_{rn}, \quad r \in REG, n \in INC, \tag{26.14}$$

$$ygovcor_o = tycor_o + ycor_o, \quad o \in COR. \tag{26.15}$$

Block 27 Equations determining institution's income

$$yhou_{rn} = \frac{1}{VYHOU_{rn}} \Big(\sum_{p \in PRF} VYHOULAB_{rnp} \times yhoulab_{rnp}$$
$$+ \sum_{c \in CAP} VYHOUCAP_{rnc} \times yhoucap_{rnc}$$
$$+ \sum_{d \in LND} VYHOULND_{rnd} \times yhoulnd_{rnd}$$
$$+ \sum_{o \in COR} VYHOUCOR_{rno} \times yhoucor_{rno}$$
$$+ \sum_{u \in REG} \sum_{v \in PINC} VYHOUHOU_{rnuv} \times yhouhou_{rnuv}$$
$$+ YHOUGOV_{rn} \times yhougov_{rn} + VYHOUROW_{rn} \times yhourow_{rn}\Big),$$

$$r \in REG, n \in INC, \tag{27.1}$$

$$ycor_o = \frac{1}{VYCOR_o} \Big(\sum_{c \in CAP} VYCORCAP_{oc} \times ycorcap_{oc}$$
$$+ \sum_{d \in LND} VYCORLND_{od} \times ycorlnd_{od}\Big), o \in COR, \tag{27.2}$$

263

$$ygov = \frac{1}{VYGOV} \Big(\sum_{c \in CAP} VYGOVCAP_c \times ygovcap_c$$

$$+ \sum_{d \in LND} VYGOVLND_d \times ygovlnd_d$$

$$+ \sum_{o \in COR} VYGOVCOR_o \times ygovcor_o$$

$$+ \sum_{r \in REG} \sum_{n \in INC} VYGOVHOU_{rn} \times ygovhou_{rn}$$

$$+ VYGOVTAX \times t0rev + V1OCT\_j \times octrev \Big). \qquad (27.3)$$

Block 28 Equations of household expenditure and disposable income

$$yhoud_{rn} = \frac{1}{VYHOUD_{rn}} \Big(VYHOU_{rn} \times yhou_{rn} - VYGOVHOU_{rn} \times ygovhou_{rn},$$

$$- \sum_{u \in REG} \sum_{v \in INC} VYHOUHOU_{rnuv} \times yhou_{rnuv} \Big), \quad r \in REG, \ n \in INC, \quad (28.1)$$

$$yhoudr_{rn} = yhoud_{rn} - xiitem_{rn}, \quad r \in REG, \ n \in INC, \qquad (28.2)$$

$$chou_{rn} = yhoud_{rn} + apc_{rn}, \quad r \in REG, \ n \in INC. \qquad (28.3)$$

Block 29 Equations for GNP and balance of payments

$$gnpexp = \frac{1}{GNPEXP} \Big(VITEM\_krn \times chou\_rn + PUR5\_is \times oth +$$

$$VSAV \times sav \Big), \qquad (29.1)$$

$$sav = \frac{1}{VSAV} \Big(\sum_{o \in COR} VSAVCOR_o \times savcor_o$$

$$+ VSAVGOV \times savgov + \sum_{r \in REG} \sum_{n \in INC} VSAVHOU_{rn} \times savhou_{rn} \Big),$$

$$(29.2)$$

$$gnpinc = \frac{1}{GNPINC} \Big(GDPIN \times gdpinc + VNFI \times nfi \Big), \qquad (29.3)$$

$$nfi = \frac{1}{VNFI} \left(\sum_{r \in REG} \sum_{n \in INC} VYHOUROW_{rn} \times yhourow_{rn} \right.$$

$$\left. - \sum_{c \in CAP} VYROWCAP_c \times yrowcap_c - \sum_{d \in LND} VYROWLND_d \times yrowlnd_d \right),$$

$$(29.4)$$

$$1000 \times 100 \times delLON = PUR2\_isj \times inv - VSAV \times sav. \qquad (29.5)$$

Block 30 Equations of domestic savings by institutions

$$yhoud_{rn} = \frac{1}{VHOUD_{rn}} \left(VSAVHOU_{rn} \times savhou_{rn} + VITEM\_k_{rn} \times chou_{rn} \right),$$

$$r \in REG, n \in INC, \qquad (30.1)$$

$$ygov = \frac{1}{VYGOV} \left(VSAVGOV \times savgov + PUR5\_is \times oth \right.$$

$$\left. + VYHOUGOVrn \times yhougovrn \right), \qquad (30.2)$$

$$ycor_o = \frac{1}{VYCOR_o} \left(VSAVCOR_o \times savcor_o + VYGOVCOR_o \times ygovcor_o \right.$$

$$\left. + \sum_{r \in REG} \sum_{n \in INC} SYHOUCOR_{rno} \times yhoucor_{rno} \right), \quad o \in COR. \quad (30.3)$$

Appendix B   List of variables

267

Variable name	Set/sets name	Description of variables
$a2_{isj}$	COM × SRC × IND	Input-augmenting technical change for commodity i from source s for capital formation in industry j.
$a2\_s_{ij}$	COM × IND	Input-augmenting technical change for commodity i for capital formation in industry j.
$a2\_is_j$	IND	All-input-augmenting technical change for capital formation in industry j.
$a2mar_{isjm}$	COM × SRC × IND × MAR	Margin-good-m-augmenting technical change for commodity-i supply to industry j, from source s, for capital formation.
$a3mar_{ism}$	COM × SRC × MAR	Margin-good-m-augmenting technical change for commodity-i supply, from source s, for item formation.
$a4mar_{im}$	COM × MAR	Margin-good-m-augmenting technical change for commodity-i supply for exports.
$a5mar_{ism}$	COM× SRC × MAR	Margin-good-m-augmenting technical change for commodity-i supply for government consumption.
$aitem_{krn}$	ITM × REG × INC	Change in the taste of household for item k consumption by household from region r and income-group n.
$aitemlux_{krn}$	ITM × REG × INC	Change in the taste of household for consumption of item k, for luxury, by region and household type.
$aitemsub_{krn}$	ITM × REG × INC	Change in the taste of household in item k, for subsistence consumption, by region and household type.
apc_{rn}	REG × INC	Average propensity to consume of household type n in region r.
$atot_j$	IND	All-input-augmenting technical change in current production.
caprev	1	Aggregate payments to capital.
$chou_{rn}$	REG × INC	Consumption of household by region and household type.
$chou\_rn$	1	Aggregate household consumption.
$chour_{rn}$	REG × INC	Real consumption of household by region and household type.
$chour\_rn$	1	Real aggregate household consumption.
delB	1	Trade balance in billion Rs.
delLON	1	Balance of payments in billion Rs.
$drate_o$	COR	Dividend rate of corporations.

... *continued*

Table B1 continued

Variable name	Set/sets name	Description of variables
$ecorcap_{oc}$	COR × CAP	Corporations' endowment of capital by type.
$ecorlnd_{od}$	COR × LND	Corporations' endowment of land by type.
$egovcap_c$	CAP	Government's endowment of capital by type.
$egovlnd_d$	LND	Government's endowment of land by type.
$ehoucap_{rnc}$	REG × INC × CAP	Households' endowment of capital by type.
$ehoulab_{rnp}$	REG × INC × PRF	Households' endowment of labour by professions.
$ehoulnd_{rnd}$	REG × INC × LND	Households' endowment of land by type.
$erowcap_c$	CAP	Capital endowment of ROW in Pakistan.
$erowlnd_d$	LND	Land endowment of ROW in Pakistan.
exp	1	Exports earnings.
$expvol$	1	Exports volumes index.
$f1oct_j$	IND	Shift in 'other costs' input in current production.
$f1wag\_j_{rp}$	REG × PRF	Shift in real wages of labour from region and of profession p.
$f5_{is}$	COM × SRC	Shift in commodity-i consumption by government from source s.
$f5tot$	1	Shift in commodity-i consumption by government from both the sources.
fep_i	COM	Shift in foreign currency ,Freight on Board (FOB), price of exports.
feq_i	COM	Shift in volume of commodity-i exports.
$fhouhou_{rnuv}$	REG × INC × REG×INC	Shift in inter-household transfers.
$fp0pub_a$	ADM × SRC	Shift in the power of tax rate on commodities with regulated prices.
$fr0_j$	IND	Shift in rate of returns on fixed investment in industry j.
$fx1cap_j$	IND	Shift in investment (unit of capital) in industry j.
$fyhougov_{rn}$	REG × INC	Shift in income of households from government.
$fyhourow_{rn}$	REG × INC	Shift in income of households from ROW.
$gdpexp$	1	Gross domestic product; expenditure side.
$gdpinc$	1	Gross domestic product; income side.
$gdpreal$	1	Real Gross domestic product; expenditure side.
$gnpexp$	1	Gross national product; expenditure side.

... *continued*

Table B1 continued

Variable name	Set/sets name	Description of variables
gnpinc	1	Gross national product; income side.
$hsize_{rn}$	REG × INC	Number of persons per households.
imp	1	Imports bill.
impvol	1	Import volume index.
inv	1	Aggregate investments.
invr	1	Real aggregate investments.
labrev	1	Aggregate labour wage bill.
$lambda_{rp}$	REG × PRF	Aggregate employment by profession and region.
$lambda\_p_r$	REG	Aggregate employment by region.
$lambda\_r_p$	PRF	Aggregate employment by profession.
lndrev	1	Aggregate rental value of land.
$luxexp_{rn}$	REG × INC	Household luxury expenditure by region and household type.
nfi	1	Net-factor payments from ROW.
octrev	1	Aggregate 'other costs' in current production.
oth	1	Aggregate government consumption.
othr	1	Real aggregate government consumption.
$p0dom_i$	COM	Basic price (production costs) of domestic good i.
$p0imp_i$	COM	Basic price (supply costs) of imported good i.
$p0ind_j$	IND	Weighted-average price of outputs of industry j in current production.
$p0_{is}$	COM × SRC	Basic price of commodity by source.
$p1cap_j$	CAP × IND	Rental price of capital by type in current production by industry.
$p1cap\_j_c$	CAP	Rental price indice of capital by type.
$p1lab_{rpj}$	REG × PRF × IND	Wages of labour by region, profession and industry.
$p1lab\_j_{rp}$	REG × PRF	Wage-rate indices by region and profession.
$p1lab\_p_{rj}$	REG × IND	Average wage rates by region and industry.
$p1lab\_rp_j$	IND	Average wage rates by industry.
$p1labr\_j_{r_{np}}$	REG × INC × PRF	Real-wage-rate indices by profession for households by region and household type.
$p1lnd\_j_d$	LND	Rental price indice of land by type.
$p1lnd_j$	IND	Rental-price of land by type in current production by industry.
$p1oct_j$	IND	Basic price of 'other costs'.
$p1prm_j$	IND	Average primary factor cost by industry.

... continued

Variable name	Set/sets name	Description of variables
$p1_{isj}$	COM × SRC × IND	Purchaser price of commodity i, by source s, for current production.
$p1\_s_{ij}$	COM × IND	Purchaser price of commodity i, for current production.
$p2_{isj}$	COM × SRC × IND	Purchaser price of commodity i, by source s, for capital formation.
$p2\_s_{ij}$	COM × IND	Purchaser price of commodity i, for capital formation.
$p2\_is_j$	IND	Purchaser price of investment good i for industry j.
$p3_{is}$	COM × SRC	Purchaser price of commodity i, by source s, for item formation.
$p5_{is}$	COM × SRC	Purchaser price of commodity i, by source s, for government consumption.
$p3item\_s_{ki}$	ITM × COM	Purchaser price of commodity i for item k formation.
pe_i	COM	Foreign currency (FOB) price of exports by commodities.
$perconr_{rn}$	REG × INC	Real *per capita* consumption.
phi	1	Exchange rate; Rs. per US dollar.
$pitem_k$	ITM	Purchaser price of item k.
pm_i	COM	Foreign currency (CIF) price of imports.
q_{rnp}	REG × INC × PRF	Number of households by region and household type with profession p.
q_p_{rn}	REG × INC	Number of households by region and household type.
q_r_{np}	INC × PRF	Number of households by household types and profession.
$r0_j$	IND	Rate of return on fixed investment by industry j.
rtot	1	Average rate-of-return on fixed investment.
sav	1	Aggregate savings of domestic institutions.
$savcor_o$	COR	Corporations' savings.
savgov	1	Government savings.
$savhou_{rn}$	REG × INC	Savings of households by region and household types.
t0	1	Power of sales tax on all commodities and users.
t_{is}	COM × SRC	Power of sales tax on commodity i, from source s.
$t1_{isj}$	COM × SRC × IND	Power of sales tax on commodity i, from source s, for current production in industry j.

... *continued*

Table B1 continued

Variable name	Set/sets name	Description of variables
$t1\_i_{sj}$	1	Power of sales tax on all commodities for current production.
$t1\_e_{ij}$	COM × IND	Power of sales tax on commodity i, for current production in industry j.
$t2_{isj}$	COM × SRC × IND	Power of sales tax on commodity i, from source s, for capital formation.
$t2\_i_{sj}$	1	Power of sales tax on all commodities, for capital formation.
$t2\_e_{ij}$	COM × IND	Power of sales tax on commodity i, for capital formation in industry j.
$t3_{is}$	COM × SRC	Power of sales tax on commodity i from source s, for item formation.
$t3\_i_s$	1	Power of sales tax on all commodities, for item formation.
$t3\_e_i$	COM	Power of sales tax on commodity i for item formation in specific.
$t4_i$	COM	Power of sales tax on commodity i for exports.
$t5_{is}$	COM × SRC	Power of sales tax on commodity i, from source s, for government consumption.
$t5\_i_s$	1	Power of sales tax on commodity i, for governmen consumption.
tm_i	COM	Power of import tax on commodity i.
t0rev	1	Total indirect tax revenues.
$t1rev\_i_{sj}$	1	Total indirect tax revenues from current production production.
$t2rev\_i_{sj}$	1	Total indirect tax revenues from capital formation.
$t3rev\_i_s$	1	Total indirect tax revenues from item formation.
$t4rev\_i$	1	Total indirect tax revenues from exports.
$t5rev\_i_s$	1	Total indirect tax revenues from government.
$tmrev\_i$	1	Total indirect import-tax revenues.
$tycor_o$	COR	Income tax rates for corporations.
$tyhou_n$	INC	Income tax rates for households.
$ucap\_j_c$	CAP	Unemployed capital by type.
$ulab\_j_{rp}$	REG × PRF	Unemployed labour by profession and region.
$ulnd\_j_d$	LND	Unemployed land by type.
$utility_{rn}$	REG × INC	Utility indices of households by region and household type.

… *continued*

Variable name	Set/sets name	Description of variables
$x0_{ij}$	COM × IND	Output of commodity i, in industry j.
$x0dom_i$	COM	Total demand for domestic commodity i.
$x0imp_i$	COM	Total demand for imported commodity i.
$x1_{isj}$	COM × SRC × IND	Demand for commodity i, from source s, in industry j for current production.
$x1\_s_{ij}$	IND	Demand for commodity i, on aggregate, in industry j for current production.
$x1cap_j$	IND	Demand for capital by type in industry j, for current production.
$x1cap\_j_c$	CAP	Total capital demand by type for current production.
$x1cap\_cj$	1	Total capital demand for current production.
$x1lab_{rpj}$	REG × PRF × IND	Demand for labour by profession and region in industry j, for current production.
$x1lab\_rpj$	IND	Demand for labour, on aggregate, in industry j for current production.
$x1lab\_rpj$	1	Total labour demand.
$x1lnd_j$	IND	Demand for land by type in industry j for current production.
$x1lnd\_j_d$	LND	Total land demand by type for current production.
$x1lnd\_dj$	1	Total land demand for current production.
$x1mar_{isjm}$	COM × SRC × IND × MAR	Demand for margin-good-m, for intermediate input good i, supplied from source s to industry j.
$x1oct_j$	IND	Units of 'other costs' input in industry j for current production.
$x1prm_j$	IND	Indices of primary-factor demand, weighted by value-added, by industry for current production.
$x2_{isj}$	COM × SRC × IND	Demand for commodity i, from source s, in industry j for capital formation.
$x2\_s_{ij}$	COM× IND	Demand for commodity i, on aggregate, in industry j for capital formation.
$x2mar_{isjm}$	COM × SRC × IND × MAR	Demand for margin-good-m, for intermediate good i, supplied from source s, to industry j for capital formation.
$x3_{is}$	COM × SRC	Demand for commodity i, from source s, for item formation.

... *continued*

Variable name	Set/sets name	Description of variables
$x3mar_{ism?}$	COM × SRC × MAR	Demand for margin-good-m, for commodity i, supplied from source s for item formation.
$x3item_{kis}$	ITM × COM × SRC	Demand for commodity i, from source s, for item formation.
$x3item\_s_{ki}$	ITM × COM	Demand for commodity i, on aggregate ,for item k formation.
$x4_i$	COM	Export-demand for commodity i.
$x4mar_{im}$	COM × MAR	Demand for margin-good-m, to export commodity i.
$x5_{is}$	COM× SRC	Demand for commodity i, from source s, for government consumption.
$x5mar_{ism}$	COM × SRC × MAR	Demand for margin-good-m, for commodity i, from source s for government consumption.
$xi2$	1	Capital goods price index.
$xi3$	1	Consumer goods price index.
$xi4$	1	Export goods price index.
$xi5$	1	Government-consumption goods price index for
$xifac$	1	Factor price index.
$xigdp$	1	GDP deflator.
$xiitem_{rn}$	REG × INC	CPI by household type; by region and household type.
xim	1	Import price (CIF) index.
$ximp0$	1	Duty-paid import price index.
$xitem_{krn}$	ITM × REG × INC	Demand for item k by household type; by region and household type.
$xitem\_rn_k$	ITM	Aggregate household demand for item k.
y_j	IND	Investments in industry j.
$ycor_o$	COR	Income of Corporations .
$ycorcap_{oc}$	COR × CAP	Corporations' income from rental value of capital type c.
$ycorlnd_{od}$	COR × LND	Corporations' income from rental value of land type d.
$ygov$	1	Government income.
$ygovcap_c$	CAP	Government income from rental value of capital.
$ygovcor_o$	COR	Government income from income tax paid by corporations.
$ygovhou_{rn}$	REG × INC	Government income from income tax paid by households.

... continued

Table B1 continued

Variable name	Set/sets name	Description of variables
ygovlnd$_d$	LND	Government income from rental value of land type d.
yhou$_{rn}$	REG × INC	Income of household from region r and in household type n.
yhoucap$_{rnc}$	REG × INC × CAP	Household income from rental value of capital type c.
yhoucor$_{rno}$	REG × INC × COR	Income from dividend paid by corporations to households from region r in household type n.
yhoud$_{rn}$	REG × INC	Disposable income of households from region r in household type n.
yhoudr$_{rn}$	REG × INC	Real disposable income of households.
yhougov$_{rn}$	REG × INC	Household income from transfer payments (from government).
yhouhou$_{rnuv}$	REG × INC × REG × INC	Household income from transfer payments (from other households).
yhoulab$_{rnp}$	REG × INC × PRF	Household income from wage earnings by profession.
yhoulnd$_{rnd}$	REG × INC × LND	Household income from rental value of land.
yhourow$_{rn}$	REG × INC	Household income, from transfer payments (from ROW).
yrowcap$_c$	CAP	Income of ROW from rental value of capital employed in Pakistan.
yrowlnd$_d$	LND	Income of ROW from rental value of land in Pakistan.
z$_j$	IND	Output or activity index of industry j.

Appendix C   List of industries, commodities and items

Table C1
List of industries and commodities

No.	Industry name	No.	Commodity name
	Agriculture Sector		
1	Wheat small-farms	1	Wheat (Small-farms)
2	Wheat large-farms	2	Wheat (Large-farms)
3	Rice small-farms	3	Rice (Small-farms)
4	Rice large-farms	4	Rice (Large-farms)
5	Cotton small-farms	5	Cotton (Small-farms)
6	Cotton large-farms	6	Cotton (Large-farms)
7	Sugarcane small-farms	7	Sugarcane (Small-farms)
8	Sugarcane large-farms	8	Sugarcane (Large-farms)
9	Tobacco	9	Tobacco
10	Oil seed and other cotton seeds	10	Oil seed and other cotton seeds
11	Pulses	11	Pulses
12	Other crops	12	Other crops
13	Livestock	13	Livestock
14	Fishing	14	Fishing
15	Forestry	15	Forestry
	Oil and gas Sector		
16	Oil and gas	16	Oil
		17	Gas
	Large-scale Manufacturing Sector		
17	Coal	18	Coal
18	Other minerals	19	Other minerals
19	Grain milling	20	Grain milling

....*continued*

277

Table C1 continued

No.	Industry name	No.	Commodity name
20	Rice milling	21	Rice milling
21	Sugar refining	22	Sugar refining
22	Edible oils	23	Edible oils
23	Tea blending	24	Tea blending
24	Fish and fish preparation	25	Fish and Fish preparation
25	Confectionery and bakery	26	Confectionery and bakery
26	Other food industries	27	Other food industries
27	Beverages	28	Beverages
28	Cigarettes and other tobacco	29	Cigarettes and other tobacco
29	Cotton yarn	30	Cotton yarn
30	Cotton fabrics	31	Cotton fabrics
31	Silk and synthetic textiles	32	Silk and synthetic textiles
32	Woollen textile	32	Woollen textile
33	Hosiery	34	Hosiery
34	Thread ball making	35	Thread ball making
35	Carpets and rugs	36	Carpets and rugs
36	Other textiles	37	Other textiles
37	Footwear other than rubbers	38	Footwear other than rubbers
38	Wearing apparel	39	Wearing apparel
39	Wood, cork and furniture	40	Wood
40	Paper, paper board and products	41	Paper
41	Printing an publishing	42	Printing an publishing
42	Leather and products	43	Leather and products
43	Rubbers footwear	44	Rubbers footwear
44	Other rubber products	45	Other rubber products
45	Pharmaceutical and medicinal	46	Pharmaceutical and medicinal
47	Perfumes and cosmetics	48	Perfumes and cosmetics
48	Paints and varnishes	49	Paints and varnishes
49	Soap and detergents	50	Soap and detergents
50	Matches	51	Matches
51	Other chemicals	52	Other chemicals
52	Plastic products	53	Plastic products
55	Glass and products	61	Glass and products
56	Other non-metallic minerals	62	Other non-metallic minerals
57	Basic metal	63	Basic metal
58	Metal products	64	Metal products
59	Agricultural machinery	65	Agricultural machinery
60	Other non-electrical machinery	66	Other non-electrical machinery
61	Electric machinery	67	Electric machinery

... *continued*

No.	Industry name	No.	Commodity name
62	Bicycles	68	Bicycles
63	Auto assembly and parts	69	Auto assembly and parts
64	Ship building	70	Ship building
65	Cotton ginning	71	Cotton ginning
66	Office equipment	72	Office equipment
67	Sports goods	73	Sports goods
68	Surgical instruments	74	Surgical instruments
69	Other large scale manufacturing	75	Other large scale manufacturing
	Refinery Sector		
53	Refinery (oil refining)	54	Kerosene
		55	High speed diesel
		56	Light speed diesel
		57	Gasoline
		58	Furnace oil
		59	Other petroleum products
	Fertiliser Sector		
46	Fertiliser	47	Fertiliser
	Cement Sector		
54	Cement	60	Cements
	Small-scale Manufacturing Sector		
70	Small-Scale grain milling	76	Small-Scale grain milling
71	Small-Scale rice husking	77	Small-Scale rice husking
72	Small-Scale gur and raw sugar	78	Small-Scale gur and raw sugar
73	Small-Scale edible oils	79	Small-Scale edible oils
74	Small-Scale other food industries	80	Small-Scale other food industries
75	Small-Scale beverages	81	Small-Scale beverages
76	Small-Scale tobacco	82	Small-Scale tobacco
77	Small-Scale cotton textile	83	Small-Scale cotton textile
78	Small-Scale silk and art-silk textiles	84	Small-Scale silk and art-silk textiles
79	Small-Scale carpets	85	Small-Scale carpets
80	Small-Scale other textiles	86	Small-Scale other textiles
81	Small-Scale shoe making	87	Small-Scale shoe making
82	Small-Scale wood	88	Small-Scale wood
83	Small-Scale furniture,	89	Small-Scale furniture
84	Small-Scale steel furniture	90	Small-Scale steel furniture
85	Small-Scale printing and publishing	91	Small-Scale printing and publishing
86	Small-Scale leather products	92	Small-Scale leather products

... *continued*

Table C1 continued

No.	Industry name	No.	Commodity name
87	Small-Scale rubbers goods	93	Small-Scale rubbers goods
88	Small-Scale chemical	94	Small-Scale chemical
89	Small-Scale plastic products	95	Small-Scale plastic products
90	Small-Scale non-metallic minerals products	96	Small-Scale non-metallic minerals products
91	Small-Scale iron and steel remoulding	97	Small-Scale iron and steel remoulding
92	Small-Scale metal products	98	Small-Scale metal products
93	Small-Scale agricultural machinery	99	Small-Scale agricultural machinery
94	Small-Scale non-electrical machinery	100	Small-Scale non-electrical machinery
95	Small-Scale electric machinery	101	Small-Scale electric machinery
96	Small-Scale transport equipment	102	Small-Scale transport equipment
97	Small-Scale sports goods	103	Small-Scale sports goods
98	Small-Scale surgical instruments	104	Small-Scale surgical instruments
99	Other small scale manufacturing	105	Other small scale manufacturing
	Construction Sector		
100	Low cost residential building	106	Low-cost residential building
101	Luxurious building	107	Luxurious building
102	Rural building	108	Rural building
103	Factory building	109	Factory building
104	Public building	110	Public building
105	Roads	111	Roads
106	Infrastructures	112	Infrastructures
107	Ownership of dwelling	113	Ownership of dwelling
	Services Sector		
113	Whole sale and retail trade	116	Whole sale and retail trade
114	Road transportation	117	Road transportation
115	Rail transportation	118	Rail transportation
116	Air transportation	119	Air transportation
117	Water transportation	120	Water transportation
118	Television	121	Television
119	Radio	122	Radio
120	Telephone	123	Telephone
121	Banking	124	Banking
122	Government services	125	Government services
123	Services not elsewhere specified	126	Services not elsewhere specified

... *continued*

Table C1 continued

No.	Industry name	No.	Commodity name
	Natural Gas Sector		
112	Natural gas (gas refining)	115	Natural gas (gas refining)
	Electricity Sector		
108	Hydro power	114	Electricity
109	Combined cycle	"	"
110	Steam plants	"	"
111	Gas turbines	"	"
	Non-Competing Imports Industries[a]		
124	Other transport	127	Other transport
125	Air transport	128	Air transport
126	Insurance	129	Insurance
127	Government	130	Government
128	Other services	131	Other services

a   These industries have no inputs and output but these commodities are imported

281

Table C2
List of item names

Item no.	Item names	Item no.	Item name
1	Wheat	37	Water and other charges
2	Rice	38	Other house expenses
3	Other cereals	39	Furniture and fixtures
4	Pulses	40	Kitchen equipment
5	Milk products	41	Crockery and cutlery
6	Edible oils	42	Other household effects
7	Meat	43	Personal care
8	Fish	44	Medical care
9	Fruits	45	Education
10	Vegetables	46	Recreation durable
11	Spices	47	Recreation non-durable
12	Mill sugar	48	Transport equipment
13	Gur and other sugar	49	Transport non-durable
14	Tea	50	Telephone and telegraph
15	Cigarettes	51	Laundry
16	Cigars	52	Domestic help
17	Pan and accessories	53	All other items
18	Other tobacco		
19	Miscellaneous food		
20	Cloth		
21	Garments		
22	Household textiles		
23	Footwear		
24	Personal effects		
25	Dung-cake		
26	Kerosene		
27	Charcoal		
28	Coal		
29	Natural gas		
30	Electricity		
31	Matches		
32	Other fuels		
33	Rent		
34	Rent free accommodation		
35	Owner occupied house		
36	Repair and improvement		

Appendix D   Conversion formulae[1]

Using first principles, a levels equation, for example:

$$Y = X2 + Z,$$

is turned into percentage-change form by first taking total differentials:

$$dY = 2XdX + dZ.$$

Percentage changes x, y, and z are defined *via*:

$$y = 100\frac{dY}{Y} \quad \text{or} \quad dY = \frac{Yy}{100}, \quad \text{similarly} \quad dX = \frac{Xx}{100} \quad \text{and} \quad dZ = \frac{Zz}{100}.$$

Thus our sample equation becomes:

$$\frac{Yy}{100} = 2X\frac{Xx}{100} + \frac{Zz}{100}, \quad \text{or} \quad Yy = 2X^2x + Zz.$$

In practice such formal derivations are often unnecessary. Most percentage-change equations follow standard patterns which the modeller soon recognises. Some of these are shown in Table D1.

The third alternative form for example 10 shows how ordinary and percentage changes may be mixed. It is based on the identity $Yy \equiv 100\Delta Y$. See also example 5.

Variables can only be added or subtracted (as in examples 9 and 12) where they share the same units. In adding quantities, we can normally identify a common price (often the basic price). By multiplying through additive expressions by a common price, we can express the coefficients of percentage-change equations as functions of flows, rather than quantities, thus obviating the need to define physical units (compare examples 9 and 11).

283

Examples of percentage-change forms

Example	Original or levels form	Percentage-change form
1	$Y = 4$	$y = 0$
2	$Y = X$	$y = x$
3	$Y = 3X$	$y = x$
4	$Y = XZ$	$y = x + z$
5	$Y = X/Z$	$y = x - z$ *or*
		$100(Z)\Delta Y = Xx - Xz$
6	$X_1 = M/4P_1$	$x_1 = m - p_1$
7	$Y = X^3$	$y = 3x$
8	$Y = X^\alpha$	$y = \alpha x$ (α assumed constant)
9	$Y = X + Z$	$Yy = Xx + Zz$ *or*
		$y = S_x x + S_z z$
		where $S_x = X/Y$, etc.
10	$Y = X - Z$	$Yy = Xx - Zz$ *or*
		$y = S_x x - S_z z$
		where $S_x = X/Y$, etc, *or*
		$100(\Delta Y) = Xx - Zz$
11	$PY = PX + PZ$	$PYy = PXx + PZz$ *or*
		$y = S_x x + S_z z$
		where $S_x = PX/PY$, etc.
12	$Z = \Sigma X_i$	$Zz = \Sigma X_i x_i$
13	$XP = \Sigma X_i P_i$	$XP(x+p) = \Sigma X_i P_i (x_i + p_i)$

Note

[1]   This appendix has been taken from Horridge *et al.* (1993).

Appendix E Solution of the cost minimisation problem[1]

Problem: Choose inputs X_i ($i = 1$ to N), to minimise the cost $\sum_i P_i X_i$ of producing given output Z, subject to the CES production function:

$$Z = \left(\sum_i \delta_i X_i^{-\rho}\right)^{-1/\rho}. \tag{E1}$$

The associated first order conditions are:

$$P_k = \Lambda \frac{Z}{-X_k} = \Lambda \delta_k X_k^{-(1+\rho)} \left(\sum_i \delta_i X_i^{-\rho}\right)^{-(1+\rho)/\rho}. \tag{E2}$$

Hence:

$$\frac{P_k}{P_i} = \frac{\delta_k}{\delta_i}\left(\frac{X_i}{X_k}\right)^{1+\rho}, \text{or} \tag{E3}$$

$$X_i^{-\rho} = \left(\frac{\delta_i P_k}{\delta_k P_i}\right)^{-\rho/(\rho+1)} X_k^{-\rho}. \tag{E4}$$

Substituting the above expression back into the production function we obtain:

$$Z = X_k \left(\sum_i \delta_i \left[\frac{\delta_k P_i}{\delta_i P_k}\right]^{\rho/(\rho+1)}\right)^{-1/\rho}. \tag{E5}$$

This gives the input demand functions:

$$X_k = z\left(\sum_i \delta_i \left[\frac{\delta_k P_i}{\delta_i P_k}\right]^{\rho/(\rho+1)}\right)^{1/\rho},$$

(E6)

or:

$$X_k = Z\,\delta_k^{1/(\rho+1)}\left[\frac{P_k}{P_{ave}}\right]^{-1/(\rho+1)},$$

(E7)

where:

$$P_{ave} = \left(\sum_i \delta_i^{1/(\rho+1)} P_i^{\rho/(\rho+1)}\right)^{-(\rho+1)/\rho}.$$

(E8)

Transforming to percentage changes (see Appendix D) we get:

$$x_k = z - \sigma\left(p_k - p_{ave}\right),$$

(E9)

and:

$$p_{ave} = \sum_i S_i p_i,$$

(E10)

where:

$$\sigma = \frac{1}{\rho+1} \quad \text{and} \quad S_i = \delta_i^{1/(\rho+1)} P_i^{\rho/(\rho+1)} \Big/ \sum_k \delta_k^{1/(\rho+1)} P_k^{\rho/(\rho+1)}.$$

(E11)

Multiplying both sides of (E7) by P_k we get:

$$P_k X_k = Z\,\delta_k^{1/(\rho+1)} P_k^{\rho/(\rho+1)} P_{ave}^{1/(\rho+1)}.$$

(E12)

Hence:

$$\frac{P_k X_k}{\sum_i P_i X_i} = \delta_k^{1/(\rho+1)} P_k^{\rho/(\rho+1)} \Big/ \sum_i \delta_i^{1/(\rho+1)} P_i^{\rho/(\rho+1)} = S_i,$$

(E13)

i.e, the S_i of (E11) turn out to be cost shares.

With technical change terms, we must choose inputs X_i so as to:

minimise $\sum_i P_i X_i$ subject to: $Z = \left(\sum_i \delta_i \left[\frac{X_i}{A_i}\right]^{-\rho}\right)^{-1/\rho}.$

(E14)

Setting $\tilde{X}_i = \frac{X_i}{A_i}$ and $\tilde{P}_i = P_i A_i$ we get:

(E15)

minimise $\sum_i \tilde{P}_i \tilde{X}_i$ subject to: $Z = \left(\sum_i \delta_i \tilde{X}_i^{-\rho}\right)^{-1/\rho}$, (E16)

which has the same form as problem (E1). Hence the percentage-change form of the demand equations is:

$$\tilde{x}_k = z - \sigma\left(\tilde{p}_k - \tilde{p}_{ave}\right), \qquad (E17)$$

and:

$$\tilde{p}_{ave} = \sum_i S_i \tilde{p}_i. \qquad (E18)$$

But from (E15), $\tilde{x}_k = x_i - a_i$, and $\tilde{p}_i = p_i + a_i$, giving:

$$x_k - a_k = z - \sigma\left(p_k + a_k - \tilde{p}_{ave}\right). \qquad (E19)$$

and:

$$\tilde{p}_{ave} = \sum_i S_i (p_i + a_i). \qquad (E20)$$

When technical change terms are included, we call z and $\tilde{p}_{ave}$ *effective* indices of input quantities and prices.

Note

1   This appendix has been taken from Horridge *et al.* (1993).

Appendix F Derivation of the welfare index

Equation (6.11.2.2) can be written as:

$$w^{\tau} = \sum_{r \in REG} \sum_{n \le INC} S_{rn} \; PERCONR_{rn}^{\tau} \qquad \text{if } \tau \le 1 \text{ and } \tau \ne 0, \text{ (F1)}$$

where S_{rn} is defined as:

$$S_{rn} = \frac{POP_{rn}}{POP}, \qquad\qquad r \in REG,\; n \in INC \;\text{ (F2)}$$

$$POP_{rn} = Q_{rn} \times HSIZE_{rn}, \qquad\qquad r \in REG,\; n \in INC. \text{ (F3)}$$

HSIZE is the household size of the group rn and Q is the number of households in this group. In linear percentage change form, equation (F3) becomes:

$$\tau \times w = \sum_{r \in REG} \sum_{n \in INC} \frac{S_{rn} \; PERCONR_{rn}^{\tau}}{\displaystyle\sum_{r \in REG} \sum_{n \in INC} S_{rn} \; PERCONR_{rn}^{\tau}} \Big(s_{rn} + \tau$$

$$\times perconr_{rn}\Big),$$
$$\tau \le 1 \text{ and } \tau \ne 0 \qquad\qquad\qquad \text{(F4)}$$

The variables in the above equations are in the lower-case and represent percentage changes, while coefficients are in upper-case and represent data flows in the base year (see Appendix D for linearisation rules). Hence, $perconr_{rn}$, and s_{rn} represent percentage changes in real *per capita* consumption and population-share of group rn respectively, while w represents the percentage change in the social welfare.

By taking the linear percentage form of equation (F4), we arrive at:

$$s_{rn} = q_{rn} + hsize_{rn} - pop. \tag{F6}$$

The percentage changes in total population and household size, *i.e.*, pop and $hsize_{rn}$, are zero since total population is assumed exogenously fixed and the household size does not change in a policy simulation. Therefore, we can replace s_{rn} in equation (F4) by q_{rn} using equation (F6). Equation (F4) can now be written as:

$$\left(\sum_{r \in REG} \sum_{n \in INC} S_{rn} PERCONR_{rn}^{\tau} \right) \times w = \sum_{r \in REG} \sum_{n \in INC} S_{rn} PERCONR_{rn}^{\tau}$$

$$\times \left(perconr_{rn} + \frac{q_{rn}}{\tau} \right),$$

$$\tau \leq 1 \text{ and } \tau \neq 0. \tag{F7}$$